NEW HORIZONS

Healing and Hope After the Pain of Divorce

Stephen J. King

Clarke Books

Anna Maria Island, Florida

Claᴙke Books

Cover design and book layout by Blue Harvest Creative Concepts
www.blueharvestcreative.com

ISBN-13: 978-1478329169
ISBN-10: 1478329165

Printed in the U.S.A.
First Printing July 2012

The Table of Contents

A Personal Word From The Author...

This is a book about hope, healing, and new beginnings. It is specifically for anyone who has struggled through a painful divorce and is now trying to start over.

My life took a dramatic turn a few years ago when my wife decided to divorce me after 19 years of marriage. To be fair, I don't blame her for the decision. While there had been problems in our relationship for years, my actions just prior to the divorce were irresponsible and caused us to be permanently wedged apart.

In the span of a few short months, my life completely fell apart. My family split up as I moved out of my house and, regrettably, apart from my three children. I resigned my position as the pastor of a prominent church in the community and left the ministry, surrendering my ordination credentials to the United Methodist Church. Ridden with guilt, I made the mistake of choosing not to hire an attorney and gave everything I had to my wife in the divorce settlement. Fighting depression and in financial ruin, I secluded myself away from anyone and everyone who loved me or tried to help. I lost my identity, personally and professionally, and entered into an emotional tailspin from which I almost didn't recover. There were moments when I questioned whether or not it was worth it to go on.

But I did go on and, eventually, I healed and recovered. It wasn't easy and it didn't happen quickly, but it did happen. I addressed the issues that I had to address and worked hard to improve my situation. As a result, I was able to make a new beginning in my life. My goal now is to help others who want and need to do the same.

If you've been through the pain of divorce and are struggling to put the pieces of your life back together, or if you are wandering through life feeling lost, hopeless or alone, then this book is for you. Born out of my own experience in starting over and offering the practical wisdom of my 25 years as a professional counselor and pastor, *New Horizons* can guide you as you take the steps to improve your life, heal, and move forward.

I don't pretend to have all the answers, but I do understand the issues and I know the right questions to ask to help you. I've been where you are. I understand the tears, fears, and doubts which can hold you back.

Whatever your circumstances and whatever your situation, I believe *New Horizons* can help you improve your life. May your heart be touched, your spirit lifted, and your soul inspired as you read. Most importantly, may God's richest blessings be upon you as you travel the path to new horizons...

With a grateful heart,
Stephen J. King
Author of *New Horizons*

This book is dedicated to my three wonderful children, each of whom means more to me than I could ever adequately express here. Caleb, Jacob, and Sarah, you are the light of my life and I am incredibly proud of each of you and who you have become. The greatest blessing in my life is being your father. I love you.

This book is also dedicated to my Mom, an amazing woman who has shown me the true meaning of unconditional love at all times and in all circumstances. Thanks, Mom, for always being there. I love you.

And lastly, this book is dedicated to the many friends who have shared my journey to new horizons and supported me as I have struggled to begin again after the pain of my divorce. My life is better because of you. Thank you.

NEW HORIZONS

Healing and Hope After the Pain of Divorce

Chapter 1

My Story...

"Only when we are no longer afraid do we begin to live"
– Dorothy Thompson –

There are some moments in life you never forget...

✻ ✻ ✻

Approximately one month before the divorce...

I took a deep breath and tried to relax before sitting down at the kitchen table with my kids for our 'family meeting'. As I prepared to share the news which would forever change their lives, I tried to get a sense of what each of them was feeling.

Chris, my oldest, was 15 and about to start his second year of high school. He was at that awkward stage where the innocence of childhood was gone but the maturity of adulthood had yet to arrive. Quiet and compassionate, he always had a heart for the less fortunate or for those out on the fringes of society. I loved that about him. At the same time, he was also the child I worried about the most. Like his mother, he rarely shared his feelings.

Josh, my middle child, was 12 years old and about to begin 7th grade. He lived life at one speed – full. Athletic and energetic, Josh was a showman who loved to perform and make people laugh. He wore his emotions on his sleeve and there was rarely a time when I didn't know exactly how he felt. I anticipated that what I was about to say would hit him the hardest.

Then there was Amanda, "Daddy's little girl". She was 9 years old and about to begin 4ᵗʰ grade. Sweet, smart, and beautiful inside and out, there was so much about our situation she didn't understand. I wanted to protect her from the painful news I was about to share, but I knew it wasn't possible.

Debbie, my soon to be ex-wife after 19 years of marriage, was at the table too. Earlier in the day, we discussed the best way to handle the conversation with the kids. We knew telling them of the divorce would be emotional, but Debbie and I decided to just say it to them as openly and calmly as possible. We both agreed there were certain things which were vital to say. First and foremost, we wanted them to know that both Mom and Dad loved them more than anything else in the whole world, and nothing would ever change that fact. Second, we wanted them to understand we would always be a family, regardless of what happened or where any of us lived. And third, we wanted to make sure they knew nothing they had done had contributed to our decision to divorce, and that Mom and I still cared for each other even though we wouldn't be married any more.

The kids sensed something was wrong as they sat down at the table. That wasn't surprising. They had been living among the tension between Debbie and I for months and they knew we were having problems.

I nervously began the conversation, fighting back tears as I struggled to speak the words. "Your Mom...Mom and I...your Mom and I have decided to get a divorce." The pain of that moment in time still sends chills up my spine and will forever be etched in my mind.

The reaction was immediate. Josh banged the table with his fist and shouted "No" as he began to cry. Amanda broke out in tears too, her nine year old mind unable to grasp the full meaning of what I'd just said. She cried harder still when she saw Josh continuing to become more upset. Chris, meanwhile, just stared off into the distance. There was no reaction, no tears, and no emotion. It was almost as if he expected it, which he probably did.

We spent the next half hour crying and hugging, and then hugging and crying some more, as I tried my best to reassure the kids everything would be okay, although I'm not sure I believed it myself at the time. No matter what,

I kept saying, we would get through this together as a family and everything would be alright.

Debbie didn't say a word the entire time we were seated at the table. Maybe she was too emotional. Or, maybe, she thought I should be made to struggle through the explanation alone since, from her perspective, it was all my fault anyway. Either way it didn't matter. I knew she was hurting inside, just like we all were.

It was one of the worst moments of my entire life.

❈ ❈ ❈

The affair proved to be too much for Debbie and I to overcome. My affair, with Jessica, the 'other woman'. It certainly wasn't the only reason for our divorce, but it definitely was the crowning blow to a relationship already teetering on the edge.

Giving up on our 19 year marriage wasn't easy. Debbie was the one who actually made the decision to divorce, but by then I also knew it was probably our best and only option. Despite our efforts to hold the marriage together after I ended the affair and confessed, neither of us had the strength to move beyond the pain of our situation.

We were a long way away from where we started 22 years before.

Debbie and I dated for two years before I finally asked her to marry me. She said yes immediately and without hesitation, just as I knew she would. Our future together was bright and promising. I was 27 and a newly ordained minister about to take my first church in Tampa, and she was a young, spirited 22 year old with a Finance Degree fresh out of Auburn University. We couldn't wait for our wedding day to arrive.

The ceremony took place in a quiet little town in south Alabama where Debbie had been raised. The quaint, downtown church reminded me of something out of a Norman Rockwell painting and provided the perfect setting as friends and family gathered from all over the south. Two ministers, both influential in my own spiritual journey, flew in from other parts of the country to officiate the ceremony.

Debbie looked gorgeous standing in the back of the church dressed in her white wedding gown with her long blonde hair falling gently upon her shoulders. She clutched her father's arm as the music rose to a crescendo and then nervously made the long walk down the aisle to meet me at the altar.

As a pastor who had performed dozens of weddings by the time I actually committed to marriage myself, I knew every word of the ceremony by heart. Still, at that moment and in that place, the sacred vows took on a new and different meaning for me than ever before. I broke down and cried as I repeated after the minister:

> *I, Stephen, take you Debra,*
> *To be my wedded wife,*
> *To have and to hold,*
> *From this day forward.*
> *For better, for worse,*
> *For richer, for poorer,*
> *In sickness, and in health,*
> *Until death do us part.*

The words came straight from my heart, just as Debbie's did from hers as well. We were certain the two of us would be together in marriage forever. We exchanged rings, received the blessing, and then embraced in that once in a lifetime kiss as we were pronounced husband and wife. It was all beautiful and wonderful, just as weddings are supposed to be.

The Early Years...

The first few years of our marriage were spent learning how to be married. We did all the normal things newlyweds usually do as we moved into a place of our own and supported each other in our careers. We spent our free time going out or hanging with friends and just having fun. It was new and exciting most of the time, and a learning process at others.

Eventually Debbie and I made the decision to start a family. Chris was born first, five years into our marriage. Josh came along three years later. Then, three years after that, Amanda was born. Each child was a blessing – special, unique, and beautiful in their own way – and we were tremendously grateful for all of them.

Along the way, however, life became busy. Very, very busy. We went through the normal ups and downs of parenthood – ranging from sleepless nights and diapering little ones to dealing with challenges of toddlers and small children – as we both continued working and moving forward in our careers. As the demands upon our time grew, we did our best to balance work, family life, school, church, baseball, soccer, recitals, sleepovers, parties, music lessons and more. The busyness of it all made for some long days and even longer nights as life became a constant juggling act. As time went on, it became more and more difficult to keep all of the balls in the air.

Somewhere along the way, the pace began to take its toll on Debbie and me. Our priorities seemed to subtly shift and accomplishing the tasks on our 'to do' lists somehow became more important than spending time together. Little problems started to develop in our relationship. Nothing major, mind you, but problems nonetheless – one line answers to questions which deserved a fuller explanation, making plans for one of us when both should have been included, or having mental tug of wars over disagreements which, in the grand scheme of things, were insignificant or unimportant. Without realizing it, it was almost as if a growing, yet unintentional, battle for control was developing.

Looking back now, I believe it was easy to gloss over those problems at the time because life was going so well in every other area. Our kids were happy, healthy, and doing well in school. Debbie and I were doing well in our careers. And our financial situation was stable and strong. The reality, however, was that most of those successes were achieved at the cost of spending less time together as a couple. Maybe we were too busy to notice back then. Or maybe we were just too afraid to actually admit it.

Our issues were no different than those that any young couples face nowadays. Life is busy when both spouses are working and even busier still when children enter into the picture. As the family dynamics change within the home, so too can the nature of the relationship between a husband and wife. The hope, of course, is that the couple will adapt and continue to make their relationship the priority. Many couples do. Some don't. Some think they are only to realize later they were mistaken.

The Tough Times...

The next few years provided some of the best memories of my life. I loved being a father and participating with my kids in their activities as they grew, and Debbie was a good mom. Our family life was fun and positive, and we had a lot of great friends. In addition, my church was exploding with growth and quickly becoming a model for other new pastors and churches within the United Methodist system. From all outside appearances, things were going well.

Yet still, something was missing. I don't think Debbie sensed it as strongly as I did, but something had changed in our relationship and we weren't 'connecting' as we once did. Neither of us was unhappy, but we weren't totally fulfilled either. Focusing on the kids or our careers became convenient excuses to ignore the ever widening gap between us.

For the first time in my life, I began to have doubts about our relationship. I went through a period when I made some choices that I ended up regretting and did some things I shouldn't have done, both of which didn't fill the void I felt or help our situation. But just like always, life kept moving.

After serving my church in Tampa for ten years, I was appointed to a new congregation 20 miles away in Palm Harbor, Florida. The move seemed to provide a spark for our marriage. We talked more, laughed more, and spent more time together. Maybe it was because we left our old situation behind, or maybe we were almost forced to depend upon each other more in our new surroundings, but either way it felt good.

The problem was we never addressed the issues in our relationship prior to the move. I think we both silently hoped they would just go away and the move would somehow magically set our marriage back on track. But it didn't. After a while, the same old problems started to return and ignoring them rather than addressing them eventually turned out to be a recipe for disaster.

❋ ❋ ❋

Approximately four months prior to the divorce...

I fidgeted uncomfortably in the church lobby as I waited for Debbie to arrive for our first appointment with the new marriage counselor. Having visited the church several times before when I was a pastor in the area, I had purposely asked for a late afternoon meeting time to avoid running into anyone I knew.

This counselor was the second we tried. After four sessions with our first counselor, Debbie decided she was put off by his advice and wanted to start the process over with someone else, preferably a female. It didn't matter to me if the counselor was male or female, but I definitely wasn't excited about having to explain how everything happened all over again. Still, understanding that both Debbie and I needed to feel good about whom we were seeing, I agreed to her request.

I wandered over to the church welcome table to read about some of the upcoming events for the congregation as I continued to wait. One brochure caught my eye immediately. The 8½ by 11 four page, full colored piece was promoting a state wide men's retreat which was happening the following month in Tallahassee. Before I had resigned from the ministry, I had greatly looked forward to attending the event for two major reasons. First, Tony Campolo was a keynote speaker and he had long been one of my favorites. And second, I too had been asked to be a keynote speaker and felt honored to be 'sharing the stage' with Dr. Campolo.

As I opened the brochure, my picture and biography had been blackened out. While it wasn't surprising in light of my situation, it was still painful to see and the page reflected what I was already feeling. I'd been deleted, erased, removed from the profession I loved and the faith community I had served for so long. I knew there was no one to blame but myself, but it still hurt to see it in print.

Debbie and I ended up meeting with the new female counselor five times over the next few months. Like most people in her profession, she was an excellent listener, which was good because Lord knows we had a lot to say. The three of us addressed the questions which had to be answered if Debbie and I were to have any hope of keeping our marriage together. Why had I been unfaithful? Was it possible for me to fully commit myself to Debbie in the future? Could Debbie get over her anger and was it really possible for her to forgive me? Did she even want to? Could both of us make a sincere effort to rebuild our relationship based on trust and mutual respect rather than on demands and control? Kids, finances, family, and personality differences – we talked about all of them during our sessions at one time or another.

In the end, the second counselor basically affirmed the same message as our first. She said I had acted selfishly and was wrong for doing what I did, a comment with which I readily agreed. She also said that my actions, in her opinion, were symptomatic of a deeper infection which seemed to have been present in the core of our relationship for quite a while. If we were serious about reconciling and remaining together, she said, I needed to accept the responsibility for my actions related to the affair and both Debbie and I needed to accept responsibility for the problems which had existed before that time. Only then would we be able to work to correct the problems and learn to rebuild our trust in one another.

What she said made sense, and I agreed with all of it. It didn't feel good to admit I was selfish or that I had acted wrongly, but it was true. I had already taken responsibility for the mess I'd created, which is why I confessed the affair to Debbie in the first place, and I had continued to take responsibility ever since. I also agreed with the counselor when she said Debbie and I were both responsible for the other problems that were in our relationship prior to that time. It certainly didn't excuse my actions – there is no reasonable excuse for what I did – but it did acknowledge that the breakdown of a marriage was something two people participated in, not just one.

Debbie, however, would have none of it. In her opinion, the reasons for the failure of our relationship were black and white without even the slightest shade of gray. Everything was my fault – before, during, and after the affair – and she denied taking any responsibility at all. She also disagreed with the results of the personality inventory which indicated she had a tendency to be demanding and controlling. From Debbie's perspective, this counselor, like the first, was wrong in her assessment of our situation.

The end result was that my options were becoming increasingly clear.

Either I could remain in our marriage with seemingly little hope of our relationship ever being fully restored, or I could consider the possibility that Debbie and I might be better going our separate ways. Both options scared me and neither was good for the kids. I felt caught between a rock and a hard place with no good alternative to choose.

❀ ❀ ❀

As the newness of our life in Palm Harbor gradually wore off, seemingly so too did the renewed sense of devotion and commitment. Soon the emotional distance returned as we became more and more like roommates who shared a bed and were committed to the cause of raising a good family rather than being a husband and wife growing in our love for one another.

Even our own families were unaware of the problems. To tell them would be to shatter the image we had created. From the outside looking in, we were doing just fine and in many ways were the model family. We did all the right things, went to all the right places, and seemed happy and content with the way things were. Yet deep within the most important of all relationships in any family – the relationship between husband and wife – a gnawing emptiness continued to build.

I remember asking myself back then if I really thought Debbie and I were still in love. It's an odd question to have to ask yourself after 15 years of marriage, but I wasn't sure of the answer. I knew Debbie cared about me, just as I did for her, and that we both wanted the best for each other. But were we still in love? It had been a long time since either of us expressed the feelings which normally are part of a healthy, loving relationship. Don't get me wrong – marriage is about much more than just feelings and emotions, but they are important.

We found ourselves in that place many couples eventually do; the place where it was became easier to stay together rather than to consider the alternatives. I've seen it happen a thousand times before with others during my years as a pastor. People stay in a relationship out of comfort, convenience, or security rather than because they truly love each other.

Some stay married for years, if not forever, in that type of situation. Maybe it's for the best. I really can't say and it isn't my place to judge. I can only tell you living under those conditions was less than ideal for me.

There were a lot of questions that ran through my mind during that time. Should Debbie and I stay together no matter what? If so, why? For the sake of our kids? Our families? Our vows? What had happened to our relationship? Was it possible to love someone one day and not the next? Do you fall out of love with someone just like you fall into it? And if you do fall out of love, is it possible to still be happy and fulfilled in a marriage? Do a few 'less than happy' years now in the present necessarily mean the next 30 or 40 years will be less than happy as well?

These are tough questions with no easy answers. Maybe you've struggled with some of them yourself. If not, count your blessings.

I believe our relationship ultimately failed because, over a period of several years, Debbie and I began taking one another for granted and stopped communicating like we once had. We talked but we didn't communicate, and there is a huge difference between the two.

We fell into the trap of not only taking each other for granted, but perhaps also our marriage. We settled for accepting less than the very best from each other, and we avoided our differences rather than addressing them. Much of that responsibility falls upon me. I saw it happening, yet I didn't do what I needed to do to change it. When the channels of communication break down, it's hard for any couple to sustain a long-term, loving relationship.

Debbie and I did eventually have some long, emotional discussions about our relationship, but even then it seemed like we were afraid to say what we really felt because we didn't want to hurt each other. As a result, I'm not sure either of us was ever completely honest. Things would always get better for a while after we talked, but it never lasted. Maybe it couldn't. Maybe we were fighting a losing battle already and didn't realize it.

Through all of our struggles, however, the 'D' word' never came up. Divorce was a scary proposition for both of us but for entirely different reasons. I feared living apart from my kids and the impact a divorce might have on my profession. Debbie, on the other hand, feared the loss of security and the uncertainty of the unknown. Coming from a conservative southern background steeped in family values, no one in Debbie's immediate family had ever gone through a divorce. You stay together to the end, no matter what. That was the expectation and anything less represented failure.

The Beginning Of The End...

This part of my story is both uncomfortable and embarrassing for me to tell, especially since I was married to Debbie and an ordained pastor in the United Methodist Church at the time. It's also painful because the events which I'm about to describe hurt many of the people I love. Yet I need to share it because, as you will see throughout the remainder of this book, it has shaped who I am and who I have become in my journey to new horizons.

I became involved with another woman and fell in love physically, spiritually, and emotionally with someone who was not my wife. I knew it was wrong and I could see it coming, but I let it happen anyway. I've wished many times since then that I could go back and rewrite the script of my life so I could change this part of my story, but I know I can't. So instead, like anyone who has ever made a life-altering mistake or done something they regret, I've learned to live with it and go on.

I had known Jessica for years before we ever became emotionally involved. She was a friend and someone I worked with. Eventually, as we spent time together and shared some of our personal struggles, our feelings for each other began to grow. Soon after, we crossed a line that we shouldn't have crossed. We both knew it was wrong, and we knew it would cause pain for many people if we were ever discovered, but we didn't stop it. I can't explain it; I can only tell you that is what happened.

Suffice it to say life became very confusing in the months which followed. When it all finally became too much for me to handle, I broke down and confessed the affair to Debbie in hopes of keeping our marriage together. Debbie didn't deserve to be put in that position and I knew it was all terribly unfair, but it was the reality of our situation at the time.

Let me be very clear on this point – there never was, is not, and never will be any justifiable excuse for what I did. My relationship with Jessica while still married to Debbie was wrong by any standard of ethics, Christian or otherwise. I knew better but I did it anyway. I mistakenly chose to put my needs and desires above those of my family and others I loved, and the end result was that I hurt everyone I cared for. Unfortunately, there are no 'do-overs' in life.

The weeks following my confession to Debbie were filled with heartache as I faced the consequences of my actions. I apologized first to my kids, then to both of our families, and then to the leadership of my church. By then the news spread like a wildfire out of control through my congregation and the community. Rumors popped up everywhere and became truth to those not directly involved. Meanwhile, as Debbie and I discussed our options for the future, I resigned from the ministry at her request.

❀ ❀ ❀

Approximately six months prior to divorce...

My knees shook as I walked to the pulpit of the Palm Harbor United Methodist Church for the final time. This church had been my home for over a decade and many in the congregation were like family to me. It was a place that I loved, a place where I belonged.

Mentally exhausted from the past two weeks, I was tense and uneasy as I was about to speak. I couldn't remember the last time I felt nervous before delivering a sermon, but then again I'd never told a congregation I was resigning as their pastor before either.

The sanctuary was full for all three services, but most of the 2600 who attended that morning were unaware of what was about to happen. The newspaper reporter from the St. Petersburg Times had graciously agreed to hold off on the printing of my story until Monday so I could talk to my congregation first, so only a select few knew of the decision I'd already made to resign.

Seated in the front row was my support system. There was my mom, always my rock in difficult times; my District Superintendent and supervisor, Dr. Kevin James; and my best friend, Mike Reeser. Debbie was there too, of course, along with several others who we were close to in the church.

As I mumbled a quick prayer under my breath before I began to speak, I found myself hoping God was still listening.

"Today will be the final time...," I tried to remain strong but the quiver in my voice betrayed me. "Today will be the final time I stand in this pulpit as your pastor. I am announcing my resignation as the Pastor of the Palm Harbor Methodist Church due to acts of unfaithfulness."

The words were painful for me to say. Audible gasps of shock and disbelief from the congregation were followed by a long, uncomfortable silence as I tried to compose myself through the tears. Suddenly, before I could begin speaking again, a single voice from somewhere in the middle of the sanctuary cried out, "We love you Steve." Then others began to chime in with shouts of love and support until, finally, I had to hold up my hand to ask them to stop. Although I appreciated their encouragement and support more at that moment than they would ever know, I was determined to say what I needed to say, what I had prepared to say, before the people I had been blessed to serve for so many years.

As gracefully as possible, I apologized to the church and expressed my sorrow and remorse for the pain I had caused Debbie and my family. I told them the last 13 years as their pastor had meant more to me than I could ever possibly explain or describe, and I wanted them to know that, even if the messenger was flawed the Gospel message I had preached throughout my time there was true. And I asked them to please respect my family's privacy as we now attempted to put the pieces of our lives back together.

I closed by affirming an important spiritual principle that I'd always believed – out of the depths of our sorrow, God always brings the opportunity for new life. Not sometimes. Not once in a while. But always. I told them I didn't know how, where, or when that opportunity would come for the church or me and my family, but I had faith that it would. As the tears streamed down my face, I let them know that I loved them and would miss them. They knew it was true. So did I.

When I finished speaking, I met Debbie at the bottom of the stairs and we began to leave the sanctuary as someone else prepared to conclude the service. It was then something happened I will never forget and that I certainly didn't deserve. In something which can only be described as a moment of spontaneous grace, people began standing and clapping for us. It was their way of saying thank you for my years of service and of showing support for my family.

I was struck by the irony of it all. There I was, a broken man who had been unfaithful to both his wife and his church, and they were giving me a standing ovation as a sign of their love. Deep down within my spirit, I knew I didn't deserve it.

❋ ❋ ❋

The newspaper article appeared on the front page of the Metro Section of the St. Petersburg Times the next day. By then, Debbie and I had already taken the kids and left town just to get away from it all for a while. Hundreds of cards and letters came pouring in over the next few weeks and our phones wouldn't stop ringing. In the chaos of it all, people wanted to help us but no one was exactly sure of what to do. Debbie and I tried to hold it together the best we could but, other than taking the kids to school, we rarely left the house. Soon the madness died down and, as it did, the early signs of depression set in for both of us. Our lives were in turmoil.

Supported by our families, Debbie and I began attending counseling sessions immediately in an attempt to save our marriage. I thought there was hope early on in the process and that we might be able to reconcile, but in the end it simply wasn't to be. Our wounds were too deep and the damage to our relationship too great.

One evening around midnight in late June, five months after I'd confessed the affair and resigned from my church, Debbie marched into my office at home and threw down the papers in front of me which needed to be filled out to begin the process of divorce. She walked out without a word. She had made her final decision.

At that moment, my first thoughts weren't about our relationship or how sad it was that we had arrived at such a tragic end to our marriage. Rather my first thoughts were about the kids. It was late at night, but I remember wanting to wake them up just to give them a hug. I didn't, but maybe I should have. My single greatest fear was about to be realized – I'd be moving out soon and apart from the three people I loved most in this world. It wasn't only my greatest fear; it was my greatest sorrow as well.

The next few days were filled with several long and painful conversations as we told our family and friends the news. Adding to the stress were the questions that I knew would have to be answered quickly. Where would I live? How could Debbie and I possibly survive financially while trying to hold down two homes? And most importantly, what could we do to help the kids through this difficult transition?

The tears fell plentiful and often in the few weeks between Debbie's decision and the day I moved out. There were moments when I thought about fighting the divorce and trying to keep my family together, but deep down inside I knew it would only postpone the inevitable. The gap between us had grown too wide and could never be bridged. Debbie would always question my ability to be faithful, and I would always question her ability to forgive.

The glow of our wedding day almost 20 years before was just a distant memory. Our dream of growing old together was dead. All that was left was pain.

❀ ❀ ❀

Shortly after moving out – six weeks prior to the divorce...

The beach was quiet and deserted, which wasn't unusual considering it was 2:00 AM on a weekday morning. I sat alone on the hood of my car with only the gentle waves rolling up onto the shore providing a break in the stillness. The moon peaked in and out of the clouds above and the dim light shone beautifully upon the water, but it seemed only the darkness covered my soul.

This night was like most others since I moved out. Battling my guilt and depression, I'd made it an evening ritual to drive to the causeway late at night to grieve, think, and cry. Mostly I cried. There were always lots of tears.

Seemingly oblivious to the time as well, an elderly couple walked along the shoreline looking at the stars and romantically holding hands. Seeing them made me feel worse, if that was possible, because they reminded me of everything I had lost in my life. I wondered what they thought about me as I sat alone with my tears at that hour of the evening. Make no mistake about it – I did feel alone. Very alone.

For 20 years I'd had a wonderful family, more friends than any one man deserved, and a respected position in the community. The phone rang at all hours of the day and night and I had trouble fitting everything I needed to do into my schedule. But not anymore. Now each day seemed to drag on with nothing to do but worry and, other than my mom, my kids, and a few close friends, no one seemed to be calling anymore. It felt like I'd dropped off of the face of the earth.

I just wanted to stop hurting, to find a way to break out of the prison of my depression, but I didn't know how. There were moments when I sobbed so violently that I could barely catch my breath. Other times I screamed out in frustration. I was grieving and completely lost, and my despair threatened to consume me.

There were even occasions when I questioned whether or not it was worth it to go on. It might be easier for everyone, I tried to convince myself, if I just curled up in a ball and died. If it hadn't been for my kids, I might have actually done it.

Instead, all I could do was cry...

❋ ❋ ❋

I moved out in July while Debbie took the kids to Alabama to visit family. After living with my mom a few weeks, I ended up renting an apartment within walking distance of my old house so the kids could come and go easily and whenever they pleased.

The divorce happened quickly. By late August, everything was completed and the court documents were finalized. Less than two months from the day when Debbie had marched into my office at home, our 19 year marriage was officially over.

The process moved quickly for a reason. Weighed down by my guilt and wanting to do everything I could to care for my kids and my now ex-wife, I decided not to hire an attorney. Instead, I told Debbie I would give her whatever she asked. Figure out what you need, I said, and I'll find a way to provide it. Although my intentions were good, the decision turned out to be a huge mistake.

Fueled by her anger at that point in our relationship, Debbie worked with her attorney to draw up an agreement which was grossly unfair. The amount of alimony and support she asked for totaled more than my annual salary in my new job which I began after I left the ministry. She also wanted sole possession of our home along with the substantial amount of equity we had in it. And finally, she requested to keep all of our furniture and belongings. In essence, I was to be left with nothing other than my car, my clothes, and the knowledge that I'd given everything I had to provide for my family. I knew the agreement was unfair, but I consented to it anyway, just as I said I would. Guilt can be a powerful emotion.

Throughout the process, my friends pleaded with me to get an attorney. They told me Debbie was taking advantage of the situation because of what had happened. They were right, of course, but it really didn't matter to me at that point. I just needed to be out of the marriage, whatever it took. I convinced myself that I would find a way to make the agreement work and still be able to provide for my Mom and myself but, in the long term, I was wrong. Two years later I was forced to file for bankruptcy. As I said before, I've learned to live with my mistakes.

The first year after my divorce was a living hell. Stressed out and exhausted, and constantly worrying about money, I went into a shell and cut myself off from everyone except my kids, my Mom, and Jessica, who reentered my life right after the divorce. People left messages but I didn't return their calls. Friends wanted to help but I wouldn't let them.

What I really wanted to do was run away and hide, just leave and start over somewhere else. But I didn't, and for one reason only. I refused to let my kids grow up without their Dad. Despite the continued problems in my relationship with Debbie and the tremendous embarrassment I felt out in the community, I remained in Palm Harbor for the sole purpose of being there for my kids. They needed me more than ever right then and I was committed to making sure they would never have to worry about growing up without a father, regardless of what happened in their lives or in mine. Debbie and I may have failed in our marriage, but it wasn't an option for me to fail when it came to caring for my children.

Over time I gradually settled into a life that was far different than the one I'd lived during my married years. Living alone in a modest one bedroom apartment, dealing with the issues of being a single dad, managing the challenges of my dire financial situation, finding a new career, and attending church as a member of the congregation rather than the pastor were all challenging adjustments I was forced to make. The good news is, after a rocky first eighteen months, I was able to make those adjustments and begin to heal.

I did my best to stay positive and remain hopeful through it all. I wasn't always, but I tried to be. The best thing I can say about that first year and a half after my divorce was that I survived. I fought my way through the circumstances and persevered. It wasn't easy, and it definitely wasn't pleasant, but I made it. I had lost my marriage, my possessions, and the career I loved, but I survived.

Life Beyond Divorce...

It's been almost four years now since my divorce. I went through a lot of tough times and experienced things that I don't ever want to experience again, but I'm a better person because of it. Thankfully, I was able to find the strength to regain control of my life, address my issues, and make a new beginning.

I've learned a lot of lessons along the way. I learned depression can rob you of life, and that guilt and anger can too if you allow them to fester and grow. I learned you have to confront your problems if you expect to move forward in life, and that running away usually only makes things worse. I learned life is ultimately what you make of it, regardless of circumstances or the situation, and that the right attitude makes all the difference in the world in determining your happiness and success. And I learned there is incredible power in the blessings of hope, love, and forgiveness, and that living life with grace is infinitely better than its alternative. Most of all, I learned starting over is possible and that new horizons are reachable.

The pages which follow are filled with lessons and experiences from my journey to new horizons. The stories are intimate and filled with emotion. Some reflect my pain and failures. Others are about joys and triumphs. I can guarantee you will see a reflection of yourself in all of them; not because our pasts are similar, but because the issues related to starting over after divorce are. My hope is, as you read, you will be encouraged to seek new horizons for yourself.

Starting over after a painful divorce isn't easy, but you will eventually find your way. The truth is that the sooner you are ready to do what you need to do to take control of your life and commit to a new beginning, the sooner it will happen. You may not feel like it right now, but there is a wonderful life on the other side of divorce, a life which can be filled with peace, happiness, and contentment.

May God's richest blessings be upon you on the journey to new horizons...

It's Your Choice...

You have a choice to make. You can allow the hurt and pain of your divorce to continue to cripple you and snuff out your joy and happiness... or...you can choose to take control of your life right now and begin to heal as you move toward new horizons.

I invite you to a new way of living, to new life, and to a new beginning. I invite you to new horizons. It's your choice...

For Your Journal...

• What is your story? Write it down in your journal in two pages or less, reflecting on good and bad times along the way.

• What is your greatest concern about the past? The present? The future? Why? How would you counsel someone if he or she was in your situation?

• Who has been hurt through the process of your divorce? You? Your former spouse? Your family? Others? How have they been hurt? Are there ways you can be helpful in positively addressing those hurts physically, mentally, or emotionally, both from your perspective and theirs? How?

• Write a personal vignette about one moment which symbolizes the pain of your divorce experience. Write a second one that symbolizes hope in the time since.

• As you begin to seek new horizons, write down the five greatest lessons you've learned through your divorce and since. Can these lessons help you move forward into the future? How?

Part One

Foundations of New Horizons –
Dealing with the Issues of Divorce

Chapter 2
Dealing With A Broken Spirit...

"Be gracious to me, O God, according to your loving kindness;
According to the greatness of your compassion, blot out my transgressions.
For I know my transgressions, and my sin is ever before me...
Create in me a clean heart, O God,
And renew a steadfast spirit within me...."
– Selected verses from Psalm 51 –

Approximately four months after the divorce and ten months after my resignation...

I was ready to back out again, just as I'd done the two days before, but this time I was determined to see it through. It felt like such a small and insignificant step in the grand scheme of everything happening in my life, but it was one I needed to take. So, I picked up my keys, left my apartment, and drove toward the movie theatres. I wasn't picking anybody up or meeting anyone there. It was just me, all by myself, going to watch a movie.

I'd never gone to a movie alone before. Other people I knew did it all the time, but not me. I was embarrassed to be by myself, especially in a place I'd always gone with friends or family in the past. Compounding the problem was the fact that I continued to feel embarrassed out in public and uncomfortable whenever I ran into someone I knew. Unfortunately, because I had been the pastor of a large church in the area for many years, it was rare for me to go anywhere without seeing someone who recognized me.

It's strange how our self-perception can change so quickly. Before my resignation and divorce, I was secure in who I was and full of confidence. Afterwards, however, my confidence disappeared and I felt like people were star-

ing at me wherever I went. I told myself that I was just being paranoid and no one stared any more now than before, but it was a hard feeling to shake. Whether it was true or not, there was a huge part of me that felt like I'd been abandoned by the community.

Looking back now, the reality was that most folks were actually very kind to me back then. They asked how I was doing and made it a point to tell me I was missed. But for every ten of those experiences, there was always the one that bothered me – the person who looked the other way when our eyes met, or who chose to go in a different direction when they saw me coming. No matter how much I tried not to let it bother me, the truth was it did.

When I arrived at the theatre, I quickly purchased my ticket and went inside, choosing to sit high in the back where I'd be less likely to be noticed. I had decided to see "The Notebook", a love story about an elderly man who cares for his dying wife, rather than one of the more popular movies which would be more crowded. I felt relieved when the lights went down and the coming attractions finally began.

The newspaper reviews of the movie had described it as a 'chick-flick' and a 'real tear jerker', and they were right. Like the other 30-40 people attending the weekday matinee, I cried hard and often in the last half of the movie as the couple struggled through their final days together. The reoccurring themes of faithfulness in marriage, always remaining true to the one you love, and living life fully rather than simply existing, all hit close to home. I couldn't help but think about Debbie and Jessica, and all that had happened in my relationships with each of them.

By the time the final credits rolled onto the screen, I was an absolute mess. My eyes were red and puffy, and there were dried tear streaks down my cheeks. I decided to wait until most of the people left the theatre before I got up to leave myself. As I stood up and began heading for the exit, I heard a familiar voice call my name.

"Steve?" The woman sounded surprised to see me.

Rhonda had been a member of my church in Palm Harbor for years. Always upbeat and energetic, she had a smile which seemed to fit her kind and gentle spirit. Like most others in the congregation, I hadn't seen her or spoken with her since my resignation ten months earlier. She and her cousin, who had attended the movie with her, waited for me by the door at the bottom of the stairs. As I gave Rhonda a hug, I noticed that her eyes were red and puffy too.

I felt awkward being alone at a movie in the middle of the day, but if I was going to run into anyone, I'm glad it was Rhonda. We spent the next few minutes talking about the movie and how our kids were doing before I gently tried to break away without being rude. Sensing I was uncomfortable, she was gracious enough to let me leave.

The afternoon sun was just setting in the west by the time I got to my car. Normally I would've talked about the movie all the way home with whoever I was with, but the problem was no one was with me.

I didn't like being alone. I especially didn't like being lonely. But, I thought to myself, I'd better learn to get used to it.

❀ ❀ ❀

Years ago I heard a story about a British naval officer named Donald Webb. Webb's first appointment as a captain was to the ship of the H.M.S. Switha and, like any newly appointed leader, he wanted to quickly earn the respect of his crew.

The Switha's first assignment under Webb's command was to check the deep water anchors attached to several strategically placed buoys on the surface of the ocean. Since the anchors were lodged on the ocean floor, the only way to successfully complete the mission was to send down deep sea divers to inspect them. To Webb's surprise, the opportunity to earn the respect of his crew came a little quicker than he anticipated when he found out the previous captain always insisted on being the first diver down. The first mate asked the captain if he planned on continuing this tradition.

Webb found himself in an uncomfortable spot. He wanted to lead by example but there was a slight problem. Webb had never actually performed a deep sea dive before. He had studied deep sea diving in officer training courses and performed several dives in controlled settings, but he had never actually completed a deep sea dive in the middle of the ocean.

Unable, or at least unwilling, to admit his lack of experience, Webb wrestled with his pride as the first mate waited for an answer. Perhaps he would be able to complete the dive successfully based on what he knew, he thought to himself. After all, he had seen divers dive many times before and he knew the basics. Not wanting to disappoint his crew, Webb ended up giving into his pride as he let it get the best of him.

"Of course I'll go down first", Webb said with a false sense of bravado. "I wouldn't have it any other way!"

Webb reconsidered his decision as he put on the heavy body suit, leaded shoes, and oversized metal helmet in preparation for the dive, but by then he felt it was too late to turn back. Just a short time later, against his better judgment, Captain Webb stepped off the ship to cheers of encouragement from his crew and slowly sank to the bottom of the ocean.

His problems only worsened when he arrived on the ocean floor, for it was then he discovered that he couldn't walk or maneuver in the heavy gear. Despite years of naval training which taught him to remain calm and in control in the face of adversity, Webb panicked and fell face first into the slimy ocean bottom near one of the anchors. To make matters worse, he accidentally let go of his life line as he fell, even as the words of his crew were ringing in his head, "Whatever you do Captain, don't let go of this life line. If you need help, just give her a tug."

Unable to communicate with the ship, Webb felt completely help-less and alone on the bottom of the ocean. "This is it", he thought to himself. "This is how it all ends for me – lost and abandoned at the bottom of nowhere."

In what seemed like an eternity to Webb but, in reality, was just a few minutes later, Webb felt a tug on his shoulder. The crew realized some-thing had gone wrong when the life line was released and a team of divers had been sent to check on their fearless captain. Picking Webb up from the ocean floor, the divers returned his life line and began to teach their captain how to walk in his new and unfamiliar surroundings.

Face Down In The Muck And Mire Of Life...

We've all been there, haven't we? We have all had those moments when we were unsure of what to do or where to go, yet our pride wouldn't allow us to ask for the help we so desperately needed.

We worry about what others might think or say if they realize we don't know how to do whatever it is we are trying to do. We don't want them to know we are incapable, or that we are somehow less than what we should be. And we definitely don't want them to know we are afraid. So, instead of admitting our limitations and asking for help, like Captain Webb we try to go it alone and hope we will be able to find our way. Sometimes we do, but there are other moments we can't. If we still fail to ask for help at that point, then we will soon find ourselves face down in the muck and mire of life, feeling lost and uncertain at the bottom of nowhere.

I've had those moments, plenty of them, both during my divorce and after. There were moments when I desperately needed help but my pride got the best of me and I was too embarrassed to ask. I know the pain of sleeping on a pillow wet with my own tears after struggling to get through another day or being completely overwhelmed by problems and fears to the point where I felt like giving up. I know what it's like to be face down in the muck and mire of life. Maybe you do too.

You want to believe life will get better. There will come a time, you tell yourself, when the hurting and heartache will stop, and the healing will begin. But that time is in the future, and the pain is real now. So, you continue to cling to your life line and hope that help is on the way.

❀ ❀ ❀

Less than one month after my divorce...

Sometimes all we need is a little bit of help and encouragement to make it through the day...

A few weeks after the divorce, I scheduled an appointment with the same counselor that Debbie and I had used back when we were still trying to save our marriage. In my opinion, she had been effective then, despite the fact that Debbie and I ended up in a divorce, and I appreciated both her candor and insights when we met. Since she already knew my story, I also thought it would be my best opportunity to quickly get the help and advice I needed. I have to admit, however, that the question she asked as our session drew to a close caught me completely off guard.

"Steve, as you look back on everything – your relationship with Jessica, the problems between you and Debbie, and the unsuccessful attempt to save your marriage – do you think you did anything wrong?"

I wanted to laugh out loud at the implication that maybe I didn't, but I couldn't because I was fighting back the tears. Then again, how could I blame her for asking? All she knew about me was that I'd been a successful minister who had an affair, resigned from my church, and ended up in a very public divorce. We had spent four or five hours together in previous counseling sessions, mostly talking about the problems between Debbie and me, but she had no way of really knowing my personal ethics or my sense of right and wrong. I would have asked her the same question if our roles had been reversed. Still, I was offended by the implication and the question ticked me off, especially in light of everything I'd done to try to keep my family together and to support Debbie. It showed in my response.

"Did I do anything wrong? Are you kidding? What kind of question is that? Of course I did things wrong. In fact, whatever wrong is, I went way beyond it. I was unfaithful to my wife, I deceived people who loved me, and I hurt my family and friends. I ran the full gamut of wrongs and I've ruined a lot of lives because of it. And now I'm angry at myself because there isn't a damn thing I can do about it. I couldn't possibly feel any worse. I've asked for forgiveness a thousand times, I've given everything I had to make sure Debbie and the kids are alright, and I've prayed until I'm blue in the face, but none of it matters. None of it helps."

My counselor already knew I had taken responsibility for my actions long before then. I had made some bad choices, and then I had followed up those choices by making others which were questionable as well. The more I had tried to hide what was going on, the worse things got. That's usually the way sin works. It grows and grows, like a snowball rolling downhill out of control, until it finally bumps up against something solid and explodes.

Despite my emotional response to her question, the session turned out to be exactly what I needed. We spent most of the time talking about how I could help my kids, but she also had some strong words for me concerning what I needed to do to help myself.

"I need for you to listen to me closely, Steve, because I want to help you and I'm going to say some things you need to hear. I'm a pretty good judge of character and I believe you are a good person who has a good heart and wants to do the right thing. You love your kids and your Mom, and you care about other people, which is why all of this is ripping you apart inside. I believe in you and I'm convinced you'll bounce back from this, but it's going to take some time. In fact, I wouldn't be surprised if you turn out to be an even better person and pastor than you already are just because of it.

I need to tell you something else, too, before we wrap up. I disagree when you said you have 'ruined a lot of lives.' That simply isn't true. Yes, your actions have caused a lot of pain and I certainly don't want to minimize their impact on Debbie, Jessica, the kids, or your church, but the truth is you haven't ruined anyone's life. Their lives aren't yours to ruin. The only way their lives will be ruined is if they decide to allow them to be."

"I'm not going to lie, it won't be easy for any of them. But eventually, they will each come to realize that they, like you, are ultimately responsible for themselves and their own healing. Setbacks happen for everybody, and some are more difficult than others, but in the end we all have to choose how we respond to adversity ourselves."

"You have a decision to make too, Steve. You can allow this to 'ruin' your life, or you can do what you need to do to heal and make things better. I know you feel terrible right now but you're only wounded, not dead. You have to start taking care of yourself, for you and your kids, if you expect things to heal."

I needed to hear those words. I needed to hear what my counselor had to say and that she believed in me. I needed to stop carrying the weight of the world around on my shoulders and act on her advice to take care of myself. Most of all, I needed to believe she was right.

❀ ❀ ❀

Healing Principle #1: Accept Who You Are

Any professional counselor will tell you that it's difficult to make progress with a client who has an addiction unless the counselee comes to the point where he admits he has a problem. In other words, the client must take responsibility for his actions and be accountable for his future if there is any chance for healing and recovery.

Think about a man, a husband and a father, who is addicted to alcohol. His family sees that his life is being destroyed by his drinking, and they have urged him time and again to seek the help he needs, but the man refuses to acknowledge that he has a problem. Instead he makes excuses for his behavior and lives in his private world of misery and denial, all the while falling deeper into the throws of the addiction. Unless the time comes when he is honest enough with himself to admit his problem and accept the help he needs, nothing will ever change. Eventually he will die.

How does this example relate to us as we deal with the hurt and heartache of divorce? Here's how – until we are honest enough with ourselves to admit that our spirit is broken and we are in pain, it is difficult for us to accept the help we need to heal. Make no mistake about it – a broken spirit isn't an addiction, but it is a problem.

Most of us don't want to admit that we are broken or that we hurt deep inside. We're too embarrassed or we can't stand the thought of people feeling sorry for us. So instead, we mask our feelings and put on a smile to try to convince the world that we are fine. But we aren't fine, and ignoring the problem rather than addressing it won't make it go away.

I struggled with this issue myself. For most of my adult life, my congregations and family saw me as a strong leader and person who could handle just about anything. Yet, despite being a good father, husband, and pastor, I ignored my personal issues and kept them hidden away. I knew they were there, of course, but I didn't want others to know and, as a leader in the community, I was too embarrassed to seek help. In time those issues, both within and outside of my marriage, caught up with me. The result was I experienced some difficult and desperate times. I should've addressed them earlier. I should have asked for the help I needed.

Only when we admit our brokenness can we actually address it. And only when we address the pain within can we begin to accept ourselves for who we are and move into the future with hope.

❋ ❋ ❋

Approximately three months after my confession and resignation...

Dressed in my black clergy robe, I felt strangely out of place as I stood in front of the 80 or so people who were gathered for the wedding in Times Square. It wasn't the location that bothered me. After all, I'd done hundreds of weddings in all kinds of places and settings during my years in ministry. What made me uncomfortable was the fact that this was the first ceremony I'd officiated since my resignation as a United Methodist pastor a few months earlier. I had been credentialed by another organization since, but I questioned whether or not I should even be performing the wedding after all that had happened.

Lisa, the bride to be, was a good friend of mine. Until she moved up north a few years before, she had been a member of my congregation in Palm Harbor. When she fell in love with Randy and he proposed, she called me a few days later and asked if I would consider flying to New York in the spring to perform the ceremony. I gladly accepted the invitation at the time, but only a few months later I confessed to Debbie and resigned from the ministry. When I called to explain the situation to Lisa and Randy and to offer my help in finding another minister for their ceremony, they were adamant about the fact that they still wanted me to officiate. Only because of our friendship, I agreed.

Other than Randy, Lisa, and a few members of their immediate family, no one at the wedding even knew me or was aware of what had happened in my life. To most there, I was just Lisa's pastor from Florida, a good friend who had flown to New York to do the service. No one questioned my character or integrity, and no one judged my worthiness. But they didn't have to because I was doing a pretty good job of questioning those things on my own. Leaving the United Methodist Church had been difficult enough, but it had also caused me to have an identity crisis personally and professionally.

I was still trying to figure out why it all happened, who I was, and who I was becoming.

Life is funny sometimes. As I waited for Lisa to come down the aisle and the ceremony to begin, I suddenly and randomly thought about a book I'd read 25 years earlier in seminary, entitled 'The Wounded Healer' by Henry Nouwen. I'm not sure why I thought about it right then, but I couldn't help but to wonder if it was a sign or some type of message. It could have been just a coincidence, but maybe, just maybe, it was something more. As I stood in front of a group of people I didn't know, 1500 miles away from my home in one of the biggest cities in the world, maybe the still small voice within my spirit – the one which some call the voice of God – was speaking to me.

That's when it hit me. The title of that book – 'The Wounded Healer' –was meant for me. It was who I was right then and there. I had been wounded deeply by the events of my life, but I was now being given the opportunity to speak words of faith, hope, and life, the words of a healer. If there was anything positive I could pass on based on my experiences, then perhaps what I went through would have some type of redemptive value and help others not to make the same mistake I did.

It was as if I'd had an epiphany. My calling in life, my purpose from that point forward, was to be a wounded healer.

My spirit calmed as the wedding march began and Lisa came down the aisle to join Randy beside me, both of them anxious and nervous. They had a right to be. They were about to embark on a new chapter in their lives, one that was unfamiliar and unlike any they had ever experienced before. What I wanted to tell them then but couldn't, was that I could relate to how they felt. In my own way, I was doing the exact same thing.

The wedding, by the way, turned out to be beautiful.

❀ ❀ ❀

Healing Principle #2: Find Positive Outlets For Your Stress

Not surprisingly, studies show that stress and anxiety negatively impact our mental, physical, and emotional health. Also not surprisingly, those same studies also show that divorce ranks first or second among all life events in terms of causing stress and anxiety. It is rivaled only by the loss of a loved one in death. For those of us who have been through a divorce, it's easy for us to agree.

Divorce can create stress in many ways. As if the grief of losing a marriage partner isn't enough, there are family issues, relational chal-lenges, financial problems, and legal battles which must also be addressed as the divorce occurs. Dealing with any one of these issues on their own can be frustrating enough, but facing them together all at once has the potential to create the type of stress that can overwhelm us.

Sadly, there are some moments when we become despondent and look for a quick fix to relieve the tension. We soon discover, however, that some of the outlets we choose do nothing but add to our anxiety.

❋ ❋ ❋

A little over one year after the divorce...

I woke up in the early afternoon with my head throbbing. The angry gurgle in my stomach reminded me it wasn't too happy either with what I had consumed the night before. I didn't want to move, think, or feel. I just wanted to fall back to sleep and make the world go away.

I've never been much of a drinker. Oh sure, there were times in college and since when I'd had a few too many beers or a little too much wine, but rarely was I ever sick because of it. Even then, those times always revolved around happy occasions with family and friends. For the life of me, I couldn't ever remember a day when I drank too much for the sole purpose of escaping emotional pain. But as the saying goes, there's a first time for everything.

When I did finally open my eyes to meet the day, the first thing I noticed was the affects of the tornado that evidently had blown through my bedroom.

There was a broken lamp hanging half-cocked on the nightstand beside me, and the alarm clock and candle that used to be there were on the floor. There was a broken glass on the dresser, although I had no idea how it became broken, and my clothes were scattered across the floor. As I staggered to the kitchen for some Advil and a glass of water, I noticed things didn't look much better in there. Slowly, but surely, memories of the night before started coming back to me. They weren't pretty.

The evening began innocently enough. I was passing time on the computer and looking forward to going out with Jessica. We had begun to see each other again after the divorce and, at that point in time, she was one of the few bright spots in my life. Then the phone rang and Jessica told me she had a family commitment and had to cancel. I understood, but I didn't like it. The thought of another night alone dwelling on my problems was more than I could deal with. I felt sorry for myself and her call had put me over the edge.

Maybe I'd heard too many country songs about the virtues of 'drinking away your problems' but, for whatever reason, I opened a bottle of Jack Daniels and decided to give it a try. The funny thing is I don't even like whiskey, or any other hard liquor for that matter. The bottle had been a gift from a friend almost a year ago and it had remained unopened ever since. But it was available that night and that seemed to be all that really mattered. I drank alone into the wee hours of the morning.

After the first hour or two of drinking, there wasn't much I remembered about the evening. I did remember a few things, like lying on the floor unable to get up and knocking over the lamp as I stumbled into bed. I wished that I could somehow forget those memories too. I knew one thing for sure, however. Nothing that could have happened during the evening could have possibly been as bad as the hangover I woke up with the next morning. I felt terrible the entire next day.

I learned a lesson from my little binge drinking episode, and I hope it's one I'll remember for the rest of my life. No matter how much or you try to escape your pain through a bottle of whiskey or any other drink or drug, it doesn't work. The pain doesn't go away. It only multiplies.

The signs were there. For the first time in my life, I was engaged in a battle with depression and I needed help – real help. Not the kind that comes from a bottle in the middle of the night, but the kind that reaches into the soul and heals the spirit.

Jack Daniels is not my friend. Damned whiskey.

❋ ❋ ❋

Stress and anxiety feed off of each other. Anxiety causes nervousness, tension, worry, and fear, which then creates the internal pressure we feel known as stress. As stress levels increase, we become run down mentally and physically, and feel tired and fatigued. If we ignore the problem instead of finding ways to deal with it appropriately, we run the risk of allowing stress and anxiety to take control of our lives.

So what do we do? What can we do? How can we lower our stress level and put safeguards in place to ensure we remain in control of our lives rather than letting the stress and anxiety control us?

There are many helpful ways to deal with stress, but let's begin here – remember the lessons life has taught you. You've dealt with stress effectively in the past, so think about how you did it and what you learned, and use those lessons to help manage stress now.

When I did this myself, I uncovered several lessons which I found to be helpful. For example, I recognized the happiest and most contented times in my life were not when stress was absent, but rather when I was able to manage well the stress I did have. Furthermore, those times in my life had several elements in common. If I could recapture and recreate those elements which had helped me to manage stress in the past, then I surmised that I would be better prepared to handle stress effectively now and in the future.

For example, I discovered my stress level usually decreased when I was with people I loved and trusted. I tended to dwell on my problems more and to worry more when I was alone. Recognizing this pattern, I realized how important it was for me make time for my family and friends when I felt stressed or pressured, rather than to push them away as I'd done often after my divorce. For me, spending time with the people I loved and trusted has always been helpful in decreasing my stress.

It was also clear that I had a much greater sense of peace and satisfaction when I felt that I was in right relationship with God. That term – 'in right relationship with God' – can mean many different things to people, but for me it meant taking the time to nurture my spirit through Scripture reading, prayer, and devotions. Somehow I let those important spiritual habits slip away from me as I went through my divorce and I knew that I needed to practice them regularly again. Spiritual development had always been a stress breaker for me in the past.

Lastly, I recognized there had always been for me a direct correlation between taking care of my body and feeling good about myself. When I exercised regularly and ate well, I usually felt good mentally and physically, which then enabled me to deal with my stress more effectively. And when I didn't, the level of stress just seemed to compound. Physical activity, good eating habits, and taking care of my body have always been important stress breakers in my life.

I knew recapturing these elements would help me deal with the stress of my post divorce situation, but reinstituting them into my life turned out to be a difficult challenge. I wish that I could tell you it was easy and that all of my stress suddenly disappeared, but it wasn't and it didn't. In fact, during my battle with depression, I resisted change of any kind, even when I knew the changes would help me. You might think the opposite would be true, but it wasn't. I was so entrenched in my world of misery and pain that I didn't care what happened to me or what was good for me. As a result, I literally had to force myself to do the things that I needed to do to help myself. Thankfully, with the help of some people who cared about me, I was able to do just that.

I started spending time with my friends and family, even when I didn't feel like it. I set my alarm 30 minutes earlier in the morning and had devotionals before I went to work. I forced myself to go to the gym three days a week to exercise. None of it was easy to start but, as I began to see positive results, I was encouraged and dedicated myself even more. If I missed a workout or a devotion because of my schedule, I just started over again the next day and tried even harder to not let it happen again.

Over time, these habits and routines became a normal part of my life once again and, as they did, I noticed that my level of stress subsided.

The biggest challenge any of us has in making meaningful changes is simply getting started. Do something, anything, no matter how small or insignificant it may seem, which will help manage your stress. Start with simple routines and build from there, and you'll be surprised at how quickly you see results. Divorce is stressful, I know that, but you've dealt with stress effectively in the past and you can do it again.

Healing Principle #3: Time Will Help You Heal

As a general rule, we are impatient people. We live in a world which craves convenience and instant gratification. ATMs, smart phones, technological gadgets, and drive through windows are par for the course. We don't like waiting in lines or being put on hold. Overall we live in a society in which quicker and faster are perceived as better.

Some of you may remember the fictional television character, Yakov Smirnoff. Smirnoff was a Russian immigrant who was enamored with the abundance and rapid pace of American society. He usually ended his monologues about the United States with his famous phrase, "What a country!"

In one of his routines, Smirnoff described his first visit to an American grocery store. Amazed by the countless 'instant items' on the shelves, Smirnoff found it fascinating that people could just add water to create a product they desired. What surprised him most, however, was when he walked into the next aisle and, right there on the shelf in front of him, was the item labeled Baby Powder! Confused momentarily, he finally stepped back and, as a huge grin broke across his face, proclaimed, "What a country!"

Wouldn't it be great if there was a magic powder which could instantly bring healing after the pain of divorce? Wouldn't it be amazing if all we had to do was add water and a product would be created that would take away our hurt and heartache?

Unfortunately, it's not that easy. There is no miracle remedy that can do those things instantly. It takes time to heal, and it rarely happens as fast as we wish it would. We only set ourselves up for disappointment if we believe otherwise.

Yet we also need to realize that we aren't helpless when it comes to the process of healing. The sooner that we decide to start doing what we need to do to bring about mental and emotional healing, the sooner it will happen. It is our responsibility and the onus is squarely on us. If we don't do the things we need to do or should do to heal, then by default we have made the decision to allow the hurt and heartache to continue.

What does that mean? How do we take responsibility for ourselves in order to facilitate our healing, and what does the road to healing look like? I can't define your road to healing exactly anymore than you could have defined mine, but I can offer some suggestions based on what has helped me.

- First, get counseling. This is a difficult step for many, especially men, to take because their ego and pride get in the way. Too many people think that counseling is only for the weak, but that simply isn't the case. In fact, I would argue the opposite. People who seek counseling are there because they are strong enough to admit they have a problem and wise enough to seek help in dealing with it. The strength required to address a problem is always far more significant than the strength it takes to ignore it.
- Keep in mind that not every counselor is right for every person and, like in any other profession, some are better than others. Look around until you find the counselor who is right for you. In all likelihood, you'll know in your first session together. If you aren't comfortable with the counselor's approach or you don't like him or her, then don't be afraid to keep searching. After all, it's your life, your time, and your money.

- But whatever you do, don't give up! It's important to differentiate between the 'counseling' and the 'counselor'. You may not like what your counselor says, but that doesn't necessarily mean that you've picked the wrong one. Counselors are there to help you, not just tell you what you want to hear. Most of them have your best interest at heart and are highly trained professionals who can help you see things from a new perspective if you will allow them. The right counselor can be a tremendous asset as you seek to heal and recover.

- Second, find a support group with people who are dealing with issues that are similar to yours. Churches, synagogues, or other religious institutions usually have a variety of classes specifically designed for this purpose. So too do community centers, YMCA's, and other educational organizations. I'd never participated in a support group as a student until I enrolled in my 16 week Divorce Recovery class on the recommendation of my counselor. I don't mind telling you that I was hesitant at first, but the group soon became an important part of my road to healing. Together we covered topics such as family relationships, forgiveness, emotions, lifestyles, dating, finances, and more. Hearing the stories of others who were facing some of the same issues as me was extremely helpful and taught me a lot. If you are recently divorced, I highly recommend that you find a Divorce Recovery group in your area.

- Third, create a plan. As the saying goes, "Fail to plan, plan to fail". The best way to facilitate your own healing is to devise a plan to care for yourself physically, emotionally, mentally, and spiritually. Healing emotionally is often the first priority in the first few months after a divorce, but it certainly isn't the only one. Each of these four areas is important and each relates to the others, so make a plan to heal which includes all of them.

- Once again, start simple. Create a plan with goals which you can reach rather easily, but which are also challenging enough to be meaningful. Work toward positive results so that you will be encouraged by your progress and continue to move forward.

- Also, remember to be patient. The healing process is just that – a process. It takes time and won't happen overnight. Said another way, it's a marathon, not a sprint. Strive to keep moving forward and to do the best you can. If you miss a commitment, allow yourself the grace to accept it and move on. Tomorrow will be a new day and give you the opportunity for a fresh start. Strive to stay committed to your plan and to keep moving forward and soon you'll see that your successes will build on one another.

It is said that 'time heals all wounds'. I believe this is true, but how much time it takes depends on us. If we use our time wisely and do what we need to do to facilitate our healing, it will happen quicker than if we don't. It only makes sense. Make a plan, focus on your goals, and be patient. Healing will come.

Healing Principle #4: From Brokenness Comes A New Creation

We've all heard the stories before. They are the stories of everyday people just like you and me – co-workers, friends, and family members – who went through difficult times in life but who have now healed and live peacefully and happily once again. The good news is, one day soon, you'll have a story like this to tell as well.

I was surprised at how many people shared stories of their personal tragedies in life as I went through my divorce. Some of these stories involved divorce and finding love again. Others involved a strained or broken relationship with a parent, a child, or a good friend, which eventually reconciled over time. Still others shared stories of personal mistakes, bad decisions, or financial failures which left them destitute, but from which they were eventually able to recover.

I appreciated the people who shared their stories with me and I'm convinced they did it to encourage me as I went through my period of darkness. They wanted me to understand that, in time, life would get better. Every story was unique, but all of them contained the common thread of hope. If each of them was able to rebound after what they went through, then I knew that I could too. Even in the worst moments of life, there is always hope.

❀ ❀ ❀

Three months after the divorce and nine months after my resignation...

I sat alone in the tiny prayer chapel of the Palm Harbor Methodist Church. My eyes were fixated on the beautiful stained glass image of a young child kneeling in prayer. The image was special to me for many reasons. As I tried to memorize every detail, I realized that way too much time had passed since I'd last seen it.

I used to come to this chapel almost every day back when I was the pastor of this church, but this was my first time back here since I resigned nine months before. Sitting in the very spot where I had counseled and prayed with so many people in the past, I allowed my mind to drift back to the memories of happier times.

The chapel, like the rest of the buildings on the church campus, was only a few years old. During my tenure, the congregation had boldly made the decision to leave its original location, where it had been for 70 years, in order to move to a larger property that would provide the room we needed for our rapid growth. First we built a large multipurpose building for worship, education, and administration. Then, a few years later, we built classrooms, offices, and a library for programming and a new school which we eventually began. And finally, a little over a year before I resigned, we completed the crowning jewel of our campus, our new sanctuary and chapel. The increased space allowed us to comfortably accommodate the nearly 2000 people who were coming to worship each Sunday morning.

While the sanctuary and chapel were under construction, a couple in the congregation surprised me by generously building and donating the stained glass piece of the child praying in my honor. What made the gift extra special was that they had used a picture of my daughter, Amanda, as the model for the design. Then and now, I was amazed at how they were able to capture the essence of Amanda's spirit in the art of stained glass. In my mind, there wasn't a more beautiful piece of art in the entire world.

That was why I had come to the chapel today. There were other places I could have gone, but none of them were quite like this one. The chapel represented so much of what had been good and right in my past, and I knew that if there was anywhere I would sense God's presence in my life, it would be here. As it turned out I was right, though it happened in a way I didn't expect.

The message of hope I was seeking didn't come through reading Scripture or my time of prayer, as meaningful as both of those were to me in that setting. Rather it came just as I was about to leave when I stopped one more time to look at the stained glass image of my daughter.

At that moment I realized something that I knew but had never really stopped to think about. The beautiful stained glass creation of Amanda praying was actually made up of nothing more than broken pieces of colored glass which had been skillfully shaped together by a master artist. The beauty had come from brokenness, and from that brokenness a new creation was made possible. More importantly, without those specific pieces of broken glass, the beautiful image would have never come into being at all.

In the quietness of my spirit, I heard the message loud and clear as I knelt back down at the altar to pray. Help me Lord, I said aloud, to fully depend on you – the Grand Master Artist – to take the broken pieces of my life and shape them into something new and beautiful. I couldn't do it alone.

There was a peace in my spirit as I left the chapel that I hadn't felt for a very long time. Somehow, someway, I knew God would answer my prayer. I didn't know how or when, or perhaps even why, but I knew that He would.

It was the power of hope, the power of faith. I knew God would eventually shape my life into something beautiful and new. All I had to do was believe.

Help me, Lord, to trust You – always, everywhere, and at all times. Amen.

※ ※ ※

It's Your Choice...

It's up to you. You have the choice to address the issue of your broken spirit by accepting yourself as you are, doing what you need to do to facilitate the healing, and trusting that the broken pieces of your life will one day be shaped into something beautiful and new...or...you can choose to remain face down in the muck and the mire of life, do nothing, and fail to take responsibility for yourself.

The opportunity to become a new creation – not in spite of your brokenness but specifically because of it – is yours. It's your choice...

For Your Journal...

- To be 'broken', or to experience 'brokenness', is part of the human condition. What do those terms mean to you? How is your spirit broken right now?

- Describe what it means to you to be face down in the muck and mire of life. Have you ever been there? Are you there now? Have you asked for help? Why or why not?

- Create a plan to heal. To begin, list two goals in the areas of your physical health, emotional health, mental health, and spiritual health. Now list how you will achieve those goals. Write down a starting date as you begin.

- Imagine you are the one whose image is in the stained glass image from the final story in this chapter. What would that image look like and what would you want it to communicate? Does the vision of your image affect the way you will live life now and in the future?

- List three lessons you've learned as you have passed through, or are passing through, this season of brokenness. What do those lessons teach you as you move towards new horizons?

Chapter 3
Dealing With Emotional Pain...

"Hear my cry, O God; give heed to my prayer.
From the end of the earth I call to you when my heart is faint..."
– Psalm 61:1-2a –

We hurt. On the inside we hurt. Deep down in the core of our spirit, there is a pain that won't let go and won't go away. It's not like the physical pain created by a cut, a bruise, or a broken bone. This pain runs deeper. This pain is in the heart. We can't just stitch it up or put a cast on it and hope for it to heal in a day, a week, or a month. Instead, this pain continues to linger, at times even for years after the wound is first opened.

We want to heal and be well. We want to stop hurting and leave the pain behind, but we don't know how. It follows us wherever we go and whatever we do, like a tattoo etched upon our soul, always present day and night. Sometimes sleep is our only respite, if indeed we are able to sleep at all.

In our worst moments, we wonder if we'll ever feel good again, ever feel normal. Please, someone, help us. Tell us what we need to do. Tell us we will be okay.

❀ ❀ ❀

Approximately 18 months after the divorce...

I saw the pain in Jessica's eyes before she spoke. We'd been through a lot together in the last couple of years and it wasn't difficult for me to recognize when something was wrong. I had a strange feeling I didn't want to hear what she was about to say.

"I love you, Steve...but I'm not sure if I love you enough..." Her voice trailed off in silence as tears began to fall. Meanwhile, my heart felt like it was being ripped from my chest.

So this was it. This was the moment we had fought so hard to avoid. After all the love and laughter of our relationship on one side, and all the pain and heartache on the other, Jessica was finally calling it quits. She was telling me it was over – really over – this time. We were done. Finished.

I've had a lot of regrets in my life, but loving Jessica wasn't one of them. I regret we had an affair. I regret we hurt our families and many of the people we loved. And I regret the consequences which resulted from our relationship. But I don't regret loving her. Perhaps in another time or place, well... who knows?

Jessica and I were involved in our relationship for over a year before I finally confessed. Our friendship existed for years before then, however, and I had always admired her kind heart and the way she treated people with dignity and respect. Eventually, we fell in love. As I said earlier, we crossed a line we shouldn't have crossed. It shouldn't have happened, but it did.

I think part of the reason we fell in love, other than the many ways we were attracted to each other, was because we each filled a void in the other's life. Even though the guilt was overwhelming at times and we knew the relationship was wrong, it wasn't enough to keep us apart. It's hard to explain or understand unless you've been there yourself, but it was the reality of our situation.

As time went on, both of us knew something had to change if we were going to move beyond the predicament we were in. That something turned out to be my decision to confess and to tender my resignation at the church. Because I'd been the pastor of Palm Harbor Methodist Church for a long time and developed many deep connections within the community, most of the congregation naturally rallied around Debbie and me. Meanwhile, Jessica grieved alone. Except for the help of a few family members and a good friend who lived next door, Jessica struggled to put the pieces of her life back together. We cut off all communication with each other after I confessed, knowing it was something we simply had to do.

During the six months between my confession and divorce, although unbeknownst to me at the time, Jessica became involved with another man – the next door neighbor who helped her through the crisis and was able to be there for her when I couldn't. In time, their relationship eventually evolved into something more than supportive neighbors. I guess we all need someone to lean on at one time or another...

After Debbie decided to divorce me and I moved out of the house, I called Jessica to see if she would be willing to meet and talk. It had been a long time since we'd seen each other and meeting that evening reminded me of why I had fallen in love with her in the first place; why I was still in love with her even then.

For whatever reasons, Jessica didn't tell me about her neighbor friend that evening, but we did talk about everything else. She told me how painful it was when I decided to try to keep my family together instead of remaining with her, even though she knew it was the right choice for me to make, and how embarrassed she felt among her family and in the community. I knew it was difficult for her because I was going through the same things. We also talked about us, and whether or not there was still a chance for our relationship to work. Neither of us knew if it was possible, but I asked if I could see her again.

Jessica and I continued to date for the next 18 months or so after that night, but our relationship never quite returned to the same level where it had been before. Maybe that was inevitable in light of how we first began. I'm not sure. I only know I wanted us to be together.

"I love you, Steve, but I'm not sure if I love you enough to stay together...I just don't see how it can work." Then, for the first time, Jessica was completely honest with me as she talked about the feelings she had for her neighbor. She had finally come to the point where she needed to make a decision between us and, unfortunately, it wasn't to be me.

Some might say it was poetic justice – the one who was unfaithful to his wife was then left by his lover for another. Maybe. Once again, I don't know. The only thing I was sure of was that I hurt inside and felt betrayed, whether I had a right to or not.

When relationships end badly, hurt is inevitable, regardless of the circumstances. It's just the way life works.

❋ ❋ ❋

Emotional pain usually comes into our lives two ways. Either it comes as the result of factors beyond our control, such as when loved ones die or the actions of others hurt us, or it comes as the result of factors we do control, such as our own bad choices and decisions. Either way, the pain is real.

The Difference Between Death And Divorce...

We hurt inside when someone who we love dies. There is no getting around it.

My Dad passed away over twenty years ago, yet I remember it like it was yesterday. He wasn't supposed to die when he did, but isn't that the way it always seems to happen when we lose someone close to us?

Dad was in his late sixties when he went the hospital in Gainesville, Florida, for surgery. The operation was designed to 'clean out' the major arteries in his legs and improve his blood circulation. According to the doctor, my Dad's problems were primarily caused by his heavy smoking and drinking through the years. I made the two and a half hour drive each way from Tampa every day for almost a week to be there with him before, during, and after the surgery.

The operation turned out to be more extensive than the doctor originally anticipated. Although he deemed it successful in accomplishing its purpose, the doctor cautioned us Dad had a difficult time and that his recovery would not be easy. The chances of him pulling through were good, he told my brother and me, but there were no guarantees.

Hearing those words – "his chances of pulling through were good, but there were no guarantees..." shook me to the core. Didn't the doctor understand that this was my Dad he was talking about? Pulling through wasn't *an* option, it was the *only* option. We had known the surgery was to be invasive, but we never actually thought it would be life threatening. Surely he could do something, I pleaded. Although my Dad was heavily medicated, I couldn't wait to see him and make sure he was okay.

As a pastor, I'd logged hundreds of hours in hospitals and emergency rooms through the years. I knew what to expect when I saw someone in ICU after a major surgery, their bodies often discolored and seemingly almost lifeless from the trauma. But this was different. I wasn't prepared to see my own Dad lying in one of those beds. What I saw shocked me.

My Dad was strapped to the bed to restrict movement. His body looked like a human pin cushion with needles and tubes sticking out in every direction. His skin was pale, and there was a huge plastic tube down his throat. The constant beeping sounds of monitors along with the drone of the oxygen pump seemed to drown out any of the voices of the nurses caring for other patients. Despite the drugs, I could tell from the look in his eyes that he was scared. So was I.

Right then and there, even though I felt sure my Dad couldn't under-stand what I was saying in his current state, I said a prayer and asked God to heal him. But it wasn't to be. Two days later, my Dad's heart failed and he died. He never made it out of the ICU.

I'll never forget the last time I saw him. On the day my Dad died, I leaned down and kissed his head as I was getting ready to drive back home. "I love you Dad. See you in the morning." Unable to speak because of the tube still in his throat, he took the pencil and pad I gave him and wrote, "Love you too". He didn't have to. I already knew. Once again, I could see it in his eyes.

Exhausted from a long day and the drive home, the phone was ring-ing as I walked through the door of my house. It was my brother. I could tell right away by the tone of his voice that something was wrong. Dad just died, he said. I hung up the phone, hugged my wife and baby, and sat down on the couch and cried, realizing I'd never again be able to talk with my Dad; not in this life anyway.

I've never been shy about saying I love you to my family and friends, but I'll always be especially grateful for saying those words to my Dad on the day before I left the hospital on the day he passed away. It reminded me of a valuable lesson. Life is too short and the future is too unpredictable for us not to take every opportunity we have to say "I love you" to those we care about. There are many things in life I don't understand, but I can guarantee this to you for sure – if you make it a habit of telling your family and friends that you love them everyday, you'll never, ever, regret it.

I have a question for you to think about. Which is more painful emotionally – losing someone you love to death or going through the heartache of a bitter divorce? I've been asked that question myself and, based on my experience, I don't know if there is a definitive answer.

Death and divorce are similar in many ways. Both can be draining physically, mentally, and emotionally. Both mark the end of an important relationship which has helped to shape our lives. And both can cause a tremendous amount of grief and mourning, sometimes for months or even years after they happen. Yet for all of their similarities, there is at least one significant difference, and that difference has to do with the process of closure.

Closure is about coming to terms with the reality of what has happened, accepting the implications, and then finding a way to move on mentally and emotionally in a healthy manner. The sense of sadness and loss may continue to remain, but there comes a time when we have to move forward and get back to living life. Many times it takes a while, but we eventually do. We must.

Family and friends, counseling and support groups, and a host of other things can help us move toward closure, but none of them guarantee that it will happen quickly. Even society has its traditions in place to help us. A funeral, for example, is such a ritual designed for the living, not the dead. When we gather to mourn, we affirm that death in this world is final and that we, the living, need to symbolically 'close' our relationship with the deceased forever. The memories remain, of course, but the funeral serves as a stark reminder that the individual is gone and that we must move on.

The process of closure related to divorce, however, is very different for several reasons. While there is a physical separation between spouses, both are usually still involved in each other's life at some level. A final decree signifies the end of the marriage and is often helpful in moving toward closure, but the relationship is rarely ever 'closed' completely at this point.

Full and final closure is almost impossible when children are involved. Visitation, school functions, birthdays and holidays, sporting events, and a host of other activities virtually guarantee the ex-spouses will continue to see each other and communicate regularly in some way. Financial obligations, such as alimony and support, keep the former couple connected as well. Even when the kids grow up there are graduations, weddings, and grandchildren, all of which but ensure involvement with each other occasionally. Though the former partners may hope that divorce means the end of their time together forever, life usually dictates otherwise. Instead of the "my spouse is gone once and for all" so many anticipate, the future becomes a series of adjustments and readjustments to the relationship as the years go by.

I once officiated a wedding in which the parents of the bride had been divorced for ten years but were still visibly angry and bitter toward one another. They refused to talk to each other for the entire weekend, instead choosing to communicate only through their kids or an occasional text message. The feud made for some awkward moments at both the rehearsal and the reception. What a shame. Their daughter was experiencing one of the most memorable moments in her life, yet her parents couldn't set aside their differences long enough to allow her to enjoy it. Even after ten years apart, neither of the former spouses had achieved closure.

As the divorced father of three, I'm grateful Debbie and I have been able to communicate regularly about them. Despite the issues which separated us, the love we both have for our kids has been stronger than any selfish desire either of us might have had in terms of one another. Like most former spouses, we simply want the best for our kids. The only way for that to be accomplished is to keep the lines of communication open and to work together when necessary. It hasn't always been pleasant when we've had to talk, but there are no other options. Our children need both of us.

I'm fully aware that Debbie and I will probably never have full and complete closure when it comes to our relationship. It's just not possible. We will always be connected by our children and our desire to be active in their lives. I am committed to doing whatever I can do, whatever I need to do, to make the best of the situation, and I will always make the effort to be as positive, helpful, and kind as I can be when I talk to her. Fostering anger and bitterness in our lives never does anyone any good. More importantly, it only hurts the ones we love the most – our children.

The Grief Process...

Grief is the mental anguish we feel deep within our soul when a tragedy occurs in our lives. Depending on how close we are to the situation and how severe the event is, our grief can last anywhere from a matter of days to several years. The grieving process itself is often marked by several distinct and definable stages as we move toward healing and closure.

Understanding these stages can be helpful to us for two major reasons. First, it helps us to identify the stages we've already been through and allows us to recognize that grief is a normal, even predictable, process. In other words, we aren't crazy for experiencing the feelings we have had. Second, understanding the stages of grief can help us prepare for the future and what we are yet to experience. Knowledge is the key. When we understand the normal progression of the grief pattern, we are better able to anticipate what will happen and make the appropriate choices which lead to healing.

Elizabeth Kubler Ross, the highly respected author of *On Death and Dying,* has long been considered one of the foremost authorities on the grief process. Although her work focuses primarily on grief related to death or the loss of a loved one, the five stages she has identified also has relevance for us who have gone through divorce. For our purposes here, let's examine each stage of grief from that perspective.

1. **Denial** – The first stage of the grief process. Denial is the reaction we often have before or during the divorce as we refuse to believe what is actually happening. We don't want to believe it and, as a result, we ignore it or cling to the feint hope that everything will be okay and somehow work out. But it isn't okay and it doesn't work out and, soon, we are forced to accept the fact that our marriage is really ending.

2. **Anger** – The second stage of the grief process. Once we've acknowledged that the divorce is real, or in many cases soon after it has occurred, anger sets in. We become angry at our ex-spouse, angry about our circumstances, angry about our financial situation, and angry about nearly everything else. If we internalize the anger, we soon come to learn that it has the power to control our lives and be destructive both to ourselves and others, causing problems for years to come.

❀ ❀ ❀

Approximately two months before the divorce...

I stayed on the computer longer than I needed to. Or I shuffled through papers on the desk that I had already shuffled though a dozen times before. Or I made a futile attempt to find something meaningful to do or convinced myself I actually cared who won the meaningless game on TV. Any excuse would work. I just didn't want to go to bed.

As the months passed and Debbie and I struggled to keep our marriage together, it became apparent to me that her anger wasn't going away. If anything, it was just the opposite. It was getting worse and seemed progressively more intense as the weeks went by.

On most nights, we ended up talking about our problems when we finally went to bed. Actually, 'talking' may not be the right word to describe those conversations – arguing was probably more like it. The pattern rarely varied. First, we would begin to talk about our issues. Then, I'd say something that she didn't like or agree with. And finally, she would become angry and begin to sling insults and accusations my way. Eventually I'd get tired of it all and defend myself, and before long we'd both say things which shouldn't have been said. The evenings rarely ended well.

I certainly couldn't blame Debbie for being angry. Anyone would be in that situation. Regardless of the problems in our marriage prior to that time, I was wrong to do what I did. I'd put everything that Debbie and I had worked for in jeopardy and, at least in the first few months after I confessed to her, I knew that I deserved everything she said to me.

But after three or four months of the same verbal beat downs every night, I'd come to the point where enough was enough. Deserved or not, I simply couldn't take the arguing anymore. If our marriage was going to heal and we had any hope of working things out, something had to change. I had my issues to work on and I felt like I was making progress, but I felt that she needed to address some of her issues too. In my opinion, her anger was at the top of that list.

She was hurt and needed my patience. I was ridden with guilt and needed her understanding. But at that point in our relationship, neither of us was able to offer what the other needed. It was becoming clear that we might not make it...

❋ ❋ ❋

3. **Bargaining** – The third stage of the grief process. As the emotional pain wears on us and takes its toll, we look for relief wherever we can find it, and sometimes even in places that we can't. We bargain with God, others, and even ourselves in a desperate attempt to find a way to make things better. We make promises we can't keep and chase after things we shouldn't be chasing, all in the elusive search to find peace for our soul. We just want to feel better, like we did before the hurt and heartache set in, but it isn't possible and our efforts to bargain away the grief only add to our frustration.

4. **Depression** – The fourth stage of the grief process and, quite possibly, the most dangerous of all. Sometimes our depression is acute. We don't want to get out of bed or we have trouble concentrating. We feel physically tired and emotionally drained all the time. Even the simplest of tasks seem to require a monumental effort to complete. At other times, our depression is more severe. Chronic depression, they call it. We withdraw and want to be left alone to drown in our self pity. We don't care what happens to us. It isn't unusual for thoughts of suicide to cross our mind. Our personalities change. Attitudes change. We change. Others recognize the depression in us often before we see it in ourselves. When chronic depression sets in, professional help is needed.

5. **Acceptance** – The fifth and final stage of the grief process. When we arrive here, it doesn't mean the grief is completely gone or the pain is fully behind us. What it does mean, however, is that we have accepted the reality of our situation and are ready to make the best of it. Despair gradually fades and the pain lessens in time. We become active in life once again and begin to enjoy doing the things we've always done. We spend time with friends and family and, ever so gradually, our perspective shifts from the tragedy of the past to hope for the future.

As you read about each of these five levels of grief, I'm guessing you thought about your own situation, perhaps trying to judge where you are in the continuum. If so, good for you. Self-examination and reflection are always healthy and positive steps on the way to new horizons. But allow me to offer a caution.

The five stages are not an exact formula. There are always exceptions to the process and to every stage in the process. While this may be the typical pattern for most people who grieve, your personal journey may be very different than what is summarized here. You may find your experience is that the stages appear in a different sequence or that, perhaps, you seem to skip one or two of them altogether. If so, that's fine. There is no wrong way to grieve and no two people are exactly alike. It's only natural there will be differences since each of us is unique and different ourselves. If your experience doesn't match up exactly with the stages above, then draw whatever lessons you can from the material and move on.

One other word of caution. It's important to understand that there is no definitive timetable for any of these stages, individually or collectively. One stage may last a week, another for a month, and still another for a year or more. Or you might find that two stages overlap or bleed into each other. It would be great if we were able to mark off each stage as we went through it as a way of charting our progress, but we can't. The human psyche doesn't allow it.

Understanding the five stages can help you better understand your grief now and in the future. Regardless of where you currently are in the progression, remember that the goal for each stage is always the same – heal and move forward toward a new beginning.

Guilt And Regret...

A sense of loss is not the only source of emotional pain. Sometimes – in fact, many times – our emotional pain results from guilt or regret. Either can be a roadblock on the path to healing, and both of them must be addressed if we expect to be healthy and whole.

Guilt results when our actions or decisions clash with our value system. We feel bad for acting in a manner that is contrary or inconsistent with what we believe or who we are and, depending on the act in question, our guilty feelings can range from a simple twinge within our conscience to an overpowering emotion that can rack our soul for years to come. In extreme cases, unresolved guilt has the ability to destroy a person.

Regret, on the other hand, is a deep seeded feeling of sorrow or remorse, usually resulting from an action or decision we wish we would have done differently or that would have turned out differently. These actions and decisions which cause regret may not have clashed with our value system at the time, but we would gladly choose to do them over if we could. For example, perhaps you regret your decision to get a divorce. Or maybe you regret not getting a divorce sooner. Or you regret something in the past which caused trouble or strife in a relationship with a friend. None of these regrets may have resulted from things you did wrong, but the outcomes were less than you wanted them to be. If you live long enough, you're bound to have some regrets. Everyone does.

Arthur Miller's "Death of a Salesman" has been widely acclaimed as one of the greatest American plays of all time. While the story is unique to the play itself, the lessons it teaches about guilt and regret are universal in their application.

The main character in the play is a salesman named Willie Loman. Willie is coming to the end of his life recognizing that he is a self-proclaimed failure. As the events unfold, we discover his self-indictment is the direct result of the guilt and regret which has plagued his soul for years.

On a sales trip early in his career, Willie had an affair with a woman in another town. As fate would have it, Willie's son, Biff, happened to stop by his father's hotel for a surprise visit at the same time and caught his father with the other woman. The event threw Biff into an emotional tailspin from which he has yet to emerge some 15 years later when the play is set. Meanwhile, Willie has carried the burden of his sin ever since.

Nowhere in the play is the power of guilt more evident than in the dramatic scene where Willie is talking to his adoring wife as the woman of his adultery slowly saunters across the stage, invisible to all but Willie himself. Though he is separated from the affair by both time and distance, his grief is still so intense that he can only hear the words of his lover and none from his wife.

Guilt can do that to a person. So can regret. Left unaddressed, they have the power to shred the soul and rip the spirit, causing emotional pain which can last a lifetime.

So how can we address the grief and emotional pain which results from our guilt and regret, and how do we begin to move forward? These questions are answered in a variety of ways throughout this book and depend on your situation, but let's begins by looking at steps that we need to take to deal with the problem right here and now.

Steps To Moving Beyond Emotional Pain...

Divorce creates a wealth of emotions including grief, guilt, and regret. That's a given.

What is not a given, however, is how we react to the emotional pain created by these things. It's entirely up to us. Furthermore, how we choose to deal with the emotional pain in the present will determine how quickly we are able to heal in the future. There are steps we can take – steps which we need to take – that can help us begin to put our lives back in order.

Several factors come into play as we heal from emotional pain. Forgiveness – granted and received – is always important. So is hope for the future. The love of family and friends, a positive attitude, and making good choices are all important too. But before we get to these things and many more in the chapters ahead, let's consider some preliminary steps we can take to help ourselves immediately.

Step #1: Identify The Source(s) Of Your Pain And Change What You Can

Identify the problem and deal with it – that's the basic premise of this step.

When we are physically ill, we go to a doctor for help. The doctor identifies the source of our illness, makes a diagnosis, and prescribes a treatment. If we ignore the doctor's advice, i.e. if we don't take the medicine he prescribes or we continue to do whatever it was that made us sick in the first place, we won't heal as quickly as we would otherwise.

The process is the same in this step except the goal is to identify the source of our emotional pain rather than physical pain. And, instead of using a doctor to diagnose the problem and prescribe treatment, we are going to do it ourselves.

Identifying the sources of our emotional pain isn't really that difficult. For most of us, those sources revolve around people, actions, or personal behaviors which have negatively impacted our lives through the years. In all likelihood, some probably relate to our divorce in one way or another.

The problem isn't in identifying the sources of our emotional pain – that part is usually fairly easy – but rather the problem is in addressing them or doing something about them. Too many times we ignore the problem or try to deny the pain it causes. That has to change if we expect to heal and get better. We have to deal with them is such a way as to minimize their impact or resolve the conflict.

When we avoid doing what we need to do to address the problem, or when we continue doing what we shouldn't be doing in the first place, we allow the problem to persist and a dangerous pattern develops. We begin to rationalize our behavior as we try to justify our actions, both to ourselves and others. As a result, nothing ever changes and our pain continues. All of our rationalizations and justifications become nothing more than a coping mechanism designed to ease our conscience or relieve our guilt as we avoid the truth.

My relationship with Jessica created a tremendous amount of pain for me emotionally because I knew it was morally and ethically wrong, yet I entered into it anyway. To cope with the inner turmoil I felt, I justified my actions and convinced myself that somehow it was okay. The longer it continued, the easier it became for me to do. Eventually I got to the point where I was totally misrepresenting the truth just to draw the conclusions I wanted to believe.

I loved Jessica and she loved me – that was true. I had problems which had existed for years in my marriage – that was also true. And I deserved to be in a loving relationship which could fulfill me physically, spiritually, and emotionally – once again, true.

All of the statements were true, yet I was living a lie. I twisted reality to selfishly care for my own needs and desires, and ignored the damage that I knew it would cause for others. Right and wrong became relative to me and I convinced myself everything would work out in time. But I was wrong. It didn't work out and, in retrospect, all of my empty justifications only delayed me from addressing the greater truth involved, namely that I was hurting myself and others.

When we rationalize a wrongful behavior, it's easy for us to become psychologically dependent upon it. Every time we return to it, however, we only renew the cycle of dependency and emotional pain. The only way we can break that cycle is to change it.

Once we've identified the sources of our emotional pain, then the tough part begins. The next step is for us to limit or eliminate our exposure to the source so we can break the cycle of dependency. This can be difficult to do, but it's necessary if we are going to actually change our situation. Only in limiting or eliminating our exposure to the source of our pain can we free ourselves from 'the chains that bind'.

Assuming some sources you've identified are people, it's important to understand that every relationship is different and, therefore, every situation must be handled individually. Don't lose sight of the goal, however, because you need to minimize or eliminate contact with the people who drag you down, negatively impact your life, or create your emotional pain. Nothing will change in your life with regards to these people until you make the decision to change it. It's that simple.

Sometimes it's impossible to eliminate contact completely with certain people on your list, especially if that person is your former spouse or a family member. But even when eliminating contact isn't possible, you need to recognize that you still have the ability to determine the type of contact you have as you make the effort to control the direction of the relationship. If a conversation with that person goes badly, walk away and talk to him or her at another time. Use phone messages, texts, or emails to communicate if you have to, instead of meeting face to face. Do whatever you can, whenever you can, to define the parameters of your relationship in ways which will be helpful to you.

Clearly the relationship I had with Debbie after the divorce was one of my primary sources of emotional pain. The volatile nature of our conversations and emails only added to the stress and frustration I was already feeling. I knew that it would be impossible for me to heal and move forward unless I somehow limited our contact with each other. So, for the sake of my own well-being and for hers, that's exactly what I did. I decided to communicate only when it was necessary, such as when we needed to discuss the kids or something related to our financial agreement. Even then, I left messages whenever possible or used emails to communicate if I could. Eventually, as our communication lessened, so also did my stress and emotional pain.

There were other individuals with whom I needed to limit contact as well. One was a friend who wasn't good for me to be around. Another was someone who continually dwelled on what had happened and was counterproductive for me as I tried to move on. None were easy to pull away from, but in each situation I strategically committed to minimizing or eliminating our contact for the purpose of my own healing.

You always have a choice in determining the direction of your relationships. You're not running from a problem when you decide to limit the contact you have with someone, rather you are proactively taking care of yourself. In some cases, you may want to talk with these people again in the future in order to reconcile or bring closure, but those conversations should only happen when you are ready, and not before.

To this point we've focused on people as the source of our emotional pain, but there may be other sources you need to address as well. Unhealthy behaviors, like drinking or using drugs, bad habits and negative attitudes, or doing things you shouldn't do, all have the potential to be destructive patterns and create pain. Again, the key is to minimize or eliminate these behaviors in an effort to heal and move forward.

I certainly had my issues to address. While I recognized the need for change in certain areas of my life for years, it took the pain of my divorce to finally move me to action. Through counseling and my Divorce Recovery group, both of which I never thought I'd be attending, I was able to make changes I should have made years before. I should have sought help before my crisis, but I didn't. Lesson learned.

I still have plenty of issues to work on as I move forward, but I'm proud of the changes that I have been able to make. I'm back on the right path and I am headed in a positive direction. It's time for you to do the same. Don't make the mistake of putting off or ignoring your problems and waiting until it's too late like I did. Change the patterns and behaviors you need change now. There is no time like the present to begin.

If you think new horizons will magically appear without making any changes in your life, then you are only fooling yourself. Limit or eliminate the contact you have with people who bring you down. Change your behaviors that are harmful and destructive. And for the sake of yourself and those who love you, do it now.

Step #2: Accept What Can't Be Changed

I've got good news and bad news for you.

The good news is that your emotional pain will decrease over time as you limit or eliminate your exposure to the sources listed in step one. You may not feel like it right now, but the day will come when you will be happy and whole once again. In the meantime, it is your responsibility to do what you can do to make that happen. Time – the precious healer in life – will do the rest. That is the good news.

Now for the bad. Your healing will come, but some scars will always remain. The hurt will eventually fade, but the painful memories won't. Even if you do all the right things from this point forward, you'll soon realize that you have to simply accept certain things that can't be changed.

Somewhere deep down in my core, I'll always have a dull ache as I think about the turmoil and pain I caused through the events which led to my divorce. I have been forgiven by God, and I've finally learned to forgive myself, but I know that I'll always feel a sense of guilt and regret at some level. I can change a lot of my relationships and behaviors to make things better or to improve my situation, but I can't erase the past. It will always impact who I am and how I live.

I'm sure the same is true for Debbie as well. She will never fully recover from the sense of betrayal she felt, and it will probably impact her for the rest of her life. That's a heavy burden to carry, for both of us. She deserves better and, despite what happened between us, Debbie is a good person and I want the best for her. Her healing will come, but the memories of what happened will be with her forever.

I'm guessing you have memories which have left their mark on your soul too. No doubt they are different than mine, but they are just as real and hurt just as much.

What can we do about the relationships, experiences, and events of our past which can't be made right? And what can we do when we've done all we can to improve the situation but the hurt still remains?

At that point, there's really only one thing we can do – accept it for what it is and move on. We don't stop trying to improve the situation and we don't abandon the hope of being fully healed, but we also remember that healing isn't necessarily synonymous with the absence of pain.

Practically speaking, here is what 'accept it' really means. First, we do everything within our power to right the wrongs of our past. Second, we address the emotional fallout and deal with the feelings of hurt and heartache to the best of our ability. And third, we make the intentional decision to accept things as they are as we commit ourselves to moving forward anyway. Anything else only hinders our ability to heal.

Granted, there are some experiences in life that are easier to accept than others. Generally speaking, the greater the negative impact of the experience or relationship upon us personally, the more difficult it is for us to accept. And if we feel personally responsible for what went wrong, it's even harder still.

One of the reasons it is so difficult for us to bounce back from divorce is that we often feel personally responsible, at least in part, for what happened. As a result, the hurt and heartache are more intense. Sometimes we beat ourselves up mentally or emotionally. We constantly replay in our minds the things we could have done, might have done, or should have done which may have led to a different outcome. In the end, however, we come to realize that what happened has happened, and the best we can do is to learn from it. We have to accept it and move on, taking control of the things which we can control, and leaving the rest to God. There is no other way to forge a new beginning.

Step #3: Let It Go

There is one more important step in the process of addressing our emotional pain. Once we've identified the sources and begun to change the relationships and behaviors which need to be changed, and once we have accepted those things which can't be changed, then it's time to let it go.

To 'let it go' doesn't mean that we forget what happened, ignore our feelings, or pretend that those relationships and experiences don't matter. They do matter, as is evidenced by the impact they have had on our lives. What 'letting it go' does mean, however, is that we refuse to allow grief to define our lives anymore.

To 'let it go' is the next step beyond acceptance. Whereas acceptance implies that certain things in life cannot be changed, letting it go acknowledges that we still have control of our response to those relationships and experiences, and we can make the decision to release the negative feelings which are holding us back. It's not easy, but it is a step we need to take to reach new horizons.

I've counseled dozens of couples who have lost loved ones to death through the years. The most difficult of those experiences, bar none, were when I talked with parents who had just lost a young child. There simply are no right words to say in a moment like that, and certainly none which can take away their pain.

I've never had a child of my own pass away. I can only imagine the hurt and pain a parent must feel or the sense of loss which continues to linger. We all know that life is unfair sometimes but, in my opinion, nowhere is this more evident than in the moment a mom or dad stands crying over the grave of their baby. My heart aches for anyone who has ever endured that type of pain.

In the months which follow the death of their child, parents typically go through the stages of grief we discussed earlier as they attempt to cope with the crisis. First there is denial followed by anger as they face the reality their child is gone. Then there is bargaining, usually with God, as they deal with their life ahead. And often there is a period of depression as their anger and pain turns inward.

Only when they move to the acceptance stage can they begin to release the negative feelings and emotions which create their grief. And only when they release those are they able to let it go and move on with life. Sadly, if they never arrive at this stage, they will likely continue to live with their grief and pain indefinitely.

The same principle applies for us when we experience the pain of divorce. The event which causes our pain is very different from losing a child, of course, but the sense of loss as our family breaks up is just as real. At some point we must accept it, let it go, and give ourselves permission to live again.

❋ ❋ ❋

A little over two years after the divorce...

I felt silly when I answered the question. Perhaps a little embarrassed too. But I was telling the truth. The clerk asked me who the three red helium balloons were for and I told her honestly that they were for me. She kind of cocked her head disbelievingly, as if she expected me to say they were for my kids or a birthday party, but they weren't. She would have thought I was crazy, I thought to myself, if I actually told her how I planned to use them. So, I just smiled, paid, and walked out the door.

The idea to purchase the balloons had come to me earlier in the day as I was driving. For some reason, I thought back to a funeral I had officiated years ago, one in which I buried an unborn child who died in his mother's womb. The mom and dad were devastated, as any parents would be. Because they were personal friends, I wanted even more than usual to make the service special. I was well aware that words alone couldn't possibly bring them the peace and comfort they deserved, so I decided to try something a little unusual.

As I stood at the gravesite doing the service, surrounded by dozens of family and friends of the couple, I told the story of another family who had a son that died at the age of one. To help their four year old daughter under-

stand her baby brother was in heaven, the parents gave their daughter a red helium balloon to release in his honor. They told her it would rise up all the way to heaven for her little brother. As they watched it climb into the air, the little girl innocently asked if her brother would be able to play with it that day. Unable to speak through the tears, the parents simply nodded. I had to control my own emotions as I told the story.

Just before the final benediction, I took my friends whose unborn child had died by the hand, along with their daughter and son, and led them to a spot away from the crowd. I asked everyone else to remain seated so the family could have a personal moment. The funeral director then brought me a red helium balloon for each family member. I had purchased the balloons on the way to the funeral and had them hidden out of sight.

Not far from the place where their child would be eternally laid to rest, I invited the family to pray and then to release their balloons into the sky. Together we held hands and watched in silence as the balloons rose up into the air and danced in the wind, tears streaming down each of our faces. I'd like to believe those balloons made it all the way to heaven that day, although the realist in me knows better. Regardless of whether they did or not, it was a beautiful moment which helped the family deal with their grief.

I couldn't help but to think about that funeral once again as I drove away from the party store with the three red helium balloons bouncing around in my backseat. My crisis wasn't anything like the ones my friends had experienced, but I needed the same type of emotional release. Although the worst days involving Debbie and Jessica were behind me, every now and then the pain still reached out and gripped my soul. Trying to let it go once and for all, I'd decided to have a balloon release of my own.

I turned off the causeway and parked in the sand by the beach road. The air was chilly, but several sunbathers and jet-skiers were enjoying the day. I felt a little out of place in my jeans and sweatshirt, holding on to my balloons, but it didn't matter. This was something I needed to do.

I walked down the beach until I was just about as far away as I could get from anyone else there. After I took a few moments to look out on the water, and to pray, I released the first balloon.

"I'm letting you go, Jessica" I said aloud, trying to convince myself of what I was saying. "Forgive me for holding on to the pain and know that I've forgiven you too. I'm letting go of the heartache and my hope of us being together. Live well and be happy."

I watched as the winds coming off the Gulf waters forced the balloon to dance and weave upward into the bright blue sky until it was only a tiny red speck high above. Then I released the second balloon. "I'm letting you go, Debbie. I'm sorry for the hurt and pain I've caused you. Please forgive me. I only want the best for you and the kids. Heal and be happy."

Again the balloon rose into air as I watched it sail out over the water. Finally, I released the third balloon. "Forgive me, Lord, for what I've done and for the people I've hurt. Please take away my guilt and pain. I don't want to hold on to them anymore. Help me Lord, please, to let it go. Amen."

As the last balloon drifted out of sight, I slowly walked back to my car and sat on the hood to take in the cool air and beautiful sunshine. Some people on the beach probably though that all I did was to release some silly red balloons into the air, but in my heart I knew it was more than that. Those balloons were symbols of my grief, and letting them go, I hoped, would allow me to release those emotions once and for all.

No doubt about it. It was time for me to move on.

❀ ❀ ❀

Stephen J. King

It's Your Choice...

You have a choice. You can address the emotional pain created by your grief, guilt, and regrets, and move beyond it...or...you can continue to let it burden your soul and control your life.

Seeking new horizons is about making a fresh start and new beginning. Dealing with your emotional pain from the past is an important step in that process. It isn't easy, but it is empowering. I encourage you to take the steps you need to take to heal. It's your choice...

For Your Journal...

- Think of a time when someone close to you died. Compare the emotions you felt then with the emotions you feel with respect to your divorce. What were the similarities? What were the differences? Which experience hurt more? Why?

- What is your greatest source of guilt and regret? How has that experience affected you? Are there steps you can take to make the situation better? If so, write down your thoughts.

- Where do you see yourself in the grief process described earlier in this chapter? Which stages have you already been through? Which are still yet to come? How can your awareness of these stages help you prepare emotionally as you continue to move toward healing?

- List the sources of your emotional pain. Which of those sources can be minimized or eliminated completely? Make notes next to each about what you need to do to begin this process.

- What broken relationships and bad experiences from the past still cause emotional pain but can't be changed? Are you willing to accept them and to let them go? Why or why not? How can you move toward acceptance and letting go so you can move forward with life?

Chapter 4

Dealing With Forgiveness...

"Forgive us our sins, as we forgive those who sin against us"
– From 'The Lord's Prayer' – Matthew 6:12 –

Adapted from an ancient Greek Fable – source unknown...

Long ago there was an ancient tribe of people who lived
deep beneath the surface of the earth.
Their dwelling underground had been home for generations,
ever since their forefathers had fled the chaos of the war
between good and evil centuries before to find refuge in a safe place.

The tribe had adapted well to the darkness of their subterranean home,
but deep within their collective soul was the dream
of one day returning to the light of the world.
They gathered nightly around village campfires
to read amazing stories about the sun and
its power to illumine all of life.
Inspired by the sacred writings of the Book of Elders,
the people believed a divine leader would come from above in the future
to lead them out of the darkness and back to the light.

One evening a stranger mysteriously appeared in their midst.
He claimed to be the prophet of truth foretold in scripture
and said he had been sent by God
to bring the people back to the light.
Captivated by his gentle spirit of truth and grace,
the people pledged to follow the prophet wherever he would lead
and made preparations that very evening for the journey
which would forever change their lives.

The journey to the light was long and hard, as the prophet predicted it would be,
and some of the people wanted to turn back along the way.
But spurred on by the hope of a better life
and encouraged by the rest of the village,
the group continued as one until they finally reached the small opening
leading to the earth's surface.

One by one, they excitedly entered the opening and emerged on the other side
with dreams of dancing in the sun on their mind,
ready to forever escape from their prison of darkness.

But then, suddenly, tragically, the unthinkable happened.
As the people emerged from the opening
they immediately fell to the ground and covered their eyes,
crying out in anguish.
The light proved too bright
for those who had lived in darkness so long,
and the villagers frantically scrambled to find the opening once again,
this time desiring to return to comfort of the familiar darkness.
Hope turned to fear and excitement quickly to rage and panic
when the opening to the earth below could not be found,
and they demanded the prophet to take them back.
"Return with us now" they cried, "or we will surely put you to death."

But the prophet of truth refused
And he pleaded with them to remain,
explaining their eyes would adjust to the light
and the pain of the present would give way to a glorious new life
as it was intended to be lived.
But the people wouldn't listen and,
fueled by their anger and fury,
blindly hurled stones in the direction of the prophet's voice
and struck him down.

As his lifeless body lie on the ground,
a second prophet, one of darkness and deceit,
suddenly appeared for the villagers.
Stepping over the prophet of truth and light,
the evil one lead the people back through the opening
into the bowels of the earth so they would
forevermore remain lost in darkness.

Alas, given the choice between good and evil,
the village chose darkness over the light of life.

❈ ❈ ❈

My journey from darkness back into the light was painful.

For me, 'the light' represented truth, honesty and integrity, traits I'd seemingly betrayed or lost along the way in my journey. I had allowed myself to live in the darkness for too long, failing to be honest with God, others, and myself. In fact, I feared the light. I feared the day my deeds would be exposed and I would have to face the consequences of my actions. I feared bringing pain upon those whom I loved. Somehow, I convinced myself, it was easier and safer to remain in the darkness where no one could see, where no one knew.

Yet at the same time, there was a yearning in my spirit to return to the light. I knew it was where I belonged and that, for me, life in the light was ultimately better than anything the darkness could offer. One way or another, I determined, I had to find my way back, regardless of how diffi-cult or how painful the journey might be. If I didn't, I knew the darkness would consume me. It was only a matter of time.

It was then I made the decision to confess and vowed to change my life. Through the entire experience, and even still today, my greatest need was to be forgiven.

The Importance Of Forgiveness...

Nothing is more important to our spiritual, mental, and emotional health as is forgiveness. Both forgiving others and receiving forgiveness from others have the power to cleanse the soul.

Forgiveness is an act of grace in which the forgiver pardons the one forgiven from whatever words, acts, or actions created the issue or ill-will in the first place. It enables both parties to release their negative feelings and emotions, such as anger, guilt, or fear, and permits them to move on with life while being free of animosity or thoughts of retribu-tion. Forgiveness doesn't remove the consequences which result from the words, acts, or actions, but it does allow each party to know that the issue has been addressed spiritually and emotionally.

We hear the phrase "forgive and forget" quite often, as if the two words are synonymous with each other, but they are not. We can rarely forget the experiences in which we hurt others or we are hurt by them. But even though we can't forget, we can always forgive or be forgiven.

Ultimately, forgiveness is a gift bestowed upon the forgiven by the forgiver. Sometimes we give that gift to another. Sometimes the gift is offered to us. And as we move toward new horizons, sometimes we learn that forgiveness is a gift we must eventually give to ourselves.

Prerequisites To Forgiveness...

In Biblical days, people with leprosy were declared 'unclean' by the temple priests. They were banished to leper colonies away from the main-stream, away from those who were without the disease, to prevent the leprosy from spreading. While this action was understandable in light of the medical science at the time, I can't help but to empathize with those who were forced to leave their communities and to live apart from everyone they knew and loved.

We don't have leper colonies anymore; at least, that's not what they are called nowadays. Instead, we have other names that we use to describe the places which separate the 'unclean' from the 'clean'. We call then rehab centers, mental wards, and ghettos; homeless shelters, nursing homes, and any of a hundred other names. Like the leper colonies of old, these institutions separate the 'sick' from the well, the diseased from the healthy, and the unwanted from the desired. It may not be how it is explained, but it is what we do.

The pain which existed for the lepers of old still exists for those who are considered the lepers of today. Separated physically, emotionally, and spiritually from those they love, and feeling displaced or cast aside by their community, the basic message is still the same. "You are unclean, and we can't have you around us anymore". The words aren't spoken, but the message is loud and clear.

Many considered me 'unclean' after the events which led to my divorce. In more ways than I care to remember, I was thrust into the role of a 21st century leper. My leprosy wasn't physical, but the affects were the same nonetheless. I felt spiritually and emotionally separated from my church and my community, and from many of the people I loved and who loved me. As a result, I was forced to adjust to a new life, far different than anything I'd ever known before.

Hopefully your situation isn't as dire as was mine, but if you've been through the pain of a divorce and lost family or friends in the process, then you understand, at least in part, what it means to be a 21st century leper. You know the pain of rejection; the feelings of being unwelcomed, unwanted, or cast aside; and the heartache of losing people who were once an important part of your life.

Just as the lepers of old longed for physical healing, I yearned for spiritual and emotional healing following my divorce. I knew deep inside that only one thing could make that type of healing possible for me –

forgiveness. I needed to be forgiven by God. I needed to be forgiven by those I had hurt. And perhaps most importantly at the time, I needed to be forgiven by myself.

Before I could be forgiven, however, there were two things that I knew I needed to do. First, I had to admit my mistakes and take responsibility for my actions, no matter what they were. And second, I had to find a way to deal with my own feelings of guilt, sorrow, and remorse by acknowledging my desperate need to be forgiven. Until those two things happened, I knew it would be impossible for me to receive the type of forgiveness I needed in order to free my soul.

The two steps weren't unique to me or to my situation. In fact, these same two steps are prerequisites for anyone who is in need of forgiveness, regardless of their circumstances or situation. Until we admit where we have erred, become accountable for what we've done, and recognize we were wrong, we will never experience true forgiveness.

You may ask, "What do I need to be forgiven for?" Only you can answer that question. But I'm certain of one thing – all of us have said or done things that we knew were wrong. There are no exceptions to this rule. And if you've recently gone through the heartache of an ugly divorce, there's a good chance you won't have to think too long or too hard to figure out what some of those things were for you.

In my years of ministry, I've worked with scores of couples who had marital problems. Several of those situations ended in divorce. At other times the couples were able to work things out and stay together. But in all of those experiences, I never encountered a single situation in which one spouse was 100% to blame for all of the problems present in the relationship. Don't misunderstand – there were situations which seemed to be 90%-10% or maybe even 95%-5% in terms of blame, but the point is that it was always the case both spouses contributed to the problems in some way, even if only as an enabler.

No one is blameless when it comes to divorce. All of us stand in need of forgiveness for any comments we made or actions we took which were intended to hurt, criticize, or put down. To think otherwise is naïve. New horizons begin with accepting ourselves for who we are, warts and all, and being accountable for our past with no 'ifs', 'ands', or 'buts' involved.

Here's another interesting fact about the lepers of old. When lepers were approached by someone who didn't have the disease, the Law of Moses required them to cover their upper lip and cry out, "Unclean, unclean". Once again, the law was designed to protect those who were uninfected, but I imagine the psychological affects upon the ones crying out were devastating. Constantly reminded they were undesirable and realizing that physical healing was beyond their control, it was impossible to escape the reality of their condition.

The big difference between the lepers of old and us is that we do have the opportunity to facilitate our healing. Divorce can rip our world apart and the pain is very real, but we don't have to remain in our 'leprosy'. We can take the steps we need to take to get better and make the choice to heal.

There comes a time when we must stop crying out "unclean" in our words and through our actions. There comes a time when we must stop living like we are diseased. We can be accountable and seek the forgiveness we need to heal. That forgiveness begins with God. And thankfully, for both you and me, His forgiveness is always available, even when the forgiveness of others isn't.

❀❀❀

Approximately two and a half years after the divorce...

I hiked into the wooded area behind my house until I found a sturdy oak that I felt was right. As I set down my backpack, I fumbled around for some nails loosely scattered on the bottom and pulled out my old hammer, the one with half of a claw missing.

I paused for a moment, thinking about the anger I'd expressed toward my ex-wife earlier in the day – anger that had much more to do with my attitude at the time than with anything she had done – and I pounded a nail into the trunk of the tree. The echo reverberated through the woods.

Then I thought about the pain I'd caused my kids over the last couple of years. My relationships with each of them were strong, but I knew the divorce was something that would impact them for the rest of their lives. I pounded a second nail into the tree just a few inches above the first.

On and on I went thinking and pounding, then thinking and pounding some more. Each time I thought about an incident or an attitude in my life for which I needed forgiveness. I covered all the bases – family, friends, Debbie and Jessica, my former church, and many more.

Eventually I ran out of nails and stepped back to view the image I'd created on the tree. It was a cross – a cross of nails. It wasn't straight and it certainly wasn't skillfully made, but it was impossible to mistake it for anything else.

As I made my way back home, I focused my thoughts on the One who had been nailed to a tree for my sins 2000 years ago. I thanked God for making His grace and forgiveness available to me, and to anyone who is willing to ask, through the death of His Son.

I wondered if anybody would ever see that cross of nails built on a tree in the middle of nowhere. And if they did, I wondered what they might think. Maybe it would be a symbol of hope to them, as it was for me. The more I thought about it, more I wondered how they could possibly see anything else.

Thank you, Lord, for Your forgiveness. Amen.

Acknowledge your need to be forgiven for whatever you haven't been forgiven for. As important, never forget God's forgiveness is always available, always total and complete. You have no need to cry out 'unclean' anymore.

With God's forgiveness as the foundation, let's examine three other areas which are also important for our healing. Those areas are forgiving yourself, forgiving others, and seeking to be forgiven by others.

Making The Choice To Forgive Yourself...

It isn't easy to forgive yourself when you've hurt the people you love and care about. It's even harder still when you know the pain that you've caused will remain for years to come.

I accepted God's forgiveness for what happened in my life long before I was able to forgive myself. After the divorce, I beat myself up mentally and emotionally, and felt like I deserved whatever bad came my way. My guilt was like a cancer robbing me of life, especially in those first few months after my family fell apart. Those were some of the darkest days I've ever known.

I wish I could tell you that I was able to snap out of it and there was an easy way to make things right, but I can't because there wasn't. What I can tell you is this, however, – you must learn to forgive yourself to be mentally and emotionally whole once again if you want to make a new beginning. You can't change the past, but you can forgive yourself, and move beyond it. It takes time, but you can do it.

For me, forgiving myself was a process. For a long time I felt unworthy of being forgiven, by myself or anyone else. Gradually, however, over a period of several months which included counseling and some deep soul searching, I was able to finally come to the point where I forgave myself and reclaimed my life. I want you to be able to do the same.

Ina Lafoe was a friend of mine who was a member of my first church in Tampa. A wonderful, grandmotherly type of woman, Ina and I continued to stay in touch through the years as I moved on to Palm Harbor. Once a year, usually around the Christmas holidays, our families would get together to exchange presents and catch up with each other. Ina eventually died at the age of 95. I had the honor – the privilege, really – of officiating her funeral.

Ina loved my kids. Every year she sent them a birthday card with a few one dollar bills in it. I don't ever remember her missing a single one. And, of course, she always bought them gifts at Christmas, usually more than one. The presents were never fancy or expensive – that wasn't who Ina was as she lived humbly on a tight budget – but they were just a simple reminder to my kids that they were loved.

Because of issues related to Ina's health as she continued to age and my own emotional state after the divorce, there were a couple of years when we missed getting together with our families at Christmas. We talked on the phone during that time, and I visited her on two separate occasions tephen J. King

when she was in the hospital, but we weren't able to coordinate a holiday visit with everyone. I didn't realize it at the time, but Ina had continued to buy gifts for the kids each of those years and quietly tucked them away in her closet, hoping the time would come when she would see them again.

Finally, one Saturday in December just two years back, Ina felt good and we arranged a 'Christmas brunch and gift exchange' with my Mom and kids, and Ina's daughter, Beverly, at a local Sonny's restaurant. The scene was almost comical. My family brought a gift for both Ina and Beverly, but they arrived with four large plastic bags of beautifully wrapped presents for us, mostly for the kids. There were so many presents, in fact, that I could barely fit them in the trunk of my car! We had a great time talking, laughing, and opening presents that day, and I was grateful for the time together. Unfortunately, Ina passed away the following year.

I've thought about that gathering several times since Ina's passing. If we hadn't gotten together when we did, there is a good chance all of those beautifully wrapped gifts which Ina prepared for the kids would have simply remained tucked away in her closet. How sad that would have been, denying joy to both Ina as the giver and my kids as the receivers as was intended. Instead, they would have just remained in a dark corner somewhere – unopened, unused, and unappreciated.

Forgiving yourself is like opening one of those gifts, except that it is a gift you give to yourself. It's completely up to you. You can leave it packed away and unopened, never allowing it to bring the freedom and joy it was intended to bring as you continue to live with your guilt and regrets; or you can open it, forgive yourself, and give yourself the opportunity to begin again.

Open the gift. Forgive yourself. And make a new beginning. Remember, you can't erase the past, but you can make the choice to move beyond it. The gift lies wrapped before you. It's ready to open.

Making The Choice To Forgive Others...

The grace we need to forgive others is born out of the grace that we ourselves have received in being forgiven by God. Forgiving ourselves is an important step as we heal, but the ability to forgive those who have hurt us is a close second. When we harbor ill in our soul toward another human being and won't forgive them, we only end up hurting ourselves. The bottom line is that the path to new horizons is about both experiencing forgiveness and learning to forgive as well.

Think for a moment. Who do you need to forgive? Who, at the mere mention of their name, stirs feelings of anger, bitterness and resentment within your spirit? Who has disappointed you, hurt you, or treated you wrongly; or demeaned you, criticized you, or put you down?

If there is a person who came to mind when you answered those questions, or perhaps many people, then you probably need to work on forgiving them. Not for their sake necessarily – the truth is they may not care one way or the other – but for yours.

But, you say, these people have hurt you and you're not sure you want to forgive them after everything they've done to you. Maybe, even now, they continue to criticize and mistreat you. Or maybe they've completely written you off, ignored you, and made it clear they don't want to see you ever again. What about those situations? Is it still necessary, or even possible, for us to forgive then?

The answer, plain and simple, is yes. It is possible to forgive and you need to work on doing it. Whether they accept your forgiveness or not isn't the issue. This is much more about you and your emotional and spiritual health right now than it is them. It's about what is in your heart and your soul, and about making your new start in life. Their response, whether it is positive, negative, or neutral, doesn't change the fact that you need to forgive them.

I know it isn't easy to forgive. I've been there too. But it's impossible to fully heal any other way. We can't be healthy if we are holding on to bitterness, anger, and resentment. It's not possible. As when we forgive ourselves, the ability to forgive others begins with a choice and a desire to forgive them. We have to choose to work towards forgiveness before it will ever happen.

One way or another, your choice – either to forgive or to not – will affect the way you heal and begin again. Either you will release the bitterness, anger, and resentment in your heart or you won't. Just like always, it's your choice.

❀ ❀ ❀

Two years after the divorce...

Patty was once a close friend. She used to work for me as the Director of Children's Ministries when I was at the church. I always admired her creative approach to ministry with the kids and usually depended on her whenever I needed help with a special event or a program.

Patty and I were good friends outside of work as well. Because our daughters were the same age and were also good friends, our families spent a lot of time together and enjoyed each other's company.

When I announced my decision to resign after the affair, I knew a lot of people would be angry or upset with me, and I was certainly right. Six months later, when Debbie decided to divorce me, things became even tougher. As I struggled to find my way during and after that time, my close friends were there to help and support me. I anticipated Patty would be one of those friends. I was wrong.

Patty all but wrote me off after my divorce. Other than a few brief and very impersonal conversations when I dropped off my daughter at her house to play, she completely ignored me. I'm not sure why exactly. She never said. But I assumed it was because she wanted me to know she was 'siding' with Debbie. It's one of the unfortunate realities of divorce, but some people feel they have to choose sides with one ex-spouse or the other, as if they can't support both. Patty wasn't the only one who cut me off after the divorce, but I think it hurt me more than most because I thought she was a good friend.

I guess we all eventually learn to accept the things we can't change, whether we want to or not, and soon I accepted that my 'friendship' with Patty was what it was. I viewed it as just another casualty from the events of my past.

Then one day two years after the divorce, seemingly out of the blue, Patty called and asked if we could meet for lunch. She said there were some things she needed to get off her chest and she wanted to talk. At her request, we met at a restaurant several miles from where she lived, perhaps because she was worried about being seen with me.

Patty talked openly about her feelings at the time of my divorce. She said she had difficulty accepting the fact that I had an affair and that she couldn't believe it. I understood her feelings since I still had trouble believing it myself. Not only was she angry and resentful toward me back then, but she also found herself wanting to blame me for every problem that had occurred in the church since I left, whether I was actually responsible for them or not. Once again, she wasn't the only one.

She also said she had questions – lots and lots of questions. She wanted to know what had been real about my faith and our friendship and what wasn't. She wanted to know why I chose to have the affair in the first place, and how I could do that to Debbie. And she wanted to know if I had any regrets, or if I'd do anything different if I had the chance to go back in time. On and on she went with her questions, barely finishing one before she asked the next.

I answered each one honestly and told Patty, as I had said to many others before her, that there was no justification for the affair. I was responsible for my actions and I was wrong in what I did. Regardless of whether I was a pastor at the time or not, I made a series of bad choices and mistake which hurt a lot of people. I also told her I understood why she felt as she did back then and now, and I was sorry to have caused her pain.

Then it was my turn to ask a question. I asked her why she decided to meet me now, two years after everything had happened. She answered with a single word – "Closure".

I wanted to tell Patty how I felt hurt by the way she treated me back then and to ask her why she completely turned her back on me, but I didn't say any of it. It just wasn't the time. Maybe we would talk again and I would get those answers, but she had asked for this meeting and I knew she was the one who needed to be heard.

We ended up talking for over an hour, both laughing and crying throughout. Sometimes the conversation was awkward, but in my heart I was glad that we had the opportunity to reconnect for a while.

I realized something even more important as I left the restaurant after we had met. In that hour we spent together, I had forgiven Patty. She didn't ask for my forgiveness. From her perspective, she probably didn't think that she needed to. But I needed to forgive her. I needed to let go of the hurt that

I felt she had caused me at a time when I needed my friends and to let go of the negative feelings in my heart. There was no need to hold on to any of it any longer. So, I finally did what I should've done long before – I forgave her.

I'm not sure if Patty received the closure that she was looking for from our conversation, but I hope so. I know that I did. I let go of a lot of feelings that I didn't like having around.

It made me wonder why I hadn't tried to have our conversation sooner.

❀ ❀ ❀

Set your mind to working towards forgiveness for the people who have hurt you. It's the right thing to do, for you and them. And it is one of many choices which lead to a new beginning.

Making The Choice To Seek Forgiveness From Others...

Asking for forgiveness can be scary and intimidating, whether the hurt we caused was intentional or not. Ideally we would always do the right things and never put ourselves in the position of having to ask to be forgiven, but reality teaches us otherwise. If and when we do ask for forgiveness from someone else, we hopefully do it because we know that it is the right thing to do.

I attended a Bill Gothard Youth Conference a long time ago, back when I was in high school. I really don't remember much about it, but there is one lesson I learned which has remained with me all these many years later. In fact, it's a lesson I've used often when I have taught classes, preached sermons, or been in counseling situations.

The lesson is that it is important to have a clear conscience. Gothard's basic premise was this – the conscience is the window to the soul and, when it is dark and muddied by anger, bitterness, or guilt, our lives will reflect those things through our words and actions. By the same token, when our conscience is clear – when we have dealt with our hurts and mistakes to the best of our ability – then that too will be reflected in our words and actions, and we will have contentment and peace of mind.

Gothard was right. I've seen this principle at work in my life just as you probably have too. When my conscience was clear, I was generally at peace, regardless of whatever else might have been happening in my life at the time. Conversely, when my conscience was troubled, dark, and muddied, contentment and peace of mind were hard to come by.

Here's what Gothard had us do in response to that teaching. Right there in the middle of a huge auditorium with a thousand others present, he asked us to write one or more letters of apology to those we had hurt or offended in the past. Regardless of their response to the letter, he said, we would take a huge step toward having a clear conscience by knowing we had made an honest and sincere effort to seek their forgiveness. With that understanding, he continued, we would be on the way to having the peace of mind which all of us desire.

Again Gothard was right. I can still remember how good it felt to write my letters and put them in the mail. I was sure that asking for forgiveness from the people I wrote to was the right thing to do. All I needed was the invitation to do it.

The truth of that simple teaching has been affirmed and reaffirmed to me time and time again through the years. I've found there is a tremendous, life-giving power in an honest apology which also seeks forgiveness, whether it comes in the form of a letter or a face to face conversation.

When I have counseled others, I've often suggested that they write a letter of apology as the first step to seeking forgiveness from someone else. Writing a letter, as opposed to having a face to face conversation at that point, has certain advantages. The writer is able to carefully edit his thoughts to make sure that the message conveys exactly what he wants it to say. Furthermore, the reader is able to focus on the message being conveyed by the writer without the pressure of an immediate response or the conflicting emotions which are often present in a conversation. I believe that, for writer and reader alike, a simple letter of apology can be a wonderful first step in the process of forgiveness or reconciliation.

I've written several letters of apology myself over the years. Some were to directly ask for forgiveness. Others were written in an attempt to clear up a misunderstanding, or perhaps express a concern. As I said earlier,

I've also worked with many other people in counseling or other settings as they have written letters to spouses, parents, children, co-workers, or friends. There have even been a few times when I've had counselees write to someone they didn't know or, in one case, to someone who had passed away. Regardless of the issue, situation, or relationship involved, a heart-felt letter of apology which expresses the thoughts and feelings of the one who is writing is one of the most positive, non-threatening ways there is to address a problem.

But understand that a letter isn't a 'cure all, end all' in terms of the process of forgiveness. Usually the writer and reader will still need to talk at some point in order to bring the closure to the issue that both of them need. Still, a letter is an important first step. It's a beginning, a means to an end, which opens the door to the possibility of forgiveness, a clear conscience, and peace of mind in the days ahead.

❋ ❋ ❋

Over two years after the divorce...

I wrote the letter, sealed the envelope, and dropped it in the mail, wondering how Dennis would feel as he read it. We'd been friends for 20 years, ever since back in the days when he was a leader in my first church, but it had been almost a year since we had last spoken. It was time for me to set things right.

After I left my church in Tampa and moved to Palm Harbor, Dennis and his family relocated to Nashville, Tennessee, where Dennis worked for several years. Eventually he and his wife, Donna, decided to move back to Florida and bought a house in the Palm Harbor area, at least in part so they could attend my church. Unfortunately, only a few months after they had moved in, I announced my resignation.

Dennis is a generous man with a heart of gold. Successful in business and a good father and husband, he was always the first one to volunteer when somebody needed help or was down on their luck. It was no different when I happened to be that person. Dennis and Donna were tremendously encouraging and supportive as I struggled to find my place in life after the divorce.

At one point, at a time when I was unemployed and out of money, they opened their home to me and invited me to stay as long as I needed. Dennis was also the first person to urge me to get back in ministry, although I was only able to make that decision a year or two later. I'll always be grateful for the kindness that Dennis and Donna showed me during that very difficult time. They are wonderful people.

The problem arose when Dennis loaned me money on two separate occasions, both times to help me cover my alimony payments. I felt uncomfortable borrowing the money, especially since I was out of work at the time and didn't know how I would pay it back, but it was the only way I could prevent falling behind to Debbie, something I desperately was trying to avoid. A few months after receiving the second loan from Dennis, I took the advice of an attorney and ended up declaring bankruptcy. Again it was something I didn't want to do, but at that point I felt that I was out of options.

As a result of the bankruptcy, my unsecured debts, which included my loans from Dennis, were legally absolved. It was always my intention, both then and now, to pay him back regardless of whether the courts said I had to or not, but I knew that seemed like an empty promise in light of situation at the time. He never mentioned one negative word about the money and, in fact, told me not to worry until I got back on my feet, but I felt awkward about it.

We basically stopped communicating not long after. It was my fault. I was embarrassed by the bankruptcy and that I couldn't start paying him back. I also wondered if Dennis ever questioned why I borrowed the money in the first place if I knew I would end up in a bankruptcy a few short months later. The truth is I didn't know when I borrowed the money. In fact, at that point I hadn't even considered it. Only later did I decide it was the path I had to take if I was going to survive. Still, I understood how it must have appeared.

Dennis had been on my mind lately as I slowly continued to put the pieces of my life back together. Although he never said anything negative about what had happened, I felt obligated to apologize.

And so, the letter began, "Dear Dennis..."

I confessed my embarrassment, apologized for avoiding him, and asked for his forgiveness. I also took the opportunity to thank him once again for our friendship and his kindness at the time when I needed it most. Lastly, I reaffirmed my pledge to pay him back in full when I was able. I ended by telling him that I loved him and missed spending time together.

I don't know if the letter will make a difference, but I know it felt good for me to address the issue. It had been bothering for quite a while. My hope is that, at some time in the near future, we will sit down and talk things out. We'll see...

❀ ❀ ❀

We all have a tendency to avoid the things we don't like to do, and asking someone for forgiveness usually falls into that category. We don't like to feel vulnerable or exposed, which often happens when we apologize. We worry about being rejected or maybe that the person will become angry. Sometimes we even convince ourselves that the other person won't forgive us anyway, so why should we even ask. Or we tell ourselves it's not the right time to apologize, ignoring that the 'right time' just never seems to come.

However we spin it, the reality is there is no better time than right now to begin healing and to seek forgiveness from those we have hurt. We need closure. We need peace of mind.

I mentioned earlier that all I needed was an invitation when I wrote my letters and did what I already knew was the right thing to do. Sometimes a simple invitation is all we need to stop putting off what we've been avoiding. I want to offer you an invitation now.

I invite you to seek the forgiveness you need from the people you have hurt or offended. You know who they are, just like I knew mine. I invite you to 'bury the hatchet', to have the courage to help yourself, and to move toward healing and peace of mind.

How? You do it by recognizing and addressing two problems which often prevent us from taking action. The first is procrastination. The second is fear.

There is only one way to overcome our inclination to procrastinate, and that is to quit procrastinating. It boils down to this – we need to make the decision to take action and do what we need to do when we need to do it. There is no other way to overcome the problem. Make the commitment to stop procrastinating and to act now rather than later. In the words of the old Nike theme, "Just do it!" Don't wait. Don't hesitate. Don't delay and no more excuses. If you need to seek forgiveness from someone, then do it and do it now. Not tomorrow, not next week or next month, but now. Just do it!

The person you are thinking about will, in all likelihood, appreciate the fact that you acted sooner rather than later. You'll also feel better knowing that you have done what you could to try to right the relationship. Unless you have a very good reason to wait, why postpone the opportunity to heal? For your own peace of mind and theirs, just do it.

The 'just do it' philosophy can also be helpful to us as we address our fears. There is no shot of courage we can take or no pill to become braver. Courage, at least as it relates to asking for forgiveness, is simply the boldness to take action. The longer we wait, the more fear will build, and the more stress and anxiety we will feel. The result is that we will delay, which leads right back to the first problem of procrastination. If we wait for our fear to go away, then we might just be waiting forever. Once again, there is no time like the present to take action and make things right. Just do it!

Once you have dealt with your procrastination and fear, and decided to begin seeking the forgiveness you need, then it's time to get to work. How do you actually begin? Here is a guide to help you:

- **First, make a list** – Make a list of everyone you can think of who you have hurt, offended, or wronged. Next, write today's date by one of those names, perhaps choosing a person who you believe will be the most open to your apology. Then write tomorrow's date by a second name, and the date two days from now by a third, and so on and so forth until every name has a date written beside it.
- **Second, write one letter each day** – Now that you've identified and dated your list, the important work begins. Write one letter of apology each day to the person who has that date written next to their name. By the way, if you did what you were asked to do in the first step, this

means that you will actually begin today. Just do it! Take action and make it happen. The letters will become easier to write as you go along.

What should the letters say? Well, only you can answer that question based on the situation and your relationship with the individual. The contents of each letter will differ, but just make sure that every word is honest and sincere. And, of course, make sure your letters include an apology asking for forgiveness.

Rewrite or edit your letters until they say exactly what you want them to say, and in the exact way that you want them to say it. Be careful not to unintentionally accuse the person to whom you are writing of any wrongdoing. Remember, the purpose of these letters is for you to take responsibility for your actions of the past and to ask for forgiveness, not to accuse them in any way. If they have hurt or offended you also, then that is a conversation for another time.

- **Third, follow up your letter with a phone call** – Lastly, follow up your letter by calling the people to whom you have written a few days after they have received it. The timing of this call is important. You want to allow them the time they need to think about what you have written, but you also don't want to let so much time elapse that they question your intentions or misinterpret you motives. What should you say when you call? Ask them if they are willing to meet with you and tell them your sole purpose in wanting to get together is to seek their forgiveness in person. You've already done the hard part by writing the letter and sharing your feelings. When you meet, simply reiterate what you wrote and ask to be forgiven. This is the step which leads to closure. Whether they choose to forgive you or not, you will feel better in knowing that you have made an honest attempt to set things right.

Many times fear kicks in just before we make the follow up calls. That is understandable since we're never quite sure of how they will react. Sometimes our imagination is our own worst enemy. We conjure up scenarios in our mind of what could go wrong or build up the drama of the situation to the point where we hesitate calling at all.

I can't take away your fear, but I can relate to it. I've had those feelings too, many times. Based on my experience, however, I can also tell you that most of those follow up calls were far more positive than I ever imagined. That wasn't always the case, but most of the time.

One last word of advice. In the event someone does react negatively to your letter or phone call and says things you don't like, be gracious in your response. Their comments may sting at the time, but you can't control what they think or feel. They may be at a different place than you mentally, emotionally, or spiritually, or they may just need more time to process what they feel. Regardless of what they say, respond with the same compassion and dignity that you hope they show you when you call.

So just do it! Stop procrastinating, set aside your fears, and seek forgiveness from those you have hurt or offended. It's the right thing to do and, as importantly, you'll take a giant step on the path to new horizons.

❋ ❋ ❋

Almost three years after the divorce...

The dumpster was already full as I heaved the last garbage bag over the upper rim and onto the pile. Given the contents of the bag, I was eager to get rid of it.

Three years after the divorce, I had finally moved into a place of my own. It wasn't big, elaborate, or fancy – just a small two bedroom condo in the middle of a huge complex – but it was mine and it felt good to own a home again. After several days of cleaning and painting, I picked up my furniture at the storage unit and began to move in.

One of my first tasks was to set up the computer desk and file cabinets in the corner of my bedroom. Wanting to start fresh in my new surroundings, I decided to go through the boxes of papers from my storage unit and to get rid of what I no longer needed. Some of the papers were six or eight years old, dating back to the time when I was still married. It was amazing to me to see some of the junk I'd held on to through each of my four moves since.

As I unloaded one box, I came across a faded, wrinkled sheet of yellow, legal-sized paper barely attached to the pad it was from. Written across the top in capital letters was the word 'FORGIVENESS', and underneath were several names written neatly in two columns. I recognized it immediately. I had made the list not long after I resigned and used it as a guide to help me track the people I needed to contact. All of them listed were individuals I wanted to apologize to. There seemed to be more names on the list than I remembered.

Rather than just ball it up and throw it away as I'd done with so many other papers in the box, I took time to read each name on the list one by one. Scattered among them were family members and friends, people from Debbie's family and from Jessica's, and several members of my former church in Palm Harbor.

Most of the names had check marks next to them, meaning that I had written a letter to them or apologized in person, and in many cases both. Five or six names had dashes, evidently indicating that I'd had contact with them but still needed to talk further. A few of the names had no marks beside them at all. Those were the ones I had yet to contact.

In all, there were over 40 names on the list – 40 people to whom I felt the need to ask for their forgiveness. That's a lot. The number reminded me of how painful and chaotic things were in my life back then.

As I read the names I'd written almost three years before, I felt a sense of pride in knowing I'd eventually contacted all of the people on my list except two. While a few of those conversations were painful, most of them had turned out to be better than I expected. Nearly all of the people were still involved in my life today.

I finally wadded up the paper and threw it on the floor where the pile of trash was growing. I didn't need it anymore. In fact, to tell you the truth, I was anxious to get rid of it once and for all. In my mind, throwing it away represented just another step on the way to new horizons.

It felt good to finally take out the trash and start fresh.

❀ ❀ ❀

May you know the blessings of God's grace and forgiveness. May you have the strength and compassion to forgive yourself and others. And may you have the courage to seek the forgiveness you need from those you have hurt. Just do it!

It's Your Choice...

You have a choice, or rather several choices, to make. You can choose to accept God's forgiveness, to forgive yourself and those who have hurt you, and to seek forgiveness from those whom you have hurt...or...you can choose to continue to live with the negative feelings, guilt, and pain which results from the regrets of the past. No one can force you to forgive or to seek forgiveness, but ultimately it is the only choice which will lead to the healing, closure, and peace of mind you desire. It's your choice...

For Your Journal...

• Write three paragraphs. In the first, define what forgiveness means to you. In the second, identify the barriers which exist which prevent forgiveness from occurring between two people. And in the third, describe the benefits of forgiveness, whether received or granted.

• Make a list of the words, actions, and attitudes for which you need to forgive yourself. What has prevented you from forgiving yourself in the past? How does your understanding of God's grace relate to the issue of self-forgiveness?

• Make a list of people you need to forgive. Next to each name, write down the reason you haven't forgiven them yet. Then ask yourself these questions about each: Should I forgive this person now? Why or why not? How would forgiving this person positively affect me now and in the future?

• If you haven't done it yet, make a list of the people from whom you need to seek forgiveness. Write a date, beginning with today, next to every name. Commit yourself to writing one letter each day to the people on your list and to follow up with a phone call a few days later. Keep notes in your journal to describe your feelings and the interaction with each.

Chapter 5
Dealing With Family
And Friends...

"Faith, hope, love, abide these three; but the greatest of these is love"
– 1 Corinthians 13:13 –

Divorce changes our relationships. That is certainly true when it involves our former spouse, but it also changes the relationships we have with our children, family members, and friends. Many times those changes are stressful and difficult to manage. As we set our sights on new horizons, we come to realize the best thing we can do for everyone involved is to get along as peacefully and positively as possible.

❋❋❋

About a month after the divorce...

"It should have happened years ago, Mom. I haven't been happy for a while, and neither has Debbie." The words were difficult to admit, but they were true. I had finally arrived at the point where I could say them out loud.

Sitting with my Mom in the living room of her humble, one bedroom villa, my heart hurt for her. I'd always taken care of my Mom financially and in other ways, ever since I was in college. She had been through a lot in life and deserved whatever help I could give her in order to make her 'golden years' comfortable and worry free. The last seven or eight months, as I went through my resignation and divorce, had been hard on her, just as they had been for me.

My Mom is an amazing woman. She's a survivor. She dropped out of school in the eighth grade to support her family. Then she married my Dad in her early 20's. They spent 17 years together before divorcing when I was young. With no marketable job skills, my Mom provided for my brother and me by working 12-14 hours a day as a waitress and a maid. Then she received her 'big break', a job with the Hillsborough County School System cleaning offices and classrooms at a local high school. The salary allowed her to scale back to only one job and gave her health and vacation benefits for the first time in her life. She never remarried, though she did have offers, and she rarely complained, even when I used to find her late at night, exhausted and half asleep on the couch because she was too tired to make it back to her bedroom after working a double shift.

My Mom loved being with our family – Debbie, myself, and of course, the grandkids – and was always there to help us with whatever we needed, whether it was watching the kids, doing laundry, or running an errand. I tried to shield her from the problems that Debbie and I had through the years because I didn't want her to worry.

Then the affair happened, followed by the divorce. I was hurting and embarrassed, and devastated by the thought that I'd be living apart from my kids. Those early months right after the divorce were especially tough, and I opened up more with my mom and shared my feelings about everything that had happened. To my surprise, she was aware there were problems in my relationship with Debbie well before everything broke. She never said anything about them, but she knew things just weren't quite right, she said. As someone who has been through a broken relationship and a divorce herself, she saw the warning signs. I realized then that I should have talked to her earlier about some of the issues Debbie and I were facing. Maybe I could have avoided some of my mistakes. Live and learn.

I gained a whole new level of respect for my Mom through those conversations. There were moments when her encouragement kept me going during my struggles, and the advice she gave about some of the issues she anticipated would become a problem for Debbie and me in the future were right on target. But what I appreciated most of all – what I will always remember about my Mom until the day that I die – was the way she expressed her unconditional love for me.

Unconditional love – love with no strings attached and with no terms, conditions, or stipulations; a love that never quits, never dies, and never ends, no matter what. It's how God loves us and I'm proud to say it's also how my Mom loves me. I hope I'm able to follow her example in the way I love my kids.

Never was her love for me more evident than on the day I sat talking with her in the living room of her condo. "Just remember," she said, "I love you no matter what. You're my son and I'll always be in your corner. I'm sorry that everything happened as it did between you and Debbie, but life goes on and we'll make the best of it from here. More than anything, married or divorced, I want you to be happy, and I'll do anything I can to help."

No matter what life ends up throwing at you, no loves you like your mom.

❀ ❀ ❀

Let Your Family Help...

Statistics say the divorce rate is climbing. The percentages indicate there are fewer 'traditional' families – mom, dad, and 2.3 kids – now than in the past. Some argue those statistics and the rise in the divorce rate points to the erosion of the family structure in our society. It's hard to disagree. Yet I also believe it is precisely because of those statistics that family connections are more than ever. The structure of the family may be changing, but our need to feel connected, to feel a sense of belonging, has never been greater.

Starting over after divorce is easier when you have the support of your family. Not easy, but easier. Some people come from large families with lots of relatives who can provide support. Others have small families with only a few relatives to depend on. And still others have no immediate family at all, depending instead on their 'surrogate family' of close friends to help them through the hard times. Regardless of how you define family and who you consider to be part of yours, it's helpful to have them standing with you through the trauma of divorce.

My family, aside from my three children, is very small. I have one brother who is seven years older than me. Regrettably, we've never really been close. Maybe it was the differences in our ages or our different philosophies concerning life and living, but we never shared the brotherly bond that so many siblings do. I wish things were different between us. I think we both missed out on something special along the way.

My Dad, whose death I wrote about earlier, passed away over 20 years ago. He was a good man, a lifer in the Air Force who retired after 30 years. In my younger days, his career often took him away from our family for long periods of time. His divorce from my Mom when I was a child, combined with his untimely death while he was still relatively young, limited our time together. Still, I'm thankful for the years that we did share and I have a lot of fond memories of him to fall back on.

Then there is my Mom. She is in her mid-eighties and still going strong. As you gathered from the vignette above, she has had a more difficult road in life than most. But through it all, her attitude about life has remained incredibly positive. In my opinion, her attitude is the one thing which has kept her going when others might have quit, and it's still her greatest asset today. Of all the lessons she has taught me, perhaps the most important is that our quality of life is determined more by our attitude than by our circumstances. She's never said those exact words to me, but she didn't have to. She lives them everyday.

I've learned there are two types of people in the world – those who choose to live life with a positive attitude and those who don't. The ones who don't seem to always believe life is unfair and that the world is out to get them. They complain about their problems more than actually doing something about them and their negative perspective on life seems to be present in everything they do and say. Often times they are bitter and resentful, or angry and unpleasant, and they never seem to be satisfied. It's a tough way to live.

On the other hand, those with a positive attitude have all the same problems as the first group, but they react to them differently. They refuse to let bitterness and negativity control or destroy their lives, and they treat people with kindness and respect. Their demeanor is characterized by words like grace, compassion, and hope, and they are a joy to be around. They laugh more, love more, and as a result, live more.

I don't have to tell you which of these two attitudes represents how I want to live. I've seen both types through the years, just as you have too, and I have experienced a little of both in my own life during the ups and downs of the last few years. There is no doubt in my mind that a positive attitude always leads to better mental, emotional, and spiritual health than a negative one. It really is that simple.

We'll examine the virtues of a positive attitude more fully in a later chapter, but it's important to realize here and now that we always have a choice in the way we respond to the struggles of divorce. We can either allow our circumstances to control our attitude, which leads to restlessness, stress, and unhappiness, or we can decide to embrace a positive attitude, deal with our circumstances, and make the best of our situation. The first option allows outside factors to control us. The second puts us in control as we work toward the best outcome possible.

I fell into the trap of allowing my circumstances to control me for too long after my divorce, and the result was that my attitude was negatively affected. Instead of working to improve my situation, I became content to feel sorry for myself when things weren't going well and seemingly became more depressed as time went by.

Eventually I realized that I had to change my attitude if my life was going to improve. I worked hard at reshaping my perspective in a positive direction and, as I did, my general outlook on life began to change too. The problems were still there, but I dealt with them differently. And in the process, I rediscovered the lesson my Mom had exemplified – a positive approach to life always leads to better mental, emotional, and spiritual health than a negative one.

Thankfully, my Mom was there for me when I needed her and helped me to walk through my difficult times, even though there were moments when I tried to shut her out. She gave me the space I needed to find my way but was always just a phone call away when I wanted to talk. She did this not only because she loved me and we were family, but because she wanted me to heal and move on.

You have family – a mom or dad, a brother or sister, or even members of your surrogate family – who want to help you too. And they will, if you let them.

One of the oddities of the human spirit is that we sometimes push away from the people who love us the most during the very times when we need them most. Sometimes we do it out of embarrassment or pride, or because we feel overwhelmed and want to live out our misery alone, but for whatever reasons we do it, it's a mistake. Pushing away from your family while you are dealing with the trials and tribulations of divorce only denies you the opportunity to receive the help you need to heal.

Your family wants to help you, so let them. Tell them what you need and how they can help, and don't be afraid to lean on them for support. They love you and want the best for you. In good times and bad, they are there. After all, isn't that what family is all about?

Caring For Your Kids...

Like any parent dealing with a divorce, my greatest concern was for my children.

❀ ❀ ❀

A week after the divorce...

I was excited to be picking up my kids for the first time since I'd moved out the week before, but I also battled my emotions as I turned into the driveway of the place I had called home for the last 11 years. Everything in the neighborhood looked the same, but somehow it all felt very different.

Because Debbie and I had agreed that it was best for her to take the kids to Alabama as I moved out of the house, I hadn't seen my children in nearly two weeks. It seemed much longer, and I missed them terribly. I wondered what type of reception I would receive at the door. This divorce thing was new to me and I wasn't sure that I knew what to do or how to act. More importantly, it was new to the kids too.

In the past, I was always around whenever my kids needed me or wanted to talk, but I was painfully aware that was about to change. I knew that I would miss the simple, everyday times with them the most – helping with their homework, eating dinner together, waking them up to get ready for school, or tucking them in when it was time for bed. Those would be my most difficult adjustments I'd have to make. Maybe for them too.

I tried to look calm as I walked to the front door – the same front door that I'd walked right through a thousand times before whenever I arrived home. I glanced around quickly to see if any of the neighbors were watching as I knocked, a little embarrassed that I had to wait for someone to answer.

Shadow, our Black Labrador Retriever, was the first to see me through the window and immediately began barking uncontrollably. Seconds later I heard the familiar sounds of kids running wildly through the house as each tried to be the first one to answer. The difference this time was that I was outside looking in.

Amanda arrived first and greeted me with all the spunk and enthusiasm of a nine year old daughter as she jumped into my arms and yelled "Daddy!" Chris and Josh, 15 and 12 respectively, were right behind her and gave me a big hug too. For just that single moment, everything seemed right in my world once again.

We had a great time going out to eat and over to my new apartment, but the truth was that it didn't really matter what we did or where we went. The important thing was that we were together – we were a family, just as we'd always been and always would be. No matter what had ever happened or would, nothing could change that. I believed that already, but it sure felt good to have it reassured to me in the midst of the craziness of the last few weeks.

As I drove them back to the house – their house – about 10 o'clock, I gave them each one more hug and told them that I loved them. Making the short drive to my apartment afterwards, I felt a peace which had eluded me for quite some time.

I began the evening hoping that I could reassure my kids of the fact that we would eventually make it through the changes in our lives and that we would always be a family, but the funny thing was that my kids actually

*reassured those things to me. I thanked God out loud for each of them as I
drove through the darkness back to my apartment.*

❋ ❋ ❋

If you have young children and are recently divorced, then you know
the questions which inevitably invade your thoughts. Will the divorce
scar my children? Will it change my relationship with them? What can I
do to help them deal with their feelings and emotions? Should I put them
in counseling, or will that only add to their trauma? Will the divorce
cause them to become angry or rebellious, and how will it affect their
understanding of relationships and marriage? On and on the questions
go, most of them based on our fears. Some of the fears are valid. Others
are only imagined. But all of them are real and the only thing that is clear
is that there are no easy answers.

Each question needs to be addressed not only from your perspective,
but especially from the perspective of your children. They didn't ask for
your divorce, but they certainly have to deal with the fallout. Depending
on their ages – actually, regardless of their ages – they need your love,
guidance, and direction as never before.

The world your children live in is changed drastically by the divorce.
Their understanding of family life, however the concept previously
existed, is shattered and they are forced to adapt to their parents living
apart instead of together. Family routines and rituals which once were
shared by all and brought them comfort and security suddenly shift and
look radically different. Money concerns for either or both parents limit
what the children can do. And meanwhile, as these changes are quickly
taking place, your kids are trying to figure it all out and process their
own feelings and emotions, most of which they are simply too young to
fully understand.

The hope is that mom and dad can set aside their personal differences
and work together to help the children with their issues but that doesn't
always happen after a divorce, which is why you need to take the responsibility upon yourself. Work with your ex-spouse if possible but, one
way or another, figure out the best way to help your kids. Talk to their

teachers, coaches, and youth leaders let them know the situation and to ask for their support. Do the same with the parents of your children's friends. Find a 'kid friendly' counselor who has worked with children of divorce in the past. Do everything you can to provide the network of love, encouragement, and support they need in this difficult time.

Helping kids through the issues of their parents' divorce is an imperfect science, No two children are exactly alike and there are a host of other variables, such as age, maturity, and personality, that should be considered as well. But while each situation is different and unique, there are some basic, practical guidelines that should be followed always. The bottom line is life will be better for your children if you live by the principles below. And if you don't, then it won't. Once again, it's that simple.

Principle #1: Don't Criticize Your Former Spouse In Front Of The Children

This principle alone may well determine the type of communication you have with your children in the years ahead. Whatever problems you are having with your former spouse, don't criticize him or her in front of your kids. It's not right and it isn't worth it, for you or your kids.

Children become upset when they hear negative comments about their parents, but it's even more confusing to them when those remarks come from one of their parents about the other. They may not know how to say it to you, but you are putting them in a terrible position when you do it. There are no winners. Remember, your divorce isn't their 'war' and your kids shouldn't be made to feel as if they enter a battle zone every time they want to talk to you about something involving the other parent.

Do you know what happens when your children hear you constantly put down your former spouse who, by the way, they love just as much as they love you? They will stop talking to you about him or her altogether. And when that happens, you lose. Unfortunately, so do you kids. It may not be your intention, but you will have effectively shut yourself off from communicating about one of the two most important relationships that your child has in their life at that point – their relationship with their other parent.

Have you ever thought about why we criticize certain people when they aren't there? Often it's in an attempt to elevate our own status in front of the ones we are talking with. But we are mistaken. Instead of those we are talking to somehow thinking better of us because of what we say, most times the opposite affect occurs and they realize, whether they ever say it or not, that we have our own issues and insecurities to deal with.

It's easy for us to make the mistake of thinking, "If I just tell them what their dad (or mom) is really like and he (or she) really treats me, then they will be on my side." But your kids don't want to choose sides. All they really want to know is that both of their parents are on their side. Criticize your former mate too often and all your children will remember in the years ahead is that you were bitter, resentful, and angry.

Stephen Covey offers a valuable perspective on relationships and the power of communication which I think can be helpful here. Covey says that we have an 'emotional bank account" with everyone we know well and that every time we make a comment which is good, kind, or positive either to or about someone, we make a 'deposit' into that account. Conversely, every time we criticize or say something negative either to or about a person, either directly or in the presence of others, we make a 'withdrawal'. If we make too many withdrawals, soon we become bankrupt.

We need to be making deposits every day into the emotional bank accounts of our children. Yet, every time we criticize our former spouse in front of them, we make a significant withdrawal. We must realize that our children just want to love and to be loved by both parents, without feeling unfairly pushed or pulled by either.

You are the adult. You are the parent who must be responsible and set the example, for your children's sake. Don't criticize your former spouse in front of the kids. Be supportive and encourage their relationship with him or her. In the long run, it's best for them and for you. As the saying goes, "If you can't say something nice, then don't say anything at all". It's good advice – always. Focus on making deposits, not withdrawals.

Principle #2: Encourage Your Kids To Talk About Their Feelings And Be Honest With Them About Yours

Especially in the first year after a divorce, life is difficult for both us and our children. The difference, however, is that we understand what is happening and why, while they often don't. They only know their world has been turned upside down, often leaving them confused and with a variety of conflicting feelings and emotions.

Meanwhile, as our kids do the best they can to adapt, we are busy dealing with the 'adult issues' of divorce – strained relationships, money concerns, legal squabbles, and life changes. These problems can zap our energy and leave us frustrated and exhausted, causing us to focus on other things more than our children. Yet it is precisely in these times that our kids need us most. Despite the struggles and changes occurring in our lives, it is absolutely crucial that we give our children the attention and support they need. If we don't, there will be consequences down the line.

Sometimes it can be frustrating when our children don't want to talk, or won't talk, about their feelings and emotions related to the divorce as quickly as we want them to, but they eventually will if you continue to lovingly give them the opportunity. Patience and understanding are the keys.

It's important to remember that your children are going through an emotional trauma too, just like you. Furthermore, while you probably had months to prepare yourself mentally and emotionally for the divorce, they didn't and are still trying to figure out the 'what' and 'why' of it all. There is a fine line for us to walk as parents between pushing our kids to talk and not giving them the opportunity to talk at all. Both can be risky.

This much is sure, however. When your children are ready to talk, you need to be ready to listen and to allow them to share what they are feeling openly and honestly without the fear of judgment or retribution. If you make the mistake of trying to tell them how they should feel, or if you somehow express that what they are feeling is wrong, you only add to their confusion. You may be able to offer insights that will help them understand things differently in the future but, for now, their feelings are their feelings and good, bad, or indifferent, they need to be heard.

I remember being troubled in the early days after my divorce when my kids didn't want to open up and talk about what had happened. I tend to share my feelings and emotions rather easily and I wanted my children to do the same. But they weren't me, and their experience of the divorce wasn't my experience. On the advice of my counselor, I wisely backed off from trying to push them to places they weren't ready to go emotionally at the time. I had to be patient.

Yet also on the advice of my counselor, I regularly let them know that I was ready to listen whenever they did want to talk. There was nothing they couldn't say to me, I told them, and there were no 'wrong' feelings for them to have. Whatever they needed to say was okay, and I just wanted them to know that I loved them and wanted to help.

I also did one other thing that, over time, proved to be invaluable. I set up one on one times with each of my kids every week, times that were separate and apart from the weekdays and weekends we spent together as a family. Some of those times were spent going out to eat. Other times we just went back to my apartment and swam or watched TV. But whatever we did and whenever we did it, the important thing was we had time together by ourselves on a regular basis.

As those initial months after the divorce passed by, my kids did begin to talk and share their feelings. Because of the difference in their ages, their questions and understandings of what had happened also differed, yet the process was basically the same for each of them. First they asked simple questions, almost as if they were testing the waters and making sure it was okay to talk about the divorce and what happened. Then, as they became more comfortable and felt safe talking about the issues, they began to ask about things they didn't understand and to share some of their deeper fears and concerns.

I believe that the one on one times not only laid the groundwork for us to be able to talk openly about what had happened, but they also established a foundation for our communication in the future. I'm very grateful that we can talk openly about several of the issues they face in their lives today; issues which many parents and kids don't often talk about. Don't get me wrong – our communication is far from perfect and there are still plenty of the normal parent/teen clashes that almost every family has, and I know there are some difficult conversations which are yet to take place as they get older, but I feel good that we have established a pattern of open and honest discussions.

Your children will eventually talk to you about the important issues related to the divorce if you consistently give them the opportunity. Often they simply don't know how to begin the conversation, so go ahead and set the example for them. Tell them about your own feelings and fears, and let them know there are times when you have been or are confused. Ask questions, but don't push. Be patient, understanding, and open. And most of all, remind them often of how much you love them. You won't regret it.

Principle #3: You Are A Role Model For Your Kids – Live Like It

Kids learn by our example. The words we say are important, but more important still is how we live and what we do. And our children are perceptive. They see how we treat other people, how we respond to adversity, setbacks, and disappointments. We may not realize it as we go through the struggles of our divorce, but our words, attitudes, and actions provide a model for our kids in terms of dealing with adversity in life.

I made two pledges soon after my divorce was over. The first had to do with the way I communicated with my kids, as we've already discussed in the last principle above. I pledged that I would be open and honest with them about my feelings and the events which had happened, and that I would also encourage them to do the same. I knew it was my responsibility to address whatever questions, feelings, and emotions they had.

The second pledge I made was a commitment to be the role model my kids needed and deserved. This pledge wasn't new – I had always tried to be a role model for my kids since the day they were born – but it was important for me to reaffirm because of the mistakes I made which led to my divorce. I wanted my children to see me take responsibility for my actions, both my failures and my successes, but it was also more than that. I wanted them to see a positive example of how to handle tough times and adversity. It was impossible for me to change what had happened, but I did have the opportunity to show them an appropriate way to respond. As a result, I pledged to be an example of perseverance, faith, and a positive attitude.

In essence, I wanted my kids to see in me someone who was able to maintain a good attitude even when life was difficult, and someone who had faith and continued to look to the future with hope. I wanted them to see their dad always treat people with dignity, respect, and compassion, even when the people he was dealing with didn't respond in the same manner. And I wanted them to see me keep working, keep trying, and keep believing, regardless of the circumstances. I knew my example would set the stage for how they would handle their own problems and adversity in the future.

It's been 40 years since my parents divorced but, to this day, I can still remember the example they set for me in terms of how they responded to life and the way they treated each other. Most of those memories are good, several shaping who I am and how I live today. A few aren't, but they taught me painful lessons I can learn from nonetheless. And just like I still remember how my parents acted during and after divorce, my kids will also remember my example. Your kids will remember yours too.

I invite you to take the pledge to be a living role model for your children, especially now as you go through the struggles of divorce. It's the right thing to do but, more importantly, it's the best thing you can do for them. Show them a positive example of how to live and how to handle adversity. The alternative is to show them anger and bitterness instead of forgiveness and compassion, and defeat instead of hope. That is a legacy none of us want to leave.

The greatest failure for us as parents isn't when we make a mistake or do something wrong. Those things happen to all of us and none of us is perfect. Rather, the greatest failure for us as parents comes when we shirk the responsibility of caring for our kids. Make no mistake about it – you are a role model for your children. The only question that remains to be answered is what type of role model will we be?

What type of legacy will you leave behind for your children? It's totally up to you. I urge you to take the pledge and give your kids what they deserve – the best parent you can possibly be.

Principle #4: Put Your Kids First, Not Yourself...

Put the needs of your children first, even before your own. This is the penultimate rule in parenting.

Years ago there was a movie called "Brian's Song". Based on the true story of two football players for the Chicago Bears, Gayle Sayers and Brian Piccolo, the movie depicted their friendship through the struggles of life and, ultimately, death as well. Brian Piccolo died of cancer while still in the prime of his career and Gale Sayers, his ever-faithful friend, was with him until the end.

What I'll always remember about the movie was Gayle Sayers' credo for life – "God is first, my friends are second, and I am third". In other words, his goal was to put the needs of his family and friends before his own in every situation and under any circumstances.

If we take the word 'friends' out of that saying and replace it with 'children', I believe we have the perfect credo for us as parents. "God is first, my children are second, and I am third". It challenges us to put the needs of our children before our own everyday. Granted, it's not always easy when we are struggling with divorce and just trying to survive, but it should always be our goal.

How do we live by this credo in practical terms and put the needs of our children before our own on a day to day basis? Before every choice we make, every word we say, and every action we take, we ask ourselves the question, "How will this affect my children?" More often than not, the answer to that question will determine what direction we should go.

If the situation ever presented itself where you were forced to make a decision between you or your children dying, you wouldn't hesitate to sacrifice yourself. The truth is that your kids don't need you to die for them; rather they need you to live for them. They are depending on you to be the role model you should be and to show them the way. If not you, then who?

The Relationship With Your Former Spouse...

It's not unusual for one or both spouses to become angry, bitter, or resentful toward each other when a divorce occurs. No one wants their once happy marriage to end this way but, unfortunately, it often does. Sometimes the former spouses can't let go of their feelings and hold on to them for years, creating even more problems for both them and their already broken family.

If you have a supportive and amicable relationship with your former spouse, consider yourself fortunate. You are one of the lucky ones, and your journey to new horizons will be considerably easier because of it. But if you don't, if you have struggled through a difficult divorce and words like 'supportive and amicable' aren't your vocabulary when describing that relationship, then you have some choices to make.

It's not surprising that the relationship between former spouses is strained for a while after divorce. That a couple decides to permanently separate in the first place is usually a pretty good indicator that there are major problems. The final papers may end the marriage officially, but they can't take away the hard feelings or unresolved baggage from the relationship in the past.

❀ ❀ ❀

Almost two years after the divorce...

My cell phone rang as I waited at the stoplight. It was almost midnight and I was exhausted, anxious to get home and get in bed. When I saw the name of the caller on the phone screen, I thought seriously about not answering it. I didn't like talking to Debbie at that point in our relationship any more than she liked talking to me. Too many of our conversations ended badly.

Although we were eighteen months removed from the divorce, she continued to blame me for everything that went wrong in her life and the put-downs and criticisms were getting old. I knew it wasn't easy for her and that I was an easy target, but her constant negativity towards me just made things more difficult for everybody, including the kids. It was hard for me to remember the last time we had a descent discussion, which was the very reason I'd begun to limit our contact as much as possible.

Worried that there might be something wrong with the kids, however, I decided to answer the call. And as it turned out, I was right. There was a problem. Debbie was upset with Chris, our oldest son, who was just about to turn 18. The two of them had been arguing, complete with yelling and words that shouldn't have been said, and Josh and Amanda had been awakened in the process. The argument ended with Chris speeding away from the house in his pick-up truck, saying that he needed to just 'cool off', even as Debbie tried unsuccessfully to stop him.

Unfortunately, this wasn't the first time this scene had played itself out in recent months. The only difference this time was that it was Debbie calling me instead of Chris. Most of their arguments revolved around the 'house rules' and Chris not following them as Debbie thought he should; not an uncommon issue between parents and teens of that age.

The bigger problem, at least as I observed it from the outside, was the way they communicated with each other. It seemed to me that many times they argued over things that were petty or insignificant, and that somehow became blown out of proportion. Both Debbie and Chris had a stubborn streak in them, and neither ever wanted to give in to the other. Debbie would command Chris to do something she felt strongly about, and then Chris would dig in his heels and rebel. Instead of respecting each other and working together to find a solution, too many of their conversations turned into major battles.

I worried about their relationship, but I was especially concerned for Chris. Being young, it was difficult for him to understand how his mother communicated at times and, having experienced Debbie's anger myself, I knew that he needed my support. I'd often been a buffer between them when they disagreed back when we all lived together, but that was more difficult now that we were no longer under the same roof. The constant arguing between them was the main reason Chris had already decided to move in with me on the day he turned 18.

Like many of our discussions, my conversation with Debbie on the phone that evening quickly went awry. After she explained what had happened, she went on a rant saying Chris was out of control and that I'd failed to help keep him on the straight and narrow. Then she demanded that I 'fix' the situation and told me exactly what I needed to do.

I'd heard it all before – too many times, in fact – but her comments still stung. Nobody knew better than me that I had made some mistakes, but I bristled at her insinuation that the problems she had with Chris were my fault. In my opinion, she needed to take a look in the mirror and accept some of the responsibility herself. If Chris had been the only one having problems, I might have felt differently. But the truth was that I was beginning to see the same pattern develop with Josh.

I ended the call with Debbie and immediately called Chris to make sure he was okay. Not surprisingly, he was very upset too. I offered to meet him wherever he was to talk for a while, but he declined saying that he just wanted to be by himself to think. I understood.

We ended up talking on the phone for about another 15 minutes. Throughout the conversation, I tried to walk that fine and uncomfortable line between being supportive of Debbie as his mother and also letting Chris know I was in his corner. I hated being put in the middle, but that's how it is when your former spouse has the primary custody of your child. My only goal was to work out a solution that both of them could live until Chris moved in with me.

I told Chris he was wrong for speaking disrespectfully to his mom, regardless of who was right, and that he needed to apologize to her. He knew I was right but, because he was still angry, he wasn't quite ready to go back home and do it just yet. Again, having been there myself, I understood. He promised to call me when he got back to the house.

By the time we hung up it was nearly 1:00 AM. I'd been sitting in my car in the driveway for the last hour 40 minutes. I felt better after talking with

Chris, but I knew it was only a matter of time before something else would happen and we would all go through it again.
Divorce can be hell, even when it's over.

❀ ❀ ❀

People get divorced for a lot of different reasons. Sometimes their communication breaks down or they lose their respect for each other. At other times the divorce has to do with problems such as an affair or an addiction, or even finances. I've even counseled couples who are just generally unhappy with each other and have grown tired of their relationship. Sometimes one spouse wants out of the marriage and the other doesn't, while at others both spouses want to end it. Regardless of how, why, or when it happens, divorce is never easy and leads to a time of high stress and anxiety, which often opens the door for anger, bitterness, and resentment to set in.

It's hard to understand how two people who were once passionately in love and who worked so hard to create a life together can turn so vehemently against one another when the relationship ends. It doesn't make sense, yet it happens all the time, just as it did in my situation. I'm sure of this much, however – I don't want to live with anger, bitterness, and resentment in my life. I've seen too many people almost destroyed by their hatred of a former spouse. Forgiving him or her can be a challenge after divorce, but that is exactly what you need to do if you ever expect to move on and be happy once again.

Maybe you're thinking, "I agree, but if you only knew how my ex treated me or what he (or she) did, you wouldn't just tell me to forgive and move on. Believe me, my former spouse is one of a kind". You know what? You're right – your former spouse is one of a kind. Then again, so are you.

I don't know your situation but I do have the experience of living through mine. I understand the difficulties and frustrations of relating to your former spouse during and after a divorce. I also know that, while every relationship is different, the feelings and emotions surrounding those experiences are remarkably similar for all of us.

I've definitely had times when anger and frustration got the best of me and I said or did things that I later regretted. I'm guessing you have too. Those experiences are common to almost every person who has been through divorce. None of us like it, but it happens. And when it does, when we hold on to those negative feelings and emotions, it makes it even more difficult for us to start over.

The individual who holds on to their anger, bitterness, and resentment is like someone who is constantly banging his head against the wall. Banging your head against a wall hurts! Furthermore, it doesn't do anything to solve the real problem. The only thing that banging your head can do is keep you in constant pain. When the person finally figures that out, he'll stop and, eventually, the pain will go away. At that point he will realize that he was only hurting himself.

It doesn't make sense to beat your head against a wall, so why do it? If you are angry or bitter toward your former spouse, find a way to deal with it and move on. We've already discussed several options which can help, such as forgiveness (you won't forget but you can forgive), counseling, limiting your contact with him or her, or finding positive outlets for your stress. Find the one that works for you and do it. Taking action to stop the pain is always better than constantly beating your head against a wall.

Below are some helpful guidelines to help you when you communicate with your former spouse. Actually, these guidelines are helpful in any relationship of any kind, but they are especially important as you relate to the one to whom you were once married.

- **Treat your former spouse with kindness** – You were in love once. That, in and of itself, deserves to be recognized and respected. The way you treat your ex-spouse will speak volumes to your children and to others about your character and the way you treat the people in your life. Kindness and compassion are always the best options.
- **Treat your former spouse with respect** – Regardless of who did what and why, when it happened, or who this or that, don't ever forget that you and your former spouse

spent years together as both a couple and a family. Don't make the mistake of letting the good memories be wiped out or demeaned by bitterness and anger. Treat your former spouse with the same respect that you hope to be shown yourself, whether he or she actually does or not. Take the lead and set the example.

- **Don't discuss issues when you are angry** – It only leads to further frustrations and more problems down the line. If you are upset or angry, walk away from the conversation and cool down so you won't say things that you will later regret. Take time to gather your thoughts, cool down, and gain a fresh perspective. You can always talk more about the issue when you are more relaxed.

- **Think in terms of building the relationship, not dividing it** – Maybe there have been some struggles and hard times in your relationship with your former spouse in the past, but the real question for you now is where do you want to go from here? No one wants to carry around anger, bitterness, and resentment because it's a burden that does nothing but drag us and our family down. Our ultimate goal is to be peaceful and happy. So live like it. Be positive and helpful in the conversations with your former spouse, even when he or she isn't. You may not be able to control the words and actions of others, but you can always control your own. Set the example and work to build up the relationship rather than to tear it down, no matter what challenges are involved. It will help you in the present and also set the tone for your communication in the future.

- There's no better time than right now to commit to building a positive relationship with your former spouse. It may not be easy, but it is the right thing to do for you, your ex, and your family. And, it is always better than the alternative.

The Relationship With Your 'Former' Family Members...

Debbie's family, which is now my former family, is made up of a lot of wonderful people. There was rarely a time when I didn't look forward to seeing them, especially when our family would go to Alabama for the holidays or when they would come visit us in Florida.

Debbie's parents, Hannah and Papa, are about as good as they come. Outside of my kids and my own mom, they were the ones that I hated to disappoint the most with news of the affair and our eventual divorce. Papa is a quiet man who loves to smoke his pipe. He reminds me of the old E.F. Hutton commercials – when he speaks, people listen. Hannah, on the other hand, is outgoing and gregarious, full of energy and always running around at seemingly a mile a minute. Together they have raised four beautiful daughters and, like any parents, they simply want the best for their kids.

Debbie has a strong family and they enjoy their time together. They aren't perfect, of course, but no family is. One thing I've discovered in working professionally with people through the years is that there is no such thing as a 'perfect' family. A family may look perfect from the outside, but on the inside there are always issues such as strained relationships, secrets from the past, hurt feelings, or prejudices which need to be addressed. Some of these issues are discussed only within the inner circle of the family. Some aren't even talked about there. That said, however, Debbie's family certainly has fewer issues than most.

Growing up in the conservative, middle to upper middle class environment of a small Alabama town, Debbie and her three sisters are the definition of 'southern women' and traditional family values. They are all attractive, courteous, and active in their churches; and each of them also have husbands who are successful and committed to their faith as well. Some of my best family memories were spent with my former brother-in-laws. I've missed seeing them since my marriage fell apart.

Divorce had never raised its ugly head in Debbie's family until ours occurred. Naturally, everyone was shocked by what happened, especially since I was 'the minister' of the group. Despite my sorrow and heartfelt apology, I quickly became an 'outcast'. I understand family loyalties and why, but I'd be lying if I said that it didn't hurt. Other than Hannah and Papa, and Debbie's sister Kristen, no one even bothered to call me in the six months Debbie and I struggled to make things work. Maybe it was too much to ask but, after all, I had been their family too for the past 20 years.

❀ ❀ ❀

Approximately five months prior to the divorce...

I sat down with Kristen, one of Debbie's older sisters, out on the back porch of my house. In all the years I'd known her, Kristen was never shy about speaking her mind. She usually said exactly what was on her mind and I didn't anticipate that this time would be any different. Actually it was one of the things I liked about her. I didn't always agree with her opinions, but I appreciated her passion for life and the fact that she was willing to listen to both sides of any argument.

That was why we were sitting down to talk then – Kristen wanted to hear my side of the story and determine for herself if Debbie and I had any hope of putting our marriage back together. After a long time when no one in the family would even talk to me other than Debbie's parents, Kristen had come to Florida to 'extend the olive branch' and to see if she could help us stay together.

As I expected, Kristen was still angry about the affair. She wasn't the only one upset about the pain and embarrassment I'd caused for her sister and the family, but she was the only one willing to share it with me. To tell you the truth, I wasn't too happy about it all either; Debbie's family was my family and I hated that I'd hurt them.

Kristen asked if I had any hope for my marriage, and then waited patiently for me to respond. After thinking about the question, I explained there were some days I did and others when I didn't. I was pretty sure Debbie would have had the same response. My concern, I said to Kristen, was that I still wasn't sure Debbie and I had addressed the problems in our relationship which existed before the affair ever happened. I knew that I was responsible for the mess we were in, but in my opinion Debbie and I both needed to make changes if we were going to be able to remain together in the future.

Kristen didn't like my answer. Like Debbie, she too felt that the breakdown of our marriage was completely my fault, and she thought I was somehow trying to justify what I had done. I wasn't, but I understood why she felt as she did. In fact, I even expected it because she was on the outside looking in. The reality, however, is that no one knows what goes on behind closed doors when a relationship falls apart. No one, that is, except for the couple themselves.

The redemptive part of our conversation came when Kristen told me 'the family' wanted us to stay together. As if she was speaking on their behalf, she said they would be willing to forgive if I just did my part to make things right and restore the relationship to where it was before everything blew up. I didn't feel that I could say it then, but the problem was that I didn't want our relationship to be like it was before, and I knew Debbie didn't either. We both deserved better and had to make some changes if we were to be together in the future. One person, regardless of whether it was Debbie or me, couldn't do it alone, no matter how hard either of us tried.

We ended our conversation after about an hour, but I don't think Kristen was any closer to having her question answered than when we started. It was only a few months later when Debbie decided that she wanted a divorce and we all had our answer. I guess it was impossible to fix what was already broken beyond repair. Still, I've always appreciated Kristen coming to talk that day. I know her desire for Debbie and I to work things out came from the heart.

Sometimes even good people lose their way. I know; because I was one of them. I also know those same people need the support of their family and friends if they are to find their way back. They need family and friends who are willing to show kindness, compassion, and forgiveness, and who will be there to offer grace when others can't or don't. These are the people who bring hope to those who are lost, and who make second chances and new beginnings possible.

Thank you Kristen, and Hannah and Papa too, for being those types of people in my life. I'll always be grateful to you.

❋❋❋

There are bound to be awkward moments between you and your former spouse's family after the divorce. It's only natural. But if you have children or happen to live in the same town, it's important to understand that your relationship with them will probably continue at some level for years to come. And those relationships should continue. Just because you and your former spouse aren't married anymore doesn't mean that you stop caring about the people who have been your family through the years. Life is better for everyone involved – you and your family, your former spouse and his or her family, and especially your children – when those relationships continue to remain healthy, caring, and strong.

Take the high road and set the example in how you relate to your former family. If some of them have hard feelings because of the divorce, do your best to care for those people just as you always did. Ignoring them or avoiding them rarely leads to anything good. Strive to be kind, gracious, and supportive, and respect the years you have shared together. It's always better to focus on the hope of the future rather than to dwell on the hurt of the past.

Thank God For Friends...

For many people, friends are their family. I guess it's true for all of us at one time or another.

❋❋❋

Approximately eight months after the divorce...

I met Billy, Clark, and Kelly – all three of them United Methodist pastors – at the Hampton Inn in Sarasota. Although I'd spent time with each of them individually after I resigned from the United Methodist Church, this was the first time we'd all been together since.

At one point in our collective lives, we had all been pastors who served churches within a 20 mile radius of each other. It seemed like we were always together back then, whether it was for church meetings, lunch, or a round of golf. Even after they all transferred to other churches around the state – a product of the United Methodist clergy system – our friendships continued to remain strong.

What kept us connected when we became spread out in different parts of the state were the three weeks we annually set aside to attend clergy conferences together. We always roomed with each other in those settings and usually spent more time golfing and going to movies than actually attending the meetings. Those were some good times.

My resignation shocked my clergy friends and, for a while, made it difficult for us to be together. When things finally settled down a little after my divorce, the four of us decided to meet for a 'reunion' weekend to relive old times and catch up on life. Our plan was to go out on the town Friday night after we met that afternoon, and then play a round of golf on Saturday before they all had to return to preach at their churches on Sunday morning. I was envious they had a church to go to.

Despite our plans, we never made it out Friday evening. Instead, we returned to our hotel after dinner and started a conversation which ended up going deep into the wee hours of the morning. It all began when they asked me how I was doing – how I was really doing – after my resignation and divorce. So I told them.

Flip-flopping between tears and laughter, I told them the good, the bad, and the ugly of everything I'd been through as I answered every question they had and held nothing back. Right there in the Hampton Inn in Sarasota, I had a therapy session with three of the people in this world that I trusted most. The night just kind of ticked away and I think we all felt it was one of the best we had ever spent together.

People pay a lot of money for counselors nowadays, and rightly so because they are helpful. But for me, no counselor in the world could have been a better listener, more encouraging, or more supportive than my friends were that Friday night in Sarasota. Friends – true friends – are a gift from God. They stay with you for the long haul, no matter what happens in your life or in theirs, and they don't run away when times are tough, even when they know you are the one who made them that way.

This much I know – when everything in my world was stripped away and I had no home, no money, and no hope, I only made it through because of my kids, my Mom, and my friends, and not always in that order.
The very heart of God is revealed in friendship. I know, because I've seen it.

❋ ❋ ❋

Funny thing about friends – you never realize how much they mean to you until you really need them.

As I went through the struggles of my divorce, people reacted in a variety of ways. Some shied away or distanced themselves from me and the situation. Others felt caught in the middle and backed away from me so they wouldn't appear to be siding with one person or the other. Then there were my friends – my real friends – who were able to support Debbie but also stand with me and believe in me even when I had trouble believing in myself. There was no judgment or condemnation for what I had done; they knew I had suffered enough. They only wanted to help. That is what real friendship is all about.

During your hard times, let your friends be your friends. Don't close them out of your life. Like your family, they love you and want to help, but you have to let them. Lean on them when you need to, and don't be afraid to talk to them when you are down. They will understand. They want the best for you.

I believe there is a special place reserved in our hearts for those we call friend. For all of those who have walked with me through the good and bad times in my life, and to all who continue to walk with me on my path to new horizons, thank you.

It's Your Choice...

You have a choice. You can rely on your family and friends, and commit yourself to acting in the best interest of your kids, your former spouse and his or her family, and yourself...or...you can let the pain, anger, and embarrassment push you away from the people who love you and control your life. Only you can make the decision.

You will be a role model for your kids either way, and your response may well determine your path to new horizons. Once again, it's your choice...

For Your Journal...

- Which members of your family have helped you through the struggles of your divorce? How have they been supportive? Take the time to write a thank you note to each of them.

- Since your divorce, how have you been a good example for your children? In what other ways have you failed to be the example that you should be? What changes can you make right now to be the positive role model that they need and deserve?

- Write a paragraph describing the problems in your relationship with your former spouse. What can you do to improve that relationship? More importantly, are you willing to try? Write down three things you can do to make the relationship with your former spouse better.

- Write a paragraph that describes your feelings about your former family. What are the benefits for you and your children if those relationships continue to be strong in the future? What can you do to help them remain strong?

- Make a list of the friends who have helped and supported you as you have gone through the difficult times related to your divorce. Call each one just to say thank you. In what ways can your friends help you in the future as you move toward new horizons?

Chapter 6

Dealing With Financial Problems...

"For what does it profit a man to gain the whole world and forfeit his soul?"
– Mark 8:36 –

Few things are more stressful than financial problems. Believe me, I speak from experience.

✸ ✸ ✸

Approximately 16 months after the divorce...

It was just a salad and sandwich, but I was grateful for the meal. The only reason I agreed to meet Mike for lunch that day was because I knew he would pick up the tab. I wouldn't have done it otherwise. I simply couldn't afford to. If that sounds desperate, it's because my situation was at the time.

Money was tight. In fact, it was beyond tight. I literally worried about every dollar I spent. Having been unemployed for three months and with no real prospects for work on the horizon, I was just trying to find a way to survive. It was hard to believe I was in that position after everything I'd had just 24 months before, but it was true. I kept hoping that one day I would wake up and discover it was all a bad dream.

Two years earlier I had been the pastor of one of the largest churches in Pinellas County and I had a salary and benefits package which totaled $120,000 a year. I lived in a beautiful, four-bedroom home with a pool and $200,000 tucked away in equity, and I had a pension of about a half-million *dollars. Life was good. Life was comfortable. There were still concerns about money even then, of course, but that was exactly what they were – concerns, not problems. My family rarely hesitated to go on vacation or out to eat based on money alone. We weren't excessive by any means, but there was always enough to do what we wanted to do whenever we wanted to do it.*

Then the divorce happened. My salary at Metropolitan Ministries, where I worked for the first year after my divorce, was less than half of what I made at the church. I loved my job there, but I knew there was no way I could continue if I expected to meet all of my financial obligations.

The alimony and child support were my biggest concern. Together they totaled $60,000 per year – more than my entire salary at Metropolitan Ministries. In addition, according to the divorce agreement, I provided another $6,000-8,000 per year for health insurance and incidentals, such as camps and recreational activities for the kids. At the same time, I was also supporting my Mom. Her mortgage and the other bills I paid for her totaled another $10,000 per year. Adding up all of those figures together, I needed to make $78,000 a year before I could even begin to think about my own needs.

It seemed like an impossible situation, especially since I had no assets and had given up everything to Debbie in the divorce. My decision to not hire an attorney and to give her whatever she asked for turned out to be a huge mistake because, in her anger at the time, she took full advantage of me and the circumstances.

According to the divorce agreement, Debbie received half of my pension, which she certainly deserved given the fact that she had been supportive of me through most of the years I earned it. The kicker, however, was that she also demanded that she have sole possession of all of our other assets too, including our home and the entire $200,000 plus we had in equity. I knew it was unfair but, because of my guilt, I consented anyway. I left our 19 marriage with only the hope of starting over from scratch.

I was caught between two extremes back then. On one hand, I felt sorry for Debbie and what I had put her through, and I convinced myself that she deserved everything we had. And on the other, I was struggling with my own depression and felt that I deserved the worst that could happen, whatever the outcome. By the time Debbie and her attorney worked up the agreement, I just wanted out of the marriage and away from her. I would have probably consented to more if I'd had anything else left to give.

My financial problems mounted quickly. As my debts increased, I drained the part of my pension which I was able to pull out early just to get by for a few months. I applied for credit cards left and right, and quickly ran each of them to the max. I borrowed money from friends and eventually moved in with a good friend who offered me a spare bedroom because I couldn't pay the rent on my apartment. Other than my alimony payments, child support, and Mom's mortgage, my monthly bills were paid late if they were paid at all and my credit rating plummeted. I never had more than a few dollars in my pockets at any one time and, worst of all, I saw no way out of my predicament. The whole experience was frightening and took a heavy toll on me psychologically.

After working at Metropolitan Ministries for almost a year, my circumstances forced me to look for something else which could offer more money. Eventually I took a huge risk and left my job to start a new business with a friend. Six months later, however, the investment money used to begin the company ran dry and I was left unemployed and without an income. Despite a frantic search to find something to pay the bills in which I checked into every conceivable opportunity, including sales jobs, home businesses, internet businesses, and even call centers, nothing seemed to work. I felt the intense pressure of knowing I had to find something quickly or else the people who depended on me financially – my kids, Mom, and ex-wife – would end up suffering the consequences.

Mike was a rock for me throughout that time, just as he had been as I actually went through my divorce. He had been my best friend for years and was always just a phone call away. Other than Jessica, Mike was the only other person who really understood my situation and what had happened with everything I'd been through.

Just before we finished lunch and it was time to pay the bill, Mike reached across the table and handed me an envelope without saying a word. My eyes immediately welled up with tears immediately. I knew what was in it and, despite the fact that every ounce of my pride was telling me not to take it, I did.

Pride is a funny thing. Most times we don't want people to know when we are desperate and hurting, so we do our best to hide the pain and continue to struggle. We wear our pride like a badge of courage until we finally find ourselves in a position where we have to choose between pride and survival. When we get there, survival wins. That was the point where I was when Mike handed me the envelope. True to his nature, he passed it off as nothing and told me not to worry about it.

It wasn't the first time Mike had helped me, nor would it be the last. When few people understood or really cared about my situation, he did. I thanked him through my tears and stuffed the envelope in my pocket.

When I got in my car, I leaned my head back against the seat and took a huge sigh of relief before opening the envelope. The few hundred dollars that was in it would help me hang on for another week or two. I wondered, as I thought to myself, if this nightmare would ever end and I would one day get back on my feet. Truthfully, I was beginning to think it wouldn't.

My stomach was full, however, and I was grateful for that. And thanks to Mike's help, my gas tank was about to be full as well. Thank you, God, for best friends and the little blessings of life.

❀ ❀ ❀

Money isn't the most important thing in the world, but having it definitely helps. It can't solve all our problems or cure all our woes, and it may not be able to bring us long term happiness or contentment, but it sure is easier to start over after a divorce when you don't have to struggle financially to survive. If you have money, it can open doors to your future. If you don't, life can get tough.

Divorce puts a strain on our finances and it isn't difficult to understand why. The income once used by the husband and wife together to support their home is suddenly divided in two. Two homes means two mortgage payments or rents, two electric bills, two cable bills, two water bills, two insurance bills, and two of just about everything else. Throw in lawyer bills, court costs, and the other incidentals caused by a divorce, and you soon see that more money is going out than is coming in. The financial pressures mount quickly and result in tension, stress, and frustration.

Money problems are relative, of course, but they impact everyone who goes through a divorce at some level, no matter what income they make. For the individual with a large estate and a healthy financial portfolio, tough times after divorce may simply mean having fewer assets than in the past. But for the person who has little or no financial resources – no equity, cash, or investments – and who is living paycheck to paycheck already, divorce can literally mean worrying about how to pay the rent or buy groceries each month.

The issues of which spouse should pay what, how the estate should be divided, or determining the appropriate amount of alimony and child support are beyond the scope of this book. If you need that type of information, I strongly recommend that you seek the professional advice of an attorney or a financial advisor, something that I didn't do but should have. Even then, however, understand that it is highly unusual for both spouses to be satisfied with the end result. There are always concessions and compromises to be made before a final agreement is reached. Many of you reading this book have already been through that process and know exactly what I mean. It is one of the many difficult realities of divorce.

What is within the scope of this book, however, are the tools you need to begin again as you address the mental, physical, emotional, and spiritual issues which are holding you back. Regardless of money problems and your financial situation, there is hope and you can start over in life. I say that with absolutely certainty because I've been where you are now – struggling to get by, living day-to-day with uncertainty and fear, and seemingly without hope for the future – and yet I made it through to a brand new start. Because I did it, I know you can too.

❀ ❀ ❀

Two years and one month after the divorce...

Entering the United States Bankruptcy Court, Tampa Division, with my briefcase full of the financial papers and legal correspondence related to my bankruptcy filing, I was beyond nervous. In fact, I was downright scared. I'd never appeared in a courtroom before, not even for a traffic ticket or for my own divorce, and the setting intimidated me.

Three months prior to that point, I'd met with Esquire Susan Sharp and made the difficult decision to file for bankruptcy. Despite working two jobs at the time, I soon realized that I'd never be able to fully pay back the debts I'd accumulated in the two years since the divorce. Declaring bankruptcy was embarrassing, but I felt it was the only way for me to get out of the hole I had dug for myself.

Two jobs and two salaries helped, but they still didn't provide enough money for me to make ends meet. Servicing the monthly interest charges on my debts as I continued to support my kids, Mom, and ex-wife meant there wasn't enough left for me to afford even a modest, one bedroom apartment. Thankfully, I'd been living with a good friend for the past several months. Fred Zinober had graciously opened his home to me at a point when I was unemployed and unable to pay rent. Since then, my oldest son, Chris, had also moved in with me on the day he turned 18. We shared a set of bunk beds in the guest room. It wasn't ideal, but we made the best of it. Fred was incredibly generous in allowing us to live there and a God-send for me personally when I had nowhere else to go.

My credit card debts, most of which came as the result of cash advances used to pay alimony, totaled $55,000 dollars. Despite my financial struggles, I was proud of the fact that I had never once fallen behind in supporting Debbie or my Mom. The bad part of that, however, was that providing for them had caused me to fall further behind on my debts and everything else.

In addition to my credit card debts and other bills, I also had two substantive personal loans from friends who had helped me when things were at their worst. I didn't want to list them as creditors in the bankruptcy filing, but my lawyer said that I needed to and it was required by the law. Whether the bankruptcy was to be approved or not, and whether those debts were to be legally forgiven or not, I knew I had a moral obligation to pay those loans back, and eventually I would.

Susan was a 'no nonsense' attorney who was pleasant enough to make conversation but firm enough to make sure I completed the maze of documentation and paperwork required for the filing. Because of my unusual circumstances, Susan advised me to file for a Chapter 7 bankruptcy instead of a Chapter 13. The main difference, at least as I understood it in laymen's terms, was that a Chapter 7 would eliminate all of my unsecured debts while a Chapter 13 would only eliminate part of them and require me to repay a portion over time.

Susan explained that it was rather unusual for an individual like me, as opposed to a business or a corporation, to be granted a Chapter 7. However, she felt it was warranted to ask for based on the financial analysis and the commitments I already had. The fact I was working two jobs showed that I was making an effort to rectify my situation, and the reality that I was still unable to afford an apartment for myself only further proved I'd have trouble making any more monthly payments. Even so, she said, there were no guarantees the bankruptcy would be approved.

The purpose of my court appearance that morning was to have my '341' hearing, a necessary and required part of the bankruptcy process. Two people – a court appointed trustee and a representative from the US Federal Bankruptcy Court – had thoroughly examined my financial records and had prepared a variety of questions related to my debts and my financial viability.

The scheduled time for the hearing was 10 AM, but I arrived by 9:30. Susan arrived shortly thereafter. She was relaxed, upbeat, and positive but, then again, she did this type of thing every day for a living. She immediately sensed my apprehension and began to make small talk to pass the time. Her counsel was simple and straight forward – answer each question that the representatives of the court asked briefly, directly, and honestly.

As it turned out, the hearing wasn't nearly as bad as I had anticipated or imagined. There were a few uncomfortable moments for me when I had to explain how I'd fallen into debt so quickly, but both representatives were satisfied with my explanation when they reviewed my income history and weighed it against the significant amount of alimony I paid. The whole thing only took 15 minutes. As I was excused, I was told a final ruling would be determined in approximately two months, which happened to be falling right around Thanksgiving.

I felt relieved when the hearing ended. As Susan and I walked out of the courtroom and into the streets of downtown Tampa, just before we parted ways to go to our cars, she asked if she could tell me something. I said yes, of course, and she went on to say that she admired my perseverance, and respected the way I had continued to support Debbie, my kids, and my Mom after everything I went through. Too many times, she said, she had seen other people, many with financial resources much greater than I ever had, who hadn't done the same. I appreciated her kindness and comments. They made me feel good inside.

After thanking Susan for her counsel and guidance, I hopped into my car and headed back to work. For the first time in a long time, I had hope for my finances and my future.

P.S. – The bankruptcy was granted two days before the Thanksgiving holidays and my debts were discharged.

❋ ❋ ❋

I worked at Metropolitan Ministries for the first year after my divorce. The mission of the organization was to care for the homeless of Tampa and to equip them with the tools they needed to rebuild their lives in becoming self sufficient.

Homeless individuals who qualified for the program agreed to live under strict guidelines in on-campus housing for anywhere from six to 24 months as they received education in basic life skills such as personal finances, health and nutrition, cooking, and family relationships. In addition, they were also required to receive training from partnering schools and institutions in order to develop marketable job skills in a field of their choice.

Each individual or family was also assigned a dedicated counselor who charted their progress and helped them deal with any special concerns.

They were then assisted in finding a job in the community while a percentage of their salary was set aside in anticipation of the day when they would graduate from the program and move into a home of their own.

I was often amazed by the stories of those who graduated from the program and inspired by the fact that they were able to turn their lives around. Most had overcome tremendous obstacles, such as alchohol abuse, addictions, or a series of bad choices, all of which had played a part in them becoming homeless in the first place.

But every now and then, a very different type of story would be told. These stories involved people who had college degrees and once had good jobs, and nice homes. Then, suddenly, an unexpected setback arose – a medical emergency, a personal tragedy, a lay-off at work – and they were unable to pay their bills. Eventually they lost their homes and found themselves out on the streets. For them, as for the others, Metropolitan Ministries was their salvation.

Like most people hearing those stories, I often thought to myself, "That could never happen to me". Yet the reality was it almost did. Just a year and a half removed from my divorce, I found myself out of resources, without a home, and scrambling to provide for myself and those I loved. I literally had to depend on others to survive. Thankfully I had family and friends who could help me, but not everyone is that fortunate.

Living through the experience taught me a valuable lesson. Life can change quickly and unexpectedly, no matter who you are or how well off you may be. Divorce is one of those life-changing events which can leave us desperate and financially challenged like never before.

As we pursue new horizons relative to our financial situation, perhaps we can learn from those who have rebuilt their lives at Metropolitan Ministries and take the time to review some basic life skills in areas such as budgeting, goal-setting, and perspective. After all, regardless of who or where we are in life, we're never too old to learn.

Step #1: Begin With Where You Are

You can't go where you want to go until you know where you are to begin with.

❋ ❋ ❋

Approximately ten months after the divorce...

Pride had something to do with it. Denial too. But whatever the reasons, I had ignored the problem way too long. The time had come when I finally needed to address my financial situation head on. I was in a mess and, one way or another, I had to get things turned around. Ignoring the problem wasn't helping. One way or another, I had to get things turned around. The first step, I knew, was that I had to create a budget.

I rarely cuss, but I let a few choice words fly as I ripped up yet another piece of paper and tossed it in the trash can. No matter how many times I started over, the numbers just didn't change. They weren't pretty.

I had three goals in the process. First, I wanted to determine exactly where my money was going. Second, I wanted to see my expenses on paper and to determine which were essential and which weren't. And third, I wanted to see how much more I needed to make each month to cover my many bills and obligations.

In the months prior, I'd looked into nearly every type of program available to help me reduce my expenses, including debt reduction and debt consolidation programs, in hopes of finding a miracle solution to my problem. The more I researched, however, the more obvious it became that no miracles were out there to be found. All of the programs I came across only covered the sore up rather than heal it.

I had prepared budgets professionally for most of my life and knew how to put one together. In theory, it was simple. You determine the amount of your income over a defined period of time. Then you determine your anticipated expenses over that same period of time. And finally, you compare the two. If you have more money coming in than going out, you're usually in pretty good shape. But if not... uh-oh.

When your expenditures exceed your income, tough choices have to be made. Either you can find a way to make more money, which usually means changing jobs, taking a second job, or furthering your education, or you can decide which expenses to cut. Since most people either can't or don't want to take on a second job or go back to school, they usually end up trying to cut the discretionary expenses out of their life. Too many cuts, however, and you end up with a 'bare bones' budget. If you still have more money going out than coming in at that point, then you have real problems.

My budget had crossed that line several months ago, ever since I was divorced and well before I actually sat down to put the numbers on paper.

I had been falling further and further into debt in the last year and it was impossible for me to cover my obligations based on my salary at Metropolitan Ministries. Whining about it didn't help, and I certainly knew that it wouldn't solve the problem. I had to come up with a plan to address my situation or soon I'd eventually go down in flames. The bottom line was that it was up to me.

So, hopeful and determined to find a way, I tried again to make a budget, starting over for the fourth time.

❀ ❀ ❀

Debbie and I never made a detailed budget when we were married. We made some basic budgets through the years just to be aware of where our money was going, but even then those numbers were always based on abundance rather than scarcity. I don't ever remember a time in our lives when we were desperate or felt that our bills couldn't be paid. And there was definitely never a time when we went hungry or felt the threat of losing our home.

For me, the season of abundance faded quickly after my marriage ended and my financial world turned upside down. At that point, I had a choice. Either I could complain about what I lost in the divorce and become bitter about my situation, or I could try to do something about my situation, get back on my feet, and move forward with life. I chose the latter, but it took a while to see the results.

You can't resolve a problem until you identify it and are willing to address it. Maybe you are struggling right now, barely getting by from one week to the next as you try to make ends meet. Maybe you're tired and frustrated, and you don't know what to do or how you can change your situation. If so, you need to hear what I am about to say.

You can change your financial future. I know you can because I did. I'm certainly not rich by any stretch of the imagination, but I have righted the ship and things are much better than they were before. It won't be easy for you to do, and it will take time along with discipline, determination, and a commitment to succeed, but it can and will happen if you put forth the effort.

There may be a few people who win the lottery or experience a financial miracle every now and then, but the best way – really the only way – to change your financial situation short of a miracle is through planning and hard work. It may sound 'old-fashioned', but it is absolutely true

So get started. The first step is to begin with where you are and to make a budget which is realistic for you. Being as detailed as possible, make a list of all your expenditures – bills, mortgage, car, gas, food, recreation, and any other items or necessities you pay for each month. If you need help, there are plenty of budget worksheets and budgeting tools on-line that can guide you in the process.

After you've listed your expenditures, list your sources of income – net, not gross – total it up. Then compare the two. Hopefully the difference will leave you with a positive balance to work with, but if not or if the numbers are too close for comfort, then its time for step two.

Step #2: Decide Where You Want To Go

Years ago, my friend Charlie Hunt and I drove across the country in a monstrous U-Haul truck. Inside the truck were my aunt's belongings, and, in addition, her car was hitched on the back. I had never driven a truck that big before and, admittedly, I was tense as I drove in traffic on the interstate.

We were driving the U-Haul from Arizona to Florida because my aunt was moving to Palm Harbor to be close to my mom, which was also her sister. Charlie flew out to Phoenix with me the day before my aunt left so he could help me pack and then we took her to the airport and began our 2000 mile journey back to the Sunshine State. To spice things up on the long drive, we planned a few recreational stops along the way.

One of those stops was in New Orleans. Our plan was to arrive in the early evening, find a hotel on the outskirts of town, and head to Bourbon Street for a little fun. As it turned out, we arrived a few hours earlier than anticipated and ended up exiting Interstate 510 into downtown New Orleans during the late afternoon rush hour. Traffic was literally at a standstill in the sweltering New Orleans heat and, as the frustrations of drivers began to boil over, no one was going anywhere fast. Suffice it to say it wasn't fun trying to maneuver that giant U-Haul through the crowded streets of the downtown area. Every time I tried to turn or switch lanes, people seemed to get angry or honk their horns at me, with many saying things I shouldn't repeat. A few of them even gave me the infamous one-finger wave.

The worst part of it all was that Charlie and I had no idea where we were or where we were going. We didn't have a map and neither of us knew the city. As a result, our only goal during that hectic time was to make it to the next traffic light without having an accident. All of this only added to my anxiety until, finally, I found a parking lot and pulled over, deciding to wait for the madness to clear. It was almost an hour before the traffic died down and we got back on the road. Charlie and I can laugh about it all now, but it wasn't funny then.

It's no fun to be lost and to not know where you're going, whether it's in the middle of rush hour traffic in New Orleans or in life in general. That's especially true when you have money problems and don't know where to go or what to do. If you don't have a plan to guide you as you find your way, there is a good chance that you will be wandering aimlessly for a long, long time.

I know what it's like to have bill collectors calling at all hours of the day, to be overdrawn at the bank with no money for food or gas, or to feel the embarrassment of having a credit card rejected because it is over the limit. It's difficult to just inch along, minute by minute and hour by hour, stuck in a jam with seemingly no way out. Unlike my U-haul experience in New Orleans, you can't just pull over and wait for the trouble to clear, because financial troubles won't clear. Not, at least, until you have a plan to clear them.

My only plan in the first year after my divorce was to survive. I secluded myself away as much as possible and tried to ignore the world around me rather than making a sincere effort to improve and move forward. I felt powerless to change my situation at the time and, as a result, I continued to fall deeper into debt, which only created more problems and more stress in my life.

When I left my job at Metropolitan Ministries to start a business which ended up failing six months later, I was unemployed and reached a new low. Only then did I finally decide that something had to change. Either I would address my financial issues head-on and turn things around, or I would continue to go downhill which would eventually lead to someplace I didn't want to go. I knew there was no in between. My only hope was to devise a plan, take action, and reverse my direction.

I knew that I had to consider every possibility if I was serious about changing my life and moving beyond where I was. That wasn't a problem. By then, I was ready to do whatever I needed to do to improve my situation. Perhaps the most important decision I made at the time was to stop settling for less – less than what I could be, less than what I wanted to be, and less than I deserved to be.

My plan included two different options. The first option had me explore new career opportunities in the business world. Although I didn't have any previous experience in for-profit world, I knew that I had a good education and marketable skills from my years in the ministry. With executive salaries in the business world typically being higher than those in nonprofit agencies, I thought that I might be able to find a position which could provide the income I needed in my post-divorce circumstances. At the very least, it was worth a try.

My second option followed a much more familiar path. I decided to set aside the embarrassment of what had happened in the past and explore ministry or social work opportunities once again. I knew these types of positions would be personally fulfilling and provide me with the sense of purpose I wanted in a job, but I questioned whether or not I could survive on the salary they offered.

Based on my budget, I knew exactly what I needed to make to meet my obligations. I wanted to make more than just that, of course, but the key to the plan was my commitment to turn down anything that didn't provide at least the minimum amount that I needed, regardless of how tempting it might be to take the job at the time. I knew it was risky, especially since rationally it seemed that receiving some money was better than no money at all, but I also knew it was the only way I could turn things around. I refused to jump at the first thing which came along just because it offered a paycheck. The opportunity, and the salary, had to be right; otherwise I would just continue in the downward spiral I was in. Only as a last resort would I accept less than what I needed and what I believed I was worth. I was desperate, but I had to think long term rather than short.

There were no guarantees either option would succeed, but I set the plan in motion and got to work. Being patient was difficult. I went through four agonizing months of sending out resumes, having interviews, and making follow-up calls with very little success along the way. I borrowed money from wherever I could just to get by and maxed out every credit card that I had. Within the first six weeks of being unemployed, I received two job offers in retail sales. Under normal circumstances, I might have taken either one, but neither paid anything close to what I needed. So, with some hesitation, I stuck to my plan and turned both of them down. I needed money, but I knew that neither of those jobs would provide the long term solution to my problem, and I didn't have the luxury of time to work my way up the corporate ladder. Instead, I kept looking and tried to keep the faith.

Remaining committed to my plan of action was one of the most difficult things I've ever done. Many times I was discouraged and thought that things would never work out. It's hard to stay positive when the days continue to roll on by and there is no money coming in, or to be confident in your step when you end up having to borrow ten dollars from your mom so you can buy gas to make it to the next interview. But I knew I couldn't give up. There were no other options.

I don't know how desperate your financial situation is right now. I can only speak from my experience, but I will tell you this – the right opportunities will eventually come along if you are realistic in your expectations and disciplined enough to act on your convictions. They may not be the opportunities you expected, or even the ones you want at the time, but they will come if you stick to your plan and do the right things.

Here's what I know – one way or another, life somehow works out for the best for good people who are willing to work hard. Call it fate, destiny, providence, or whatever else you may want to call it, but it's true. Good things eventually happen for people whose hearts are in the right place. It's just the way life works.

After suffering through four months without an income, my plan finally paid off. I wasn't able to find a single position which met all of my requirements but, in the process of searching, a third option surprisingly presented itself. Two separate job offers came my way simultaneously, one in social work and the other in ministry. Combined they were able to provide what I needed and also offered the sense of mission and purpose I desired. I knew neither job would ever make me rich, but both of them together were enough.

Did taking on two jobs mean that I would have to work twice as hard? Yes, but I was ready and willing to do that in order to change my situation. Did it mean I would have less time and have to give up some of the things I enjoyed? Again the answer was yes, but it was more important for me to provide for the people I loved than anything else at the time. I was ready to do anything and everything that I needed to do to relieve the financial pressure and begin to move forward.

After four long months of searching for the 'right' opportunity, I received two job offers in a matter of days. One was to become the Executive Director of Meals On Wheels of Tampa, and the other was to become the pastor of Harvey Memorial Community Church in Bradenton Beach. I accepted each of them on the spot, and both have been an incredible blessing in my life ever since.

So now it's your turn. Determine where you want to go, come up with a plan to get there, and then get to work. You are the only one who can change your future and, as experience teaches us, we are always better off doing something as opposed to doing nothing at all. It may take time and there will be moments when the journey is difficult, but you've made it through tough times before and you can do it again!

Step #3: Work Hard And Dream Big

I receive them in the mail, through my television, and on my computer all the time. You probably do too. I'm talking about those ads that promise great wealth, fancy homes, new cars, and dream vacations, all while only working minutes a day!

I learned a long time ago that if something sounds too good to be true, it probably is. Maybe it is possible for someone to make millions of dollars working only minutes a day, but all that I know is I've never met anyone yet who has actually done it.

It seems to me that the most significant accomplishments in our lives – whether professional, personal, financial, or relational – always require time, effort, and discipline to achieve. They don't just happen. Instead, we have to work hard to make them happen. In the end, nothing replaces hard work and a desire to succeed.

Every year, when I was the pastor of the Palm Harbor church, we would go through the process of creating an annual budget. And every year, as we considered adjustments in an effort to balance the budget before it was presented to the congregation, our Finance Chairperson would say to me, "We only have two options – either we raise the bridge or we lower the water". It was his way of saying that we either had to raise more money or lower our expenses if we expected to get to where we needed to be. Doing nothing was unacceptable, else we would soon outspend our income and the bridge would be washed away.

Working two jobs put me in a much better position than I was in before, but it certainly didn't solve all of my problems. I was back on track professionally and it was a relief to know that I could provide for my Mom, my kids, and Debbie, but I continued to struggle with my debts. I was able to pay my bills on time, but I struggled to make anything more than the minimum payments on my loans and credit cards, which made it impossible to reduce the principal to any significant degree.

It was then that I filed for bankruptcy. After consulting with an attorney, I decided it was the only way I could start over with a clean slate. I'm not proud of the fact that I couldn't repay my debts back then, but to this day I still believe it was the right decision for me at the time. It gave me the opportunity to get my life back.

Once I was on the other side of bankruptcy, I set my sights on new goals that I wanted to accomplish. First and foremost, I wanted to own a home again. My credit rating was ruined due to the bankruptcy so I knew it would be difficult to obtain a mortgage, but I also believed that somehow I could find a way. I wanted something simple and small; some place my kids could come and I could call my own. After living with friends and moving four times since the divorce, I just wanted to lay my head down at night knowing that I was in my own bed, in my own room, in my own home.

So, once again, I made a plan and got to work. And also once again, an opportunity presented itself in a way that I never anticipated or imagined. Two people, both friends of mine from separate and unrelated eras in my life, worked together to make it possible for me to purchase the small two bedroom condo I now call home. It's amazing how life can surprise us sometimes if we are diligent in pursuing our goals and remain open to the possibilities.

There is still much more I want to accomplish in the days ahead. Eliminating my debts and purchasing a home were important first steps, but they weren't and aren't my only goals in life. I want to find a way to provide for my children's dreams, and to help them do more and be more than I've done and been in the past. I want to completely pay back the loans from those friends who showed me kindness when I was down and out. I want to provide my Mom with the life she deserves in her golden years. And I want to do something significant to help others, something big that I have yet to determine but that will make a difference in the lives of those in need. The list could go on.

I can't promise you wealth, mansions, and fancy vacations by working only minutes a day, but I can offer an alternative I believe is even better. I can offer you a hope born out of faith and believing in yourself, determination born out of discipline and perseverance, and success born out of hard work and dedication. These are the things which lead to peace and contentment within the soul. These are the things that are important in life.

If my struggles and new beginning have taught me anything, it is that you can find a way to fulfill your dreams, regardless of how humble or how grand they may be, if you work hard, focus on your goals, and never give up. Go for it!

Step #4: Get Started And Keep Things In Perspective

As I said earlier, the hardest part of accomplishing any task is getting started. How many times have you told yourself that this was the day you were going to get out of bed and begin that project, or start working out, or make those changes, only to put it off for another day? If you want to change your financial situation, the truth is there's no better time to begin than right now. And I do mean now. Pull out a pencil and a piece of paper, figure out a budget, and begin to create your plan.

What should the plan look like? That depends on what you want to accomplish but, ideally, it will define your intentions as you move from where you are now to where you want to be in the future. From a financial perspective, your plan needs to be realistic and reasonable, and it needs to include a budget within your means. Look for ways to increase your income and to cut your costs so you can begin to save money. But financial goals should only be one part of the plan. Think about your personal goals, career goals, and your dreams, and list the action steps you need to take to achieve them. Be creative and flexible, and always be open to new possibilities. Most importantly, be committed.

In order for you to truly embrace your plan, it needs to be wholly and totally yours. Family and friends may offer thoughts and ideas about what you should do and expand your thinking, but ultimately this plan is about you. It must come from your within your heart and soul, for you are the only one who can change your life. It needs to include the goals, dreams, and desires that you have for yourself, not the ones that others have for you.

Be assured that challenges will lie ahead. There will be times when you want to deviate from the path, when you want to deviate from your plan or compromise its integrity. There may even be times when you want to give it up completely. But don't you do it. Stay the course and keep focused on the future. Like anything of lasting value, your hard work will eventually pay off and bring the results you desire in time.

There is one more very important thing you can do, that you need to do, as you work hard to change your financial situation. Stay grounded and keep life in its proper perspective. Everyone faces hardships, difficulties, and struggles from time to time, but I guarantee better days are ahead. You may not see be able to envision them now, but if you keep working hard and focus on moving forward one day at a time, they will be here very, very soon. Count on it.

❀ ❀ ❀

Approximately two and a half years after the divorce...

I had an interesting conversation with Mom last week.

Every Sunday for the last year, I pick up my Mom to take her with me to the worship service at my church in Bradenton. The drive takes about an hour each way and gives us the chance to talk apart from the hustle and bustle of rest of my work week. I think I've learned more about my Mom's past in those conversations driving back and forth to Bradenton over the last twelve months than I ever knew from all of my other years combined. I've wondered occasionally why I didn't take the time to talk with her about those things more before then.

Last Sunday we started talking about money. It's not an unusual topic for us to discuss. I've supported my Mom financially at some level for the past 25 years and I have always been happy to do it. I'll never stop because she deserves it. No one is prouder of their mom than me, and I know that I could never repay her for everything she has done. Knowing that I'd had a difficult time helping her since the divorce, I think my Mom brought up the subject intentionally.

As we talked about our financial struggles, Mom started reminiscing about the house she bought after her divorce many years ago, back when I was still a small child. She said she purchased the house 'on a wing and a prayer', and she still wasn't sure how she made it through those days. I could hardly get a word into the conversation – also not unusual when I have a conversation with my Mom – as she described the times when she wouldn't answer the phone because she was afraid it might be another bill collector, or how she remembered writing checks even as she prayed that they wouldn't bounce, or how she struggled to hold down two physically demanding jobs while raising me and my brother as a single mom. I knew times were tough for her back then, but it was only when I matured that I really realized the sacrifices she had made on my behalf.

The conversation struck a nerve. As she detailed her struggles, I realized that I'd been through every one of them myself recently, including working two jobs as I was raising my boys who now both lived with me. Life was getting better slowly but surely, and I was grateful to be on the other side of most of those struggles at that point, but the painful memories were still fresh on my mind.

My Mom will never admit it, but I think that was exactly why she chose to talk about those things on the way home from church last Sunday. In her loving way, without trying to embarrass me or put me on the spot, she wanted me to know that everything would eventually work out in time for me and the kids just as it did for her. We would be just fine.

I pulled into her driveway and unloaded the groceries we had picked up on the way home before giving her a kiss goodbye. As I drove back to my condo, I had time to think about the conversation and everything she had said. Without realizing it as it was happening, the preacher had just heard a sermon from his mother and the message was loud and clear. If I could just hang in there through the ups and downs, and keep life in its proper perspective, better times were ahead of me. I could see them coming already.

My Mom isn't wealthy in terms of bank accounts, money, or real estate. In fact, she has only a few possessions that are worth anything at all in terms of worldly value. But there isn't a person alive who couldn't convince me that my Mom is rich. The kind of riches she possesses will never show up on a balance sheet or in an investment. Instead, her riches are found within the soul – in her attitude, her outlook on life, and in her perspective.

We all need money to live. There is no denying that. But given the choice between the wealth of this world and the riches of a contented and peaceful soul like my Mom's, I'll take the latter every time.

Thanks for the sermon, Mom, even though I didn't realize church was still in session.

❋ ❋ ❋

Your Worth Is Determined By How You Live, Not By What You Have

It's one of the greatest lessons in life. Our worth isn't determined by what we have or how much we make, but rather by how we live and the legacy we leave behind.

Life is about living. It's about relationships with family, friends, and God. It's about joy and sorrow, love and loss, and pleasure and pain. It's about the little things like a sunset on the water, a cool breeze on a hot day, or a nap in the middle of the afternoon. It's about all of the people, places, and experiences that shape our lives and make us who we are.

That's life. It isn't measured by your possessions or the size of your portfolio, but rather by the way you live and the difference you make in the lives of others. These are the qualities which will define your legacy.

Jesus talked a lot about money. In fact, He talked more about money in the Scriptures than he did about prayer, forgiveness, or even love. Why? I believe it was because Jesus understood, even 2000 years ago he knew, the powerful lure that money can have upon the human soul. So it was then, and so it remains today.

Jesus once shared this parable with his disciples:

> *The land of a rich man was very productive.*
> *And he began reasoning to himself, saying,*
> *"What shall I do, since I have no place to store my crops?"*
> *Then he said,*
> *"This is what I will do: I will tear down my barns and build larger ones,*
> *and there I will store all my grain and my goods,*
> *and I will say to my soul,*
> *'Soul, you have many goods laid up for many years to come;*
> *take your ease, eat, drink, and be merry.'"*

But God said to him,
"You fool! This very night your soul is required of you;
and now who will own what you have prepared?"
So is the man who stores up treasures for himself,
and is not rich toward God.
(Luke 12:16b-21)

The word "fool" may catch us by surprise, but the more you think about it, the more accurate the description is. What else do you call a man who lives as if he never has enough, whose only interest is in building bigger and bigger 'barns' rather than being with his family and friends? What other description can you use for someone who is so consumed with money and possessions that he doesn't even recognize his time on earth is coming to an end? The point of the parable is clear – there are priorities in this life which are more important than the money and riches that this world has to offer. Pity the poor person who thinks otherwise.

Money is a wonderful tool that can enrich our lives and provide security, but it's important to realize that is exactly what money is intended to be – a tool, not an end in and of itself. Wise are the people who use what they have to make the world a better place and to help others in need. Wiser still are those who grasp the truth that no amount of money is more important than life itself.

People misquote the Scriptures often when they say "money is the root of all evil". That isn't what the verse says. Instead, it says, "the *love* of money is the root of all evil". That has an entirely different meaning. Money itself isn't the problem, but the love of it is. That love can be more addictive than any drug on the street and has the power to ruin a reputation and destroy a life. It's all a matter of how you handle it. It's all a matter of keeping the value of money in its proper perspective.

Here is a good rule to live by – do the best you can to make the money you need to care for yourself, your family, and others, but guard against bowing down to the 'almighty dollar' as your priority in life. If money becomes your god, you'll pay a heavy price in the end. Some people may judge you by the size of your bank account or the type of house you live in, but don't let yourself fall into that trap.

Riches are nice to have, but we don't need to be rich to enjoy life. Some of the happiest people I've ever known were those who lived simply and within their limited means. The key to a contented life is keeping our priorities in order and understanding that the most important things in life can't be bought. Money is great when it's yours, but it doesn't determine your worth unless you allow it to.

John Wesley, the founder of Methodism, had this philosophy on money – "Make all you can, save all you can, and give all you can". These are good words. Work hard enough to make what you need, save enough to care for those you love, and give enough to make a difference in the lives of others.

May your life be rich and your worries be few. And may you always know that you are of infinite worth to God and to those who love you!

It's Your Choice...

Only you can change your financial situation. You can choose to ignore it, complain about it, and stress over it...or...you can choose to do something about it. Make a budget, determine where you want to go, and create a plan to get there.

You can change your life through hard work, determination, and a commitment to succeed, but don't ever forget that true worth is defined by how you live, not by what you have. Your perspective now and in the future will likely determine whether you control your money, or your money controls you. As always, it's your choice...

For Your Journal...

- Write a definition of success. Has your understanding of success changed since your divorce? How and why? What priorities in life are more important to you right now than money?

- Rewrite your definition of success to define what you think it should be as you move toward new horizons. What steps can you take right now to experience success according to your definition?

- Create a detailed budget. List three ways that you can decrease your spending (consolidate bills, eat out less, pay off high interest loans, cancel subscriptions or memberships, etc.) to save money.

- Now list at least two ways in which you can increase your income. Would changing jobs help? Taking on a second job? Going back to school to get an education in something you've always wanted to do? Which of these are realistic for you right now as you consider your financial situation?

- What would you like life to look like in a year? In three years? In five? What do you need to do to make these dreams a reality? Are you willing to commit yourself to doing it? Develop a plan, complete with goals and action steps, to guide you as you begin.

Part Two

Setting Your Sights on New Horizons

Chapter 7

The Greatest Strength –
Your Spiritual Foundation...

"We are not human beings going through a temporary spiritual experience.
We are spiritual beings going through a temporary human experience."
– Teilhard de Chardin –

The Story of the Prodigal Son – Luke 15:11-24...

Jesus said, "A man had two sons.
The younger of them said to his father,
'Father, give me the share of the estate that falls to me.'
So he divided his wealth between them.
Not many days later, the younger son gathered everything together and
went on a journey into a distant country,
and there he squandered his estate with loose living.

Now when he had spent everything,
a severe famine occurred in that country and he began to be impoverished.
So he went and hired himself out to one of the citizens of that country,
and he sent him into his fields to feed swine.
And he would have gladly filled his stomach with the pods that
the swine were eating, and no one was giving anything to him.

But when he came to his senses, he said,
'How many of my father's hired men have more than enough bread,
but I am dying here with hunger! I will get up and go to my father,
and say to him,
"Father, I have sinned against heaven, and in your sight;
I am no longer worthy to be called your son;
make me as one of your hired men."'

So he got up and came to his father.
But while he was still a long way off,
his father saw him and felt compassion for him,
and ran and embraced him and kissed him.
The son said to him,
"Father, I have sinned against heaven and in your sight;
I am no longer worthy to be called your son."

But the father said to his slaves,
"Quickly, bring out the best robe and put it on him,
and put a ring on his hand and sandals on his feet;
and bring the fattened calf, kill it, and let us eat and celebrate;
for this son of mine was dead and has come to life again;
he was lost and has been found."

And they began to celebrate.

❁ ❁ ❁

I know what it means to be the prodigal son.

I was unfaithful to my wife. I went through a difficult divorce and left my home. I broke the vows of my ordination, disappointed my family, friends, and church, and left the ministry. I hurt the people I loved. Yes, I know what it means to be the prodigal.

And like the prodigal, I too found myself lost and lonely in a land far away. For me, the faraway land wasn't measured in miles, but rather by an emotional and spiritual distance between myself and others, between myself and God. I understand what it feels like to be separated and alone, longing to be in my Father's presence once again. I've cried violent sobs in the middle of the night and uttered heartfelt prayers hoping for restoration, reconciliation, and redemption.

And again like the prodigal, I also know what it means to be welcomed home by the Father who awaited my return. The first time was in a church that was not my own, but there have been countless times; times when His love has been affirmed and reaffirmed to me through a variety of people, places, and events. I have experienced the blessing of being renewed by His grace, lifted by His Spirit.

And now, once more like the prodigal, I too have begun to celebrate life again. I feel alive and I've begun to live and love again. Periods of darkness still come occasionally, but they are fewer and farther between now than in the past. Despair has given way to hope, and sadness to joy. I am at peace with who I am, where I've been, and what I've done. I am a child of God – wounded, imperfect, and far from what I one day hope to be – but a child of His nonetheless.

The scars will always remain, reminding me of my time away, but they will also and always remind me of my Father's love. His is a love that never ends, never dies, and never quits. Through all the pain and heartache, and all the fears and tears, I give thanks to the Father whose love for me is greater than I can ever fully comprehend.

Everyone plays the part of the prodigal at some time. Everyone has moments when they turn away from what is good and right to follow another path, a path fraught with hurt and pain. Everyone knows what it's like to feel separated and alone, hurting and in despair, wondering if life will ever get better. The good news for us and for them is that the Father always stands ready to welcome us back. Always.

Foundations...

Up to now, we've addressed several topics which are important for everyone who has ever gone through the pain of a difficult divorce. Those topics include the healing a broken spirit, dealing with emotional hurt and pain, granting and receiving forgiveness, managing relationships with family and friends, and surviving through tough times, financially and otherwise.

We now move in a different direction. The remaining chapters of this book are dedicated to focusing on our resources as we set our sights firmly on new horizons. To begin this process, not surprisingly, we start at the beginning – with the need to recognize the importance of a spiritual foundation.

Go to any growing city and you're bound to see a new building under construction. Before that building ever started to rise from the ground, however, a foundation was poured and set in place. The foundation assures that the building will remain stable, sturdy, and strong when it is built, especially as it faces nature's storms in the years ahead.

You too have a foundation, only your foundation is spiritual instead of physical. Your foundation includes many things, including what you believe about God and His activity in this world in which we live. Your foundation is spiritual because you were created as a spiritual being, and it has constantly being shaped and re-shaped, formed and re-formed, throughout your lifetime, and continues to be even today. Just as a building's foundation is designed to keep it strong and stable through the storms of nature, your foundation gives you the strength and stability to make it through the storms of life. Divorce is one of those storms and, whether you've ever thought about it or not, your spiritual foundation impacts how you handle it, both now and in the future, and how you will heal.

No two spiritual foundations are exactly alike because no two people are exactly alike. We all walk different paths and have different experiences if life and, as a result, we all perceive the world around us differently too. Our upbringing and how we were raised is an important part of our spiritual foundation, but so are our families, our education and religious training, and our attitudes and beliefs. Yet while every spiritual foundation is unique, they all have a common purpose – they provide us with the strong and solid base by which we define and interpret life in the world around us.

I strayed away from my spiritual foundation in the years before my divorce, away from what I knew was good and right, but I was never separated from it completely. I couldn't be separated from it completely because my foundation is the core of who I am. It is woven into every fabric of my being, just as yours is in you. When the storms came and washed my world away, it was only my foundation that remained, providing me with base I needed and had to have as I made my new beginning.

Understanding the essence of your spiritual foundation is one of the keys on your journey to new horizons. That foundation, made up of everything you think, feel, and believe, will provide you with the strong and solid base upon which you will make the decisions that will determine your future. For that reason alone, it is important to understand what you believe and why.

To help you reflect upon your own spiritual foundation, I've offered the three core beliefs of mine in the pages which follow. As you read these spiritual truths, which separately and together form the essence of what I think and believe, I hope they will cause you to examine your own thoughts and beliefs.

Admittedly, and also unapologetically, the spiritual truths which form my foundation are decidedly Christian in their orientation. There is a reason, which is that I am a Christian myself and it shapes the core of who I am. But please understand that I'm not trying to convert you. Whether you agree or disagree with what I believe is really immaterial and unimportant. Either way is okay. It isn't necessary for us to think and believe exactly alike as we deal with the issues of divorce and seek to make a new beginning.

What I do hope, however, is that understanding my spiritual foundation will cause you to examine yours. Why is that important? Because the building blocks of your spiritual foundation – of what you think, feel, and believe – will influence your words, actions, and decisions for the rest of your life as you walk the path to new horizons.

Stephen J. King

My Spiritual Foundation...

I am a Christian. I believe God is the creator of the universe, Jesus Christ is the Savior of the world, and His Holy Spirit is with us for comfort and guidance.

I'm not a Christian because I was born into a Christian family or raised in a Christian home. Rather, I am a Christian because I have made the conscious, intentional decision to be a follower of Jesus Christ, despite my sins, shortcomings, and failures. I believe Jesus was and is God's Son, and that He is the way, the truth, and the life. I also believe Jesus was sent by God 2000 years ago to show us God's true nature – which is that of unlimited grace, love, and forgiveness – and to reconcile the world to Himself. Finally, I believe Jesus died on the cross as a sacrifice for our sin and proved that He was who He said he was – the Son of God – through His death and resurrection. The result is we now have the opportunity to live abundantly in this life and eternally with God in the next.

I don't pretend to have God, the Bible, or even my own faith, all figured out. I don't 'know it all' and I certainly don't have the market cornered on truth. No one does or ever will. But the Christian faith makes sense to me, even though there are many questions about God that I can't answer, despite my 25 years as a pastor and a leader in the United Methodist Church. At the same time, I'm also convinced there are certain spiritual realities which supersede those questions and lie beyond the realm of proof or explanation. The holding of those types of convictions is what we call faith.

I am neither a 'right wing' fundamentalist nor a 'left wing' liberal, but I do try to be a living witness to what I believe. Labels can be dangerous since it is impossible to fully define anyone with a term or phrase, but if I had to place a label on myself I would say I am a 'mainline liberal evangelical'. The words seem contradictory to each other even as I type them, but let me explain.

I consider myself to be 'mainline' in my understanding of God because I espouse most of the traditional Christian beliefs, although not all. Many Christians here in America would actually consider me 'liberal', however, based on my view of Scripture. The Bible, or the Judeo Christian Scriptures, is the basis for my beliefs, but I am not a literalist in interpreting it. I don't believe the Bible is perfect or that it came directly from God and is without error. Instead, I believe the Bible was written by imperfect human beings just like you and me, each who were trying to understand God's activity in the world and who were limited by their own opinions and understanding. The challenge, just as it has been for each generation before us and will be until the end of time, is to understand the eternal truths of God in what is written and to weed out that which is based on the culture at that time. God's truth is contained within the Scriptures, but not that every word of Scripture is God's truth. In my opinion, that is an important distinction.

At the same time, I also consider myself to be 'evangelical' because I believe it is important for every person to be 'connected' and in the 'right relationship' with God, however those phrases are understood. I want to encourage others to seek God's presence in their lives because I believe it is important, yet I'll never 'beat people over the head with the Bible' because no one should be coerced into making a decision for God that they aren't ready to make or don't understand. Instead, I try to be a positive example of what it means to have a meaningful relationship with God through Jesus Christ in my own life and hope others are able to recognize it. There are moments when I fail in that endeavor, of course, but it doesn't change the fact that it is my desire. We all want the best for those we love and to me that means offering the opportunity to my family and friends to have a relationship with the God who is the source of love, light, and life.

I'm secure in my faith and I'm not threatened or offended by others who see things differently than me, regardless of how radically different their beliefs and opinions may be. In fact, I believe it is healthy, both mentally and spiritually, for us to be challenged in what we believe because considering differing viewpoints forces us to re-evaluate our own faith in the process.

I realize that some people who are reading this book will disagree with what I've written based on their own understanding of God and issues of faith. At the same time, others will feel strengthened and affirmed in their beliefs by those same words. Wherever you fall along the spectrum is okay. Again, I'm not trying to convert you or to force what I believe upon you. My only purpose is to cause you to think about what you believe and why in order to better understand your own spiritual foundation. Regardless of our differences or our similarities, we are all in the same place after a painful divorce and beginning again is the common goal which unites us.

The truth is divorce knows no boundaries of religion, faith, or beliefs, and its hurt and heartache isn't limited to race, color, or creed, no matter how strong the spiritual foundation of an individual may be. Rich or poor, young or old, male or female, it doesn't matter. No one is immune to the impact of divorce upon their life.

Yet, while the strength of our spiritual foundation doesn't necessarily prevent a divorce from happening, it can and does directly affect our ability to heal and to move forward. In the end, faith offers a hope that is found no where else.

❀ ❀ ❀

Approximately nine months after the divorce...

The bold letters across the top indicated the title of the sermon, "What About Divorce?" Underneath was written the date of the service and the name of the pastor who delivered the message – Rev. Stephen King. As I pushed play to listen to the recording, I thought back to the time eighteen months before when I preached the sermon. The worship service was only a month before I confessed the affair to Debbie.

The message was one of eight in a sermon series that I preached on controversial issues in the church over a two month period. Some of the other topics included 'Homosexuality', 'Why Do Bad Things Happen to Good People?', 'Can We Really Trust the Bible?', and 'Is There Salvation for Non-Christians?' The messages proved to be of great interest in the community, as evidenced by the fact that over 2000 people were attending each Sunday. The response to my sermons had been positive as well.

Meanwhile, I continued to exist in my own personal hell. Trying to balance my calling as a pastor and my marriage to Debbie with my ongoing relationship with Jessica was nearly impossible, but I avoided coming forward with the truth because I didn't want to hurt any of the people involved.

I knew that my congregation would be devastated if they ever found out about Jessica and me. More importantly, so would Debbie and the kids. None of them deserved to be put through the pain that my confession would eventually cause, yet deep down inside I knew there was no way to avoid it. I was so entrenched in darkness that there seemed to be no way back to the light.

I had learned to compartmentalize my life back then, mostly out of self-preservation. When I was with Debbie or the kids, I did my best to be fully present in the moment and to focus only on them. And when I was with Jessica, I did the same thing. It wasn't easy to do, but it was the only way that I could survive. I also tried to do the same thing professionally, focusing only on what was best for my congregation whenever I preached or did anything at the church, but there were times I was distracted because of my personal life.

The most difficult challenge, as you might imagine, was when I preached. I tried my best to always speak words of truth, even though I wasn't living them myself at the time, and made an intentional effort to not shape my messages in a way that would attempt to justify my actions. Most of the time it was do-able. Sometimes it wasn't.

I've often thought of how hypocritical it seemed and, truthfully, I can't deny that it was. There I was, a pastor who was being unfaithful to his wife and the vows of his ordination, preaching to a congregation of wonderful people about God's love and the importance of godliness in our own lives. There is no way to rationalize what I did. I can only tell you that even the best of people, people with good hearts who want to do the right thing, sometimes find themselves in impossible situations which are without a winner. Sometimes there are no good solutions, and that's where I felt that I was. Unless you've been there yourself, faced with the possibility of hurting your kids and everyone you love, possibly destroying lives in the process, there's no way for you to fully understand. My advice is to do your best to never put yourself in that situation.

When I preached the sermon on divorce, I was well aware that I might be facing the issue myself very soon. But I didn't preach the message for me. Rather I preached it for the hundreds of others in my congregation, people who were there every Sunday, who had experience the pain of a divorce in their own lives. Some of them had moved on to a second marriage. Others were still single and questioned whether or not they would ever marry again. Some had wanted to be divorced and others had fought bitterly to keep their marriage. Many were still hurting, in some cases even years after the divorce actually occurred. Even more, I knew that our congregation was simply a microcosm of the greater society in which we lived.

Because divorce is so prevalent nowadays, both inside and outside of the church, I knew the issue was important to address. People had asked me many times through the years, "What does God really think of divorce?" It was never an easy question to answer, especially since every divorce situation is different, but my experience as a counselor told me that spouses who didn't want the marriage to end were usually the same ones who quoted the scriptures against it. Often this was done as a last and futile attempt to prevent the divorce and the pain which was sure to follow. Unfortunately, in too many of those cases that I worked with, the dye had already been cast well before then.

The Bible does speak of what some call 'unjustified divorce', i.e. divorce resulting from anything other than unfaithfulness, and many understand it to be an unforgivable sin. Furthermore, they believe the sin is perpetuated if the individual establishes a new relationship after they are divorced (based on Matthew 5:31-32). I don't believe it for a second and never have, even when I was married. In my opinion, those who interpret these verses literally are wrong and the broader themes of God's grace, love and forgiveness throughout the remainder of Scripture.

My opinion, both then and now, was the belief that divorce is unforgiveable is absurd and only creates unnecessary guilt for those who believe it. While it's true the consequences of divorce always remain for the individuals who experience it in some form or fashion, but the actual 'sin' of divorce, like every other sin we commit, is forgivable and forgiven through Jesus Christ and his death on the cross.

As I listened to the recording, I heard myself affirm that divorce is a 'sin' from the Biblical perspective because, in the simplest of terms, it represents a failed relationship, which is less than what God intends for us. I also pointed out some of the lasting consequences of divorce, such as broken families, emotional pain, and unresolved guilt, regardless of who was at fault or who made the final decision to end the marriage. Any way you look at it, I said, divorce is difficult.

But I followed those comments with the 'good news' – thankfully there is always good news in the message of the Gospel – that divorce, like any and all other sin, is forgivable through the grace of God. While its affects are unwanted and its consequences harsh, the message I read in Scripture was that nothing, not even divorce, can separate us from the love of God. His love, I proclaimed, always restores us and always redeems us, even when we don't deserve it and even when we don't believe He can. Ultimately, God always offers the opportunity for us to begin again.

When the sermon was over, I thought about how ironic it all was. I had preached the message to offer hope to those who were hurting and struggling after their own divorces, and who needed to hear the good news the Gospel and God's grace. Yet there I was some 18 months later, sitting in my bedroom by myself and at a very different place in my life than I was back then, now needing to receive the good news myself. Gratefully, I did.

❋ ❋ ❋

Three Spiritual Truths...

Three fundamental truths have served as the building blocks of my spiritual foundation through the years. Separately and together, these truths have sustained me in good times and bad, and have shaped and formed the essence of everything I believe. They affect how I live and what I say and do, both personally and professionally, and each has played a vital role in my new beginning.

The good news of these spiritual truths is for everyone, regardless of race, religion, or circumstances, who has ever opened their heart to God.

That means they are yours too, if you will accept them as your own. I invite you to consider spiritual truths as you begin your journey to new horizons.

Truth #1: God Is A God Of Love...

When I was married, our family used to go to Alabama every year to visit Debbie's family during the Christmas holidays. Since I had preaching responsibilities on Christmas Eve, we usually traveled on Christmas Day. The routine was always the same. First, we read the Christmas story around the tree and opened our gifts. Then we ate a big breakfast and packed the car. And finally, some time in late morning or early afternoon, we got on the road and made the seven hour trip, always looking forward to wonderful family times together.

I have some great memories from those trips, but there is one in particular that I will always cherish. The memory involved my youngest child, my daughter Amanda, and it happened as we were driving back home to Florida early one morning just before the New Year.

I don't recall how old Amanda was at the time, but I do remember that my wife was driving on a lonesome stretch of I-10 in north Florida near Tallahassee. Amanda was asleep on my lap in the middle seat of the van as the two boys dozed in the back. All of a sudden and for seemingly no reason, Amanda woke up quickly and sat up in the seat with her eyes wide open, trying to gather her bearings and make sense of where she was. When she realized we were still driving, she lied back down and once again put her head on my lap. I remember softly stroking her hair to help her fall back asleep.

As she rustled around to find a comfortable position, she interlocked her fingers with mine and used our secret 'father-daughter code', which she thought at the time that nobody knew in the world except us, as she squeezed my hand three times quickly to signal "I love you". I squeezed back three times in response to signal the same thing. As I looked at her sleepy blue eyes still partially opened, she whispered "I love you Daddy" and nodded off back to sleep.

That was it. That was the memory, and it will always be one of my favorites. I'm grateful for hundreds of great times with my kids and all the memories we built through the years, but that one will always be special. Why? Because, at that exact moment, I remember thinking how much I loved my little girl, and I imagined how safe she felt laying there in her daddy's lap. I'd like to believe she knew right then that I would always love her, no matter what, and that I'd always be there when she needed me, no matter where.

As much love as I felt for my daughter in that moment, I believe God loves us a million times more. No matter where we are, how we feel, or what we've done, we can never, ever, be separated from God's love. Never. We can ignore it, rebel against it, or fail to recognize it, but the one thing we can't do is change it. He loves us more than we can ever imagine, and His love is present with us always and everywhere. Nothing we can ever say or do will change that fact.

People generally grow up understanding the nature of God in one of two ways. Either they view God as some type of righteous judge who watches our every move and rewards or punishes us accordingly, or they see Him as some type of caring parental figure who loves us no matter what and who continues to forgive even when we rebel. The former understanding is based on a God of justice and judgment, and often develops relationships with God which are, at some level, motivated by fear. The latter understanding is based on a God of grace and mercy, and usually develops relationships with God that are motivated by love. I don't have to tell you which one I believe is the more accurate description of the God who created us.

Whatever else you may believe, make no mistake about this – God is love and He loves you.

The clear and consistent testimony of Scripture is that God loves us all and always will. It's the reason God sent His Son to die on the cross for us. Jesus didn't come to start a new religion or to divide people according to what they believe; rather He came to reconcile heaven and earth and to show us that God's love transcends every boundary we can ever imagine. No matter what you believe, what religion you practice, or even if you practice no religion at all, God loves you. That is the simple truth.

True love – God's love – never gives up on us and can always be trusted. We never walk alone, even when the entire world seems to come crashing down around us. He is with us in the darkness and He stands with us in our pain, No matter how lost or desperate we become, He will never leave us or forsake us. His love makes our new beginnings possible. How can I be so sure? Because I've experienced it firsthand.

God's love is everywhere. It is within you, outside of you, and all around you. It can never be fully explained or defined, only received. The real question is not whether God loves you, for certainly He does, but rather do you have eyes of faith to recognize it? I hope so.

Truth #2: God Is A God Of Grace...

Grace is undeserved mercy. Just as God's love is always present in our lives, God's grace is too. No matter how far we've wandered away from what is good and right or how far we've fallen, we are never too far away from God's grace to be restored. It is the penultimate message of hope.

God's grace doesn't magically remove the consequences of our actions, but it does affirm that He will never give up on us despite those actions and consequences. People may give up on us – in fact, many times they do – but God doesn't. Ever.

❋ ❋ ❋

Approximately two months after my divorce...

The setting was new to me, yet familiar. Strange, yet comfortable. For the first time since my divorce, I was attending a worship service on Sunday morning. And for the first time in longer than I could remember, it was in a church that was not my own.

Understand that most of my life had been spent in churches of one kind or another. I was a pastor and it came with the territory. But this church was different. I hadn't planned the service. I wasn't preaching. And no one was calling me 'Pastor Steve', my usual moniker over the years. Those opportunities had ended eight months before when I resigned from the United Methodist Church. Now I was on the other side of the pulpit, out there in the pews among the congregation, just like everyone else.

My sole purpose for going to the church that morning was to worship, nothing more. Like the hundreds of others who were gathered, I wanted to hear a message which would inspire my soul and that I could apply to my life. I wanted to have my spirit lifted and to lose myself in the music, to pray and to thank God for my blessings. While I told myself that I was no different than anyone else in the congregation, inside I knew I was like no one else there.

As I entered the sanctuary, a few people recognized me and greeted me by name, saying it was good to see me and they were glad that I'd come. In some ways it was nice to hear, but in others not so much. There was a part of me that just preferred to be unnoticed and anonymous.

What those who greeted me didn't know was that I'd had a difficult time mustering up the courage to go to church at all that morning. Church had been a low priority on the totem pole of life for me recently with everything I'd been through and most of my struggles were due to my embarrassment. I was well aware that my actions before the divorce hadn't matched up with my calling and the very faith I had professed to uphold as a minister. It was tough to put the feeling behind me.

I'd preached a thousand times about God's love and grace over the years, and always with sincere passion and conviction. It was what I believed and who I was, what I knew was true. There were several times when I had looked out from the pulpit upon some of the most generous and honorable people in the community, many of whom had confided in me about personal struggles in their own lives, and each time my message had been the same – God loves you just like you are and He offers you the chance for a new beginning. The difference between those times and now was that I was the one who needed to heed the message.

Friends tried to share it with me, but I tuned them out. Racked with pain and feeling guilty about what I had done, I felt unworthy to receive God's grace. Odd that I had trouble accepting the message I'd offered on God's behalf to so many others, but I couldn't help it. It was what I felt.

Despite my hesitation and insecurity, I was glad when the service began. I missed having my family with me, but somehow I sensed a connection in being with other believers. It felt good and right. In many ways, it felt redemptive.

I couldn't tell you the songs we sang during the service, or the Scriptures we read or the title of the sermon. There was one moment, however, that I will never forget. In fact, I'm sure I will remember it for the rest of my life. It was the moment when I received the bread and juice during the Sacrament of Holy Communion.

Anyone who knows me will tell you that I'm an emotional person. It's not unusual for me to cry at a movie or to share my feelings at a time when no one will. To be honest, I like that about myself and am glad my feelings and emotions come free and easy. But I have to admit there are some moments when I wish it were less so. The worship service that morning was one of those moments.

My hands were already sweating when I received the communion elements, and as I focused on their meaning – the bread symbolizing Christ's body broken and the juice symbolizing His blood shed – I began to tear up. Then I started to cry. Then I cried harder still. At first I tried to control my emotions and fight back the tears, self-conscious that others might be watching, but soon it just didn't matter anymore.

What happened next is hard to explain unless you've experienced it yourself. I had a 'God moment', a spiritual experience which awakened my soul. I felt God's presence right there with me. There were no hallelujah choruses ringing in my head and no grand visions of rapture, but it was real and more powerful than I could ever describe.

In that moment, as I looked at the wafer and grape juice, I accepted God's grace and realized it was meant for me. He had forgiven my sin. Not just some of it or most of it, but all of it. The proof was right there in my hands.

I ate the bread. I drank the juice. I cried. And I gave thanks.

✻ ✻ ✻

God's grace is a gift. We can't earn it or buy it, and there is nothing we can do to deserve it. He gives it to us freely and unconditionally, at all times and in all circumstances, always offering the hope of restoration and a new beginning. Our only response is to accept it and be thankful.

May His grace be yours always. Amen.

Truth #3: God Is A God Of Forgiveness...

God forgives our sin. All of our sin – past, present, and future – with no exceptions. His forgiveness is total and complete for everyone who has ever walked this earth, even when they don't want it or don't ask for it. People don't always forgive, or can't always forgive, but God does. Why? Because God is love, and true love – God's love – always forgives.

Skeptics say it can't be true. God's forgiveness can't be that easy, they say. There must be more to it. And they are right. There is more to it. The 'more', however, doesn't involve us in terms of how we act, think, or believe. Rather the 'more' has already been done for us by a loving God when He acted on our behalf.

That is what the cross of Jesus Christ is all about. It's God's love in action, God acting on our behalf, and a symbol of unbounded grace which makes forgiveness available to everyone without exception. In that one act 2000 years ago, God set His children free from the power of sin and death forever. That is good news!

Maybe the reason so many of us have trouble accepting the total and complete forgiveness of God is because the message is so simple. We want to make it more complicated or complex than it really is. But whether or not we accept God's ultimate plan of forgiveness, it doesn't change the truth. The reality is that truth is truth all the time, regardless of who believes it or doesn't.

Perhaps another reason we have a hard time accepting God's radical forgiveness is because we don't have the power to do it ourselves. It's easy to pay lip service to forgiveness on a Sunday morning in church or in a conversation among friends, but it's much more difficult when we are the ones who have been hurt. Rare are the people in this world who can truly forgive – rare and blessed.

We are imperfect people and, despite our best intentions, we've all had times when we hurt others by what we said or did, just as we have also been hurt by them. Often times our desire to forgive or be forgiven depends on our relationship with the other individual. Generally speaking, the more we love someone, the more important it is for us to grant or receive that forgiveness.

The problem, however, is that our love is limited, which in turn also limits our forgiveness. Not so with God. Because His love is limitless, so is His forgiveness. Ultimately, the act of forgiveness is rooted in love, and the reality is no one – absolutely no one – loves us more than God.

God's forgiveness, like His grace, doesn't remove the consequences of our actions or wipe away what has already been done, but it does allow us to release the guilt and emotional pain which those actions often bring. And once again, it brings with it the invitation to new life and new beginnings.

Here's the best part. I believe God's forgiveness is available to everyone because no one is excluded from His love. Christian, Jew, Moslem, or nothing at all, none are excluded. Every one of us is a child of God and, whether we realize it or not, that means we are loved and forgiven, and will be with Him forever.

I certainly understand that this understanding is a radical departure from what many in the Christian faith believe, but the universal forgiveness of God through the death of Jesus Christ is the only thing that makes sense to me. If we really believe that God created all of us and we are His children, then why wouldn't God extend the same benefits of His love to all?

The belief in conservative Christian churches is that you must accept Christ as your personal Lord and Savior to be 'saved', i.e., to have forgiveness of sin and receive the promise of eternal life. Yet this doctrine seems to me to be almost anti-God in terms of affirming His love and grace. Too many people in the world have never heard the Gospel or had the opportunity to know Christ based on where they live or how they were raised. Does that mean those people will suffer eternally in a place called 'hell' because of it? That runs contrary to everything I seem to read in Scripture about the love of God.

I understand why many Christians have this understanding based on verses like John 3:16 and a few others, but in my opinion they do a disservice to the whole of Scripture by ignoring God's desire to reconcile the world to Himself. In other words, I don't believe they are digging deep enough. No one should ever base everything they believe on one or two verses, especially when hundreds of others point in a different direction. For me, it comes down to the fact that I have difficulty justifying that an all-loving, all-powerful God would actually send His children to suffer eternally. If you were all-loving and all-powerful, would you allow that for your children?

God's love for us isn't determined by anything we say or do because His love is unconditional. If there is eternal life in heaven for some, then I believe there is eternal life in heaven for all. Not because we're good enough, or make a certain confession of faith, or belong to a certain religion, but simply because God has redeemed us anyway and made a way for all of us through Jesus Christ.

When the kids were young and our family would come home late at night after an evening out with friends, the children would inevitably fall asleep in the van. If they didn't wake up when we pulled into the garage, Debbie would go inside and turn back the sheets on their beds, and I would gently carry their sleeping bodies, one by one, into their rooms. Then we would tuck them in, give them a kiss goodnight, and say a prayer they would never hear.

One day Josh, our middle child, asked me how he ended up in his bed the night before. He remembered when we were driving home, but he didn't remember falling asleep in the van. The answer to his question, of course, was that I had carried him to his bedroom, even as he was completely unaware it was happening. Josh hadn't asked me to put him to bed – he couldn't because he was asleep – but I did it because I loved him and cared for him, just as any parent would.

In the same way, I believe all of God's children will end up with Him in heaven forever, regardless of whether they understand that in this world or not. I believe this will happen because I believe God loves us and cares for us unconditionally, and wants the best for us. And I believe it will happen because Christ gave His life for the sins of the world and everyone in it. He didn't just die for the evangelical Christians, or for the church-goers or religious folks of the world, but for everyone. That includes you and me. It also includes those people who live in other parts of the world, or who know God by a different name, or who have never heard of God at all. It even includes the people we don't want God to forgive.

Just as my son was carried to a better place by the father who loved him, we too as God's children will be brought into eternal life by the One who loves us. There is no greater affirmation of God's love, grace, and forgiveness than this.

Spiritual Development...

Spiritual development plays an important role in our lives, yet it's not something we think about very often. It strengthens our spiritual foundation and, as importantly, helps us to prepare for the challenges which all of us eventually face in life.

What is spiritual development? Perhaps it is best defined as the growth which occurs within our spirit as we develop an awareness of God. Spiritual development isn't about being 'religious', although many experience significant spiritual growth when they participate in a church, temple, mosque, or synagogue. Rather spiritual development is something which occurs within us as we make an intentional effort to relate to God and recognize His presence in the world around us.

Spiritual development typically begins when we make the commitment to grow spiritually. Let's use our physical development as an analogy. Just as our bodies grow and develop from the time we are born until the time we die, so do our spirits too. If we take care of our bodies by eating right, exercising, and getting the proper amount of rest, we usually find that we feel better and are healthier than if we don't. Once again, the same is true for our spirit. If we do the things that we can do, should do, and need to do to develop spiritually, then our spirit will generally be stronger and healthier than if we don't. The stronger the spirit, the better we feel, and the more prepared we will be to deal with the rigors of life.

The opposite is true as well, of course. If we don't take care of our bodies, or if we misuse or abuse them, we will likely have problems that we wouldn't have had otherwise. If we overeat and fail to exercise, we will struggle with obesity, stress, or fatigue. And if we smoke or drink too much, we may have problems with our heart, lungs, or liver. The list could easily go on.

Even though we know that we should care for our bodies, many times we don't. We know fast foods are bad for us, but we eat them anyway. We know we should work out, but instead we make excuses and say we can't make it to the gym. We grab something quick to eat and watch TV on the couch rather than make the effort it takes to care for our bodies and be healthy. All the while, we know there are future consequences to our actions. And so it is with our spiritual development as well.

It's up to us. If we make the effort to grow spiritually by exercising our faith and increasing our spiritual awareness, then we will become spiritually healthy over time. And if we don't, we won't.

❦ ❦ ❦

Approximately four months after the divorce...

It's an oddity of the human spirit that, even in our darkest moments, many times we resist doing the very things that we need to do to get better.

It was an ugly, rainy Monday night, and I was by myself. Not by choice, mind you, but that's the way it was. My kids were at their mom's house, my friends were home with their families, and Jessica was out somewhere with her neighbor friend. I felt alone.

Tired and depressed, and with my financial pressures mounting, I decided to stay home for the evening instead of doing what I was supposed to do. I was supposed to go to a session of my 16-week Divorce Recovery class, but I blew it off. I'd begun the classes about a month earlier on the suggestion of my counselor and I always found them helpful and encouraging, but there were still times I struggled to find the motivation to go.

Actually, I had trouble finding the motivation to do just about anything since my divorce. I felt beat-up, both spiritually and emotionally. My Divorce Recovery group had been one of the few bright spots in my life, and I knew I should've gotten my butt up off of the couch and forced myself to go, but still I didn't.

Why? I guess any of a dozen excuses sufficed – I was tired, I didn't want to spend the evening sitting in a classroom, I wasn't feeling good, I was depressed, it was raining outside, etcetera, etcetera. All of them were weak, but together they were strong enough to convince me to skip the class.

So, rather than attending a session that I really needed to attend, I wasted the evening away by killing time. I bought a pizza and a six-pack of beer as I spent money that I didn't have. I flipped through the channels aimlessly as I tried to find something worth watching on the TV. I went back and forth to the computer, pulled out my guitar, and cleaned my room, all in the hopes of finding something to do.

All in all, I did absolutely nothing – not the good kind of nothing when you are relaxed and decide to take time for yourself, but the bad kind of nothing which is born out of a restless spirit filled with worry and frustration. Everything I did that evening only reinforced the very feelings I was trying to overcome. I went to bed feeling worse off than when the evening first began.

Early the next morning, before I had even left for work, the phone rang. It was the leader of my Divorce Recovery group calling to check in with me. She said she had missed me the night before and, even though the class was good, it would've been even better if I'd been there.

I wasn't sure I believed her, but it was nice of her to say. To tell you the truth, I think the real reason she called was to make sure that I was alright. I fumbled around with a few lame excuses about why I was absent from the class, but I sensed she could see right through them. I'm sure she had heard them all before. Despite feeling awkward in our conversation, I really appreciated her call. It was good to know someone cared.

Right then and there I decided to stop making excuses for my behavior.
No longer would I allow myself to put off the things I needed to do to heal.
Either I would start taking care of myself and move forward in life, or else...
I shuddered to think about what might actually come after the 'or else'...

❀ ❀ ❀

Like so many of the things we've already discussed, spiritual development is a matter of choice. Just as when we make the decision to diet and work out in an effort to improve our physical health, we must make the decision to commit ourselves to spiritual development if we want to improve our spiritual health.

One reason we often overlook the importance of spiritual development is because it is difficult to measure. It's easy to gauge physical development. We can test our strength, step on a scale, or look at ourselves in a mirror. But there are no definitive standards we can use to measure the growth of our spirit. It's only when we are tested by the trials of life, such as in the case of divorce, that we recognize the need for a strong spiritual foundation.

I don't know where you are in your spiritual journey, but I do know you have the opportunity to grow and develop in the spiritual area of your life. I also know that your decision, whatever it may be, will impact your healing as you move toward new horizons.

Below are some suggestions that can help you grow spiritually, develop your faith, and increase your spiritual awareness. The list isn't all-inclusive, but it will get you moving in the right direction. Remember, the key is to strengthen your spiritual foundation by making a commitment to develop spiritually.

- **Find a place to worship** – Regardless of your religious background, find a place to worship. Being with others who are also interested in spiritual growth is always a positive step. A local church, temple, mosque, or synagogue is a good place to start. Find a worship service that you enjoy and which inspires you so you will look forward to going. There are many different styles of worship out there – including everything from very traditional to ultra contemporary – so keep searching until you find the one you like and that meets your needs.

- If you've never participated in a church or synagogue before, I understand it can be intimidating to go for the first time. But as someone who has spent nearly his entire life in communities of faith, I can assure you everyone there is just like you. Like most things in life, the hardest part is just getting started.

- **Find the resources you need** – Spiritual development is a broad topic, but there are a lot of resources available online, at your local bookstore, or in your community which can help you. Study aids can provide guidance as you read Scriptures. Books and interactive materials can help you study areas of interest such as your spiritual health, prayer and meditation, or spiritual awareness. Classes are available at places like YMCAs, community centers, churches, temples, and synagogues. You might even consider the possibility of finding a 'spiritual mentor', perhaps a good friend or a fellow church member who you respect for their spiritual maturity. Once again, the key is just getting started. Find the resources which interest you and get to work.

- **Have a 'personal devotion' every day** – Of the four suggestions listed here, this is the most important. Make it a priority to find 10-15 minutes each day, perhaps when you first get up in the morning or right before you go to bed at night, to read a devotional thought, spend a few moments in prayer, and give thanks for the blessings in your life. There are a host of devotional guides available, including many which focus specifically on the issues related to divorce. If you make practice this discipline daily, you will soon discover the value it has for your life.

- **Be realistic and intentional** – Spiritual development will occur in direct proportion to the time and effort you put into making it happen. The first step is to commit and the second is to be intentional about what you are doing. Don't use time, or the lack of it, as an excuse. We usually find a way to make time for the things we want to do in life and this is important.

So get started. Go to a bookstore and find a devotional guide. Set your alarm a little earlier tomorrow morning and begin your personal devotions. Check the internet to find worship times at churches and synagogues in your area. Don't make excuses and don't delay. The sooner you begin, the better off you'll be.

Seeing Truth Through The Eyes Of A Blind Man...

Regardless of whether you are a Christian or not, the New Testament story of Bartimaeus offers some wonderful insights into life and the choices we make in our desire to be made well. I share this story with you from my perspective as a pastor, but the lessons it teaches transcend the Christian faith and apply to anyone of us who has ever felt trapped by the circumstances of life, including those struggling with the issues of divorce.

According to the story (Mark 10:46-52), Jesus and his disciples were passing through the city of Jericho on their way to Jerusalem. The crowd greeting him was large, probably due to his reputation as a teacher, healer, and miracle worker.

We aren't told much about Bartimaeus except for the fact that he was blind. We can make some assumptions based on his condition, however. Like most people with physical disabilities in first century Palestine, Bartimaeus was probably a common beggar who regularly asked for alms at the city gates in order to support himself. In addition, because of his condition and the fact optical care was non-existent back then, he likely lived with the belief he would never be able to see.

Imagine that feeling. Imagine knowing you would have to beg to survive your whole life, that you would never see the faces of your family and friends, or the sun in the morning or the stars at night. For Bartimaeus, every day was like the one before, just struggling to survive with no hope of anything better on the horizon.

We aren't told why Bartimaeus was in the crowd when Jesus passed by, but it's clear he took full advantage of the opportunity. As Jesus neared, Bartimaeus began to cry out "Jesus, son of David, have mercy on me." The reaction of the people next to him was interesting. They told him to be quiet, angry and possibly even embarrassed that a common beggar like Bartimaeus was calling out to such an important person like Jesus. But Bartimaeus would not be silenced. Instead, he cried out even louder, "Jesus, son of David, have mercy on me!"

Think about it. What did Bartimaeus really have to lose? If the people around him were uncomfortable or embarrassed by his cry for help, then let them move to the other side of the road. After all, Bartimaeus probably thought, at least they could see where they were going.

There is a lesson here for us. Bartimaeus refused to let pride or embarrassment stand in the way of his asking for help. He had lived for too long with the pain and hopelessness of his situation and he was willing to do whatever he could do for the chance to be healed. Maybe Jesus couldn't help him, but Bartimaeus would never know unless he tried.

I wonder how many times we've let our pride and embarrassment stand in our way, preventing us from the opportunity to be healed or to be made well. How many times have we hesitated asking for help because we were too embarrassed? Postponed an appointment with the doctor because we were afraid to hear the results? Or refused to talk to a counselor, family member, or friend because we were too uncomfortable?

Even when we hit the proverbial 'rock bottom', something inside of us rebels against asking for help. We don't want to be perceived as a modern day beggar asking for alms to survive, so instead we quietly live in our desperation and tell ourselves we will find a way out of our mess alone. Sometimes we do. But many times we can't or don't, because we do need help, whether we ask for it or not. Eventually we arrive at the point where we either cry out for help or make the decision to continue to live in misery.

Bartimaeus would not be silenced. He continued to cry out to Jesus because Bartimaeus knew that he needed help. Then, in a beautiful moment in Scripture, we are told Jesus heard his cry and says to his disciples "Bring him to me."

Do you hear the message in that statement? In that one little phrase, we learn God hears the cry of those who call out to Him, of those who are down and out and who need His help. Jesus responded to Bartimaeus' need. When no one else could help him and others turned away, Bartimaeus cried out to the Son of God and He answered.

What happens next provides us with still another lesson. When Bartimaeus heard Jesus call, he immediately leapt to his feet, threw off his cloak, and went to the Son of God. Again, imagine the scene. Imagine this blind beggar, discouraged and without hope, suddenly springing to his feet, ready to do whatever he was asked. The help he longed for and needed was available right in front of him, and Bartimaeus wasn't about to miss the opportunity.

There is a huge difference between someone who cries out for help all the time and the person who is actually willing to rise up, throw off his cloak, and do what needs to be done to receive it. A lot of people moan and complain about their problems, but far fewer still are those who are willing to rise up and come to the place of healing.

You know the type of people I'm talking about. They love to complain but they never do anything to actually help themselves. They continue to whine about their situation instead of addressing it and finding the help they need. Instead of pursuing a solution, they ignore the advice of their doctor or counselor or, worse yet, refuse to see them for help at all. Rather than change their ways, they do nothing at all to take action and, as a result, nothing ever changes. Many times it's not because help isn't available, but rather because they are simply too 'blind' to see the possibilities. They are afraid to "throw off their cloak and come..."

To me, "throw off your cloak and come..." means we are willing to explore every possible opportunity to be made well. It means we are willing to do whatever we can, whenever we can, to be healed. God does hear our cry and help is available, but it's up to us to respond and receive it. The story of Bartimaeus ends with good news. Bartimaeus was healed and Jesus changed his life. The man who was once blind now is able to see.

I believe God wants healing for you and me as well. In fact, I know He does. He has heard my cry for help and, even now, is in the process of healing me. I've thrown off my cloak to come to Him and, while my healing wasn't instantaneous as in the case of Bartimaeus, it is just as real and life changing. I'm on the way to being made well, to being whole again. I'm on the way to new horizons. What about you?

It's Your Choice...

Your options are clear. Either you can make the commitment to spiritual development and build your spiritual foundation as you recognize God's love, grace, and forgiveness...or...you can ignore it all and deny the possibility of healing and being made well that only God can provide.

'Throw off your cloak and come...' It's your choice...

For Your Journal...

- Describe an experience in your life when you felt like the prodigal son. What caused it? What did you learn? Were you able to 'go home' again?

- Write a brief summary of your spiritual journey through the years. List the people and places which have impacted you along the way. If you made a list of the 'spiritual truths' which form your foundation, what would they be?

- Do you agree with the statements in this chapter about God's love, God's grace, and God's forgiveness? Why or why not? Write a short response to each explaining your own beliefs. How will your beliefs impact your journey to new horizons?

- How has your spiritual development in the past contributed to the person you are now? Are you willing to commit the time and effort needed in the future to care for your spirit and grow spiritually? Why or why not? If so, how will you begin?

- What does the phrase 'throw off your cloak and come...' mean for you in terms of moving toward healing and a new beginning? Are you willing to do it? Why or why not?

Chapter 8
The Greatest Constant – Change...

"The only thing that stays the same is change"
– Melissa Etheridge –

Divorce shakes up your world and, like it or not, change becomes your new and constant companion. As you leave the past behind and set out into the great unknown of new beginnings, how you respond is up to you.

❋ ❋ ❋

Approximately three months after the divorce...

The first Thanksgiving was the worst. I knew it would be. Others told me the first holiday alone would be the most difficult, but I tried to convince myself that I was ready for it. The truth, however, was that I wasn't. The day was more emotional than I anticipated.

The divorce was final in late August and, by the time Thanksgiving holidays rolled around in November, I was still reeling from the changes in my life. Being a holiday weekend, Debbie's Mom and Dad decided to come down from Alabama to spend some time with their recently divorced, and still very distraught, daughter. One of Debbie's sisters also came down with her husband. As usually happened when family came to visit, they all stayed at the house – my old house – to enjoy their time together.

Meanwhile, I was alone on Thanksgiving Day.

Earlier in the week, I thought about a friend years ago who used to invite people who were recently divorced and single to her house for Thanksgiving. It was her way of helping them and brightening their holidays. She knew it was a time of year when many who are alone become lonely and depressed. I could suddenly relate.

I had actually turned down two invitations to dinner earlier in the week, both from friends who invited me to spend Thanksgiving with them and their families. Somehow it just didn't seem right to go. I eventually decided it would be better for everyone, including me, if I just tried to make it through this first holiday on my own.

I decided to spend the morning and early afternoon at Metropolitan Ministries, volunteering to help serve the traditional Thanksgiving meal to the hundreds of 'street people' who annually showed up for the event. No matter how badly I felt about my circumstances, spending time there always seemed to put life in perspective. I couldn't help but to count my blessings when seeing so many people who were without a home or food to eat.

Just before I left my apartment, my oldest son, Chris, called and said he wanted to go volunteer too. I was glad to have his company, especially on a day when I felt somewhat 'homeless' myself. Although we didn't actually get to serve the meals, we had a great time sorting food and preparing bags for other homeless families who would be coming to Metropolitan Ministries in the days ahead. It was a simple reminder to me of how much I often take for granted.

I dropped Chris off at the house about an hour before Debbie and her family were to have their Thanksgiving dinner. As it turned out, my Mom pulled into the driveway of Debbie's house at the same time. She had wanted to fix dinner and spend the day with me, but I insisted that she eat with the kids. Besides, I wanted her to have the opportunity to spend time with Hannah, Debbie's Mom. They had been good friends throughout the years and hadn't really had the chance to be together since the divorce. I helped my Mom bring in her famous sausage dressing and mashed potatoes, both traditional favorites of our holiday meals in the past, and went through a few awkward hellos before hugging my kids and heading home.

The scene at my apartment was much different than the house. No kids. No family around. The silence was deafening. In years past, my holidays were always filled with people, activity, and more food than anyone could possibly eat in a day. But not anymore. The winds of change were blowing and I was in the eye of the storm.

I turned on the TV just to provide some background noise and heated up my day old leftovers from the Chinese dinner I'd had the night before. As I sat down on my couch to eat, I mockingly said to myself 'Happy Thanksgiving'. I don't think I even paused long enough to give thanks.

Things did get better a little later, however, for which I was grateful. The kids called and said they had saved me a plate of food and wanted me to come pick it up. I was a little embarrassed, to tell you the truth, but it was good to know they were thinking of me. Debbie was much more relaxed when I stopped by and I even sat down and talked for a while, which was nice.

Later Mom stopped by my apartment to visit and bring more food. And as the afternoon turned into evening, Jessica and a few other friends called just to see how I was doing. All in all, by the time the day was done, I felt pretty good about the way it turned out.

As I lay my head down on the pillow that night, I thanked God for helping me make it through my first holiday. Life would get better soon, I told myself. It had to, I was sure of it. I just had to focus on getting through this day. And then tomorrow. And then the day after that.

It was all part of the process called change...

❀ ❀ ❀

There is a bumper sticker which says, 'Change Happens'. Well, that isn't the exact wording it uses, but you get the idea. Whether we want it to or not, change happens. It is inevitable. We only have to look at ourselves and the world around us to understand that truth.

Our bodies change physically through the years as we go through childhood and move into adulthood and old age. We change mentally as our learning capacities increase through high school, college, and beyond. We change emotionally as we mature and learn to deal with happiness and sadness, love and loss, joy and grief. And we change spiritually as we continue to grapple with our understanding of life, God, and matters of faith.

As we go through these changes in our lives, the world around us is constantly changing too. Technological advances bring new opportunities in the way we work and communicate around the globe. Discoveries in the fields of medicine and science affect how we live. Businesses and corporations find new and better ways to serve their customers. Politics, finance, industry, travel, and almost every other area are always changing, growing, and adapting, all in an attempt to meet the needs of our society in the 21st century.

Many of these changes are good. Others, maybe not so much. But either way, we learn early on that we have to constantly adjust, adapt, and manage change if we ever expect to be happy and successful. Nowhere is this more evident in our personal lives than when we deal with the changes brought on by divorce.

Change And Divorce...

Change and divorce go together. Seemingly they are synonymous. When divorce happens, every area of life is affected and the changes are often dramatic and difficult to manage. We're forced to deal with new living arrangements, altered family relationships, a new lifestyle, and shifts in our daily patterns and routines. All the while, we are also trying to make sense of our feelings and fluctuating emotions as we redefine our lives and who we are. Complicating matters even more, all of these changes occur quickly and within a short span of time, which only creates tension, stress and anxiety.

The first year after divorce tends to be the most difficult. It is then that the fear and uncertainty are the most prominent. Sometimes we adapt quickly and move on. At others we feel confused and overwhelmed by the changes. Sometimes it's both.

People react differently. Some view change as a challenge that must be met head on and dealt with quickly. Others are intimidated by change and shy away, fearing the complications it can bring. Still others try to deny or ignore change altogether, as if things will remain just as they always have been. But things won't remain the same. They can't. It's impossible, because divorce changes everything.

Not all of the changes associated with divorce are necessarily bad, however. As a matter of fact, some of them can be very positive. For example, it's not uncommon for people to feel a sense of relief in getting away from the daily tension and pressures which usually characterizes a relationship during the final days of marriage. Many appreciate the opportunity to move in a different direction, or enjoy their newfound sense of freedom. But even then, these changes still must be managed as the individual adjusts and adapts to the new situation.

How we adapt to the changes brought on by divorce will determine how quickly we are able move forward with life when it is over. Whenever we encounter change of any kind, our goal should always be the same. We want to maximize the benefits while, at the same time, minimizing the negative affects. This is the best way – really the only way – to manage change effectively.

We typically manage change on four essential levels.

Level #1: Managing Change Through Education And Awareness

Being aware of the changes occurring in our lives and educating ourselves about the best way to deal with them is one of the most important things we can do to manage change effectively.

❄ ❄ ❄

A few weeks before the divorce...

I didn't want to go. But I had to. The class for parents who were going through a divorce and still had dependent children living at home was required by Florida Law. You had to take it before the divorce could become final. So, I set aside my attitude, swallowed my pride, and headed for the hotel where the session was held.

The rain was coming down in buckets as I pulled into the parking lot. With no umbrella available, I ran to the hotel lobby but was still drenched by the time I arrived. Dripping wet, I stopped by the bathroom to dry off as best as I could before going to the registration table.

It's hard to describe the feeling I had as I walked into the room where the class was to be held. I guess the best way to say it is that I felt like a loser, like I didn't belong there. It was a strange mix of people. One guy sat in his chair with his eyes closed, apparently trying to sleep, with his legs fully extended causing others to step over them. Another guy was in basketball shorts and a tank top, and talked quietly on his cell phone as he looked at a newspaper. A few seats ahead of him was a young woman I would have sworn wasn't old enough to be married in the first place. She just looked out into space with her New York Yankees cap pulled down low and crooked over her eyes. Each of these people were here for the same reason I was. They must have a story too, I thought to myself, but somehow I didn't seem to fit. Probably the only thing we had in common was that they never expected to be sitting in a class like this either. I quickly found a seat in the back of the room.

The music playing through the speakers was upbeat and lively, intentionally chosen, I assumed, to lift the mood of those attending. Not long after I sat down, with about 30-40 people gather in the room, the instructor enthusiastically introduced herself and off we went.

Here's what I discovered over the next three hours – I was wrong. Wrong about my attitude entering the class, wrong about thinking it would be a waste of time, and wrong about feeling as if I didn't belong there. The session was not only interesting, but it was very helpful to me as well. The instructor, who was sharp and very engaging, talked knowledgably about the importance of seeing divorce through your child's eyes. She offered advice on how to avoid the mistakes that parents so often make during that difficult time as well as several insights about the best way to communicate with your kids throughout the process. By the time class finished, I found myself glad I went.

For the first time since Debbie had told me she wanted a divorce a few weeks earlier, I realized there were resources which could help me. My situation was unique, but the issues surrounding my situation weren't. I'd just spent an entire evening being educated about how to be a better father to my kids through the divorce and, if that was so, I was sure there were other materials and resources which could help me with my depression, guilt, and financial problems. I just had to find them. After all, I thought to myself, I'd be a fool not to take advantage of anything that could help me get through what I was going through.

The rain had stopped by the time I walked back out to my car. Driving home on that muggy Florida evening, I knew I had a choice. Changes were on the horizon. Of that much I was certain. But how I chose to manage those changes – well, that was completely up to me. I could educate myself and be prepared to deal with them, or I could bury my head in the sand and stumble blindly into the future.

It was totally my choice...just as it always was.

❋ ❋ ❋

Soon after Debbie made it clear to me that our marriage was about to end, I met separately with two friends of mine who had recently gone through a divorce themselves. I asked the same questions to both of them. If you were to go through it all again, I said, what would you do differently? And what lessons did you learn along the way? Their situations were different from mine, but both helped me understand the issues I would soon be facing. Experience – whether it's ours or someone else's – is always a wonderful teacher.

And since my divorce, I've also been approached by friends who have asked me for the same type of advice. There is always one lesson I share with them. If I were to relive that very difficult period of life, I tell them, I would be more intentional about educating myself on the issues. I had spent a lot of time researching the impact of the divorce upon my children, but not nearly enough researching the other personal issues which ended up dragging me down.

If I had it to do over again, I'd study the legal intricacies of divorce agreements more carefully, particularly as they relate to alimony. I would read more about depression and find the practical help I needed to deal with it. I'd gather more information on the impact grief and depression can have on a life and find materials to help me with debt and money management. At one point or another, I did eventually research all these things, but many times it was only after they had already become a major problem for me in my situation. I should have been more prepared. I should have been proactive instead of reactive. I should have educated myself in advance.

Educating ourselves about change and the issues of divorce only makes sense. There is no need to 'reinvent the wheel' through trial and error when we can draw upon the experience of others who have already been down that road. We only set ourselves up for bigger problems in the future if we don't educate ourselves now.

So how do we educate ourselves and find the resources we need to manage change effectively through the issues of divorce? It isn't difficult, but it does involve some time and effort. Here are a few suggestions, some of which we have already talked about, which might help:

- **Read books and articles about the issues of divorce.** There are a million out there. Just perform a search on Google or take a brief stroll through the local library or bookstore and you will see what I mean. You can find whatever you need about whatever the issues are for you. Keep in mind that no one article or book will ever have all the information you need, so keep searching until you find exactly what you are looking for.

- **Find a class or a support group.** This isn't the first time I've mentioned this which probably indicates just how important my own Divorce Recovery group was for me. Hearing the stories and experiences of others who are struggling with the same issues you are can be a valuable learning experience. One tip I might offer here – make sure the class or support group you choose is issue oriented rather than socially oriented. Both are important, of course, but the priority for you right now is education and awareness.

- 'Interview' people who have been through divorce. If it's true that 'experience is the best teacher', then talk to the people with the experience. They will understand, better than most, what you are going through and what you need. They have been in similar situations before and, just as a parent can relate to the needs of a child because the parent was once a kid too, so too those who have been through divorce can offer a perspective which others can't.

Whatever you do, do something. Don't ignore the changes which are happening in your life. The first step in managing those changes effectively is to be educated, informed, and aware. Take the time to do the research and to find what you need. You won't be sorry.

Level #2: Managing Attitudinal Change

Our attitude directly impacts how we manage change. While a bad attitude can be a blueprint for disaster, a good attitude allows us to manage change more effectively as we work for the best possible outcome in our situation. Our attitude is either a drawback or an asset as we manage change, and it is up to us to decide which one it will be.

Years ago I heard a story about a Youth Director at a church in Montgomery, Alabama, who wanted to teach his group a lesson on the subject of attitude. Before he had been hired in the position, the youth group had limped along for years, declining in both numbers and in spirit. Most of the kids in the community thought of the group as boring, cliquish, and irrelevant. The new Youth Minister was hired to change that.

With a genuine desire to help kids and make a difference in their lives, and with a passion for youth ministry, the new Youth Director infused new life into the program almost immediately. He worked hard to change the culture of youth ministry in the church and tried his best to make the Sunday evening youth meetings 'the place to be' for those in the community.

His leadership was welcomed and certainly provided a spark, but it wasn't long before the kids began to gradually fall back into the same old patterns and habits they had before. As decline started to set in again and the Youth Director's level of frustration began to rise, he decided to try something unusual.

The Youth Minister talked with the Pastor about his idea and, after receiving approval, reserved the sanctuary a month in advance for a special Sunday evening service. He then sent out handwritten invitations to the event to every youth and parent in the congregation, asking each of them to attend. Finally, he also personally invited the staff and Administrative Board of the church, as well as several others from around the community.

As a result of his efforts, there were hundreds of people gathered in the sanctuary on the appointed night, although no one was really quite sure of what to expect. The service began with the Youth Director and Senior Pastor processing fully robed down the center aisle, followed by six senior high leaders carrying a casket rented from a local funeral home. To everyone's surprise, they had been invited to attend a funeral!

The 'deceased' being laid to rest wasn't a person, but rather the attitudes and behaviors of the youth and the church which had prevented them from growing and moving forward. With the casket in place before the altar, the Senior Pastor read the opening words from an actual funeral service, and then the Youth Director stepped forward to offer the eulogy. As he talked about the 'dead' attitudes and laid each to rest one by one, he symbolically placed a piece of paper representing the attitude into the coffin. Each time a leader in the youth group then stepped forward to introduce a new attitude – one which was positive, life affirming, and growth oriented – in its place.

The service ended with the casket being slammed shut as the Youth Director quoted Second Corinthians 5:17, which says, "Behold, old things have passed away and all things have become new". A cheer erupted from the youth, and then from everyone attending, which indicated they understood the message.

What an incredibly powerful way to communicate the importance of a positive attitude to a group of young people! The reality, however, is that kids aren't the only ones who need to be hear that message. You and I need an attitude adjustment every now and then as well, especially when it comes to managing the changes related to divorce. Like the group in the story above, it could be that we are holding on to attitudes and behaviors which need to be dead and buried, and then be replaced with others which are positive, life affirming, and growth oriented. Our ability to make those adjustments as we manage change may very well determine how successful we are in pursuing new horizons.

Attitudes *can* be adjusted, controlled, and even changed completely. The key is to understand this truth – we *always* have the opportunity to control our attitude rather than letting it control us. That never changes, no matter what. Regardless of our circumstances, situation, or surroundings, we always have the ability to control our attitude.

If I asked you to make a list of the attitudes which need to change in your life, could you do it? What is your attitude toward your former spouse, your divorce, or the struggles you've experienced lately? What is your attitude about life in general and your future in particular? What about toward your physical, emotional, or spiritual health? Or toward your job, your financial situation, or your...go ahead, you fill in the blank.

We will devote an entire chapter to the importance of having a positive attitude a little later, but suffice it to say at this point that your attitude impacts everything you do and say in life. It affects the way you think about yourself, treat other people, and manage change. In essence, your attitude dictates the way you live. The importance of attitude cannot be overstated.

It boils down to this – you can improve your life by improving your attitude. If you're holding on to attitudes which are bad, negative, or destructive, then it is up to you to change them. Remember, you always have the opportunity to control your attitude rather than letting it control you. You are in charge.

The question is how do you do it? How do you change a bad attitude into a good one, or a negative attitude into a positive one? The process is easy enough to understand, but it does require some effort on our part to make it happen.

First, you begin by identifying and examining the attitude which needs to change. Ask yourself why your attitude is as it is, and how it got to be that way. What experiences contributed to its development? Awareness, as was discussed in the first level, is the key here.

Second, you determine the new attitude you would like to embrace in its place. Define this new attitude in terms of how it will manifest itself in your everyday life, how it will affect what you do and say. Wanting to change a bad attitude is a good beginning but, unless you have a clear goal and direction for the future, it will be hard to do. Know where you want to go.

Finally, commit to making the change by thinking, talking, and acting in a way which is consistent with the attitude you want to embrace. This is where 'the rubber meets the road' and real change occurs. You can talk about wanting to change all you want, but until you make the commitment and actually do something to initiate action, talk is all it will be.

I noticed a disturbing change in my attitude after the divorce. Up until the time when my marriage ended, I always considered myself to be trusting of other people. I usually took them at their word and accepted them as they were. But somewhere along the line that changed, I began to be suspicious of people I didn't know well, often questioning their motives or avoiding conversations because I thought they might try to twist what I was saying or somehow use it against me. I didn't like my attitude and I hated feeling that way.

I knew my attitude wasn't what I wanted to be, yet it was exactly what my attitude had become. Worse yet, I felt it was affecting my relationships with the people I loved and cared about. I knew something had to change, and change quickly. That 'something' was my attitude. So I finally decided to do something about it.

As I tried to understand my attitude, I realized it had developed into what it was because the pain and rejection I felt during and after my divorce. No surprise there. In my attempt to keep the pain from continuing, I projected my feelings onto others and unintentionally pushed them away. I became afraid to trust. That was wrong and I knew it.

Next, I thought about the 'new' attitude I wanted to embrace, or in this case the old attitude I wanted to recapture. That was easy. I wanted to trust people again. I wanted to believe that people were basically good and honest, regardless of the mistakes in their past, and I wanted my attitude to communicate the love, kindness, and compassion which I believed was a true reflection of who I really was. That, I decided, was the new attitude I wanted.

Finally I committed to doing what I needed to do to change my attitude. I tried to consciously think through the things I said and did to make sure they were consistent with the attitude I wanted to embrace. I focused my efforts on trusting people, even when they had acted angrily or let me down in the past. The transition wasn't nearly as difficult as I thought it would be. It didn't happen overnight, but constantly focusing on the new attitude I wanted to have gave me a clear direction of what I needed to do. Gradually, over time, it became a natural part of who I was once again.

Did I get 'burned' a few times along the way by people who misused or abused my trust? Yes. And there were plenty of other times when I felt uncomfortably vulnerable and wanted to pull away from individuals. But I didn't, or at least I tried not to. I fought through the urge to back away and made the commitment to trust them anyway. It took time to change some of the behaviors which had become engrained since my divorce, but I eventually did it and I'm glad I did. It was the right thing for me, and I feel better about myself because of it.

You can change the negative attitudes in your life if you want to, and you just might find, like I did, that it's easier than you think. Recognizing that you have the power to change your attitude is empowering and the good news is you can start right now. Examine the attitude you want to change; envision the new attitude you want to embrace; and commit to making the change. You are in control.

Level #3: Managing Behavioral Change

"If you always do what you've always done, then you'll always get what you've always got". I don't know who said it, or where the quote came from, but there is a lot of wisdom in that little saying. Too many times in life we make the mistake of doing the same things we've always done and yet hope for different results. Life doesn't work that way. Different results only come with a change of direction.

❋ ❋ ❋

Approximately six months prior to the divorce...

My final conversation with Jessica, much to my disappointment, happened over the phone. I wanted to talk to her face to face but, by then, I had already promised Debbie that I wouldn't see Jessica anymore for any reason or under any circumstances. Therefore, the phone had to do.

When I explained to Jessica that Debbie and I were going to try to salvage our marriage, she knew exactly what that meant. From that point forward, there would be no more contact between us. No more personal times together. No more phone calls. No more emails, cards, or texts. No more anything. I wasn't sure if my marriage could survive with Jessica out of the picture, but I was absolutely certain it couldn't with her in it. I had to make some major changes in my life if I was going to keep my family together, and my relationship with Jessica was at the top of that list.

Jessica and I had talked about the possibility of this day coming a thousand times before, but the truth is both of us hoped it would never happen. She knew that if it did, I would try to do anything I could do to stay with my kids. But that didn't make the conversation any easier. After all, Jessica was the one who had my heart.

Our relationship, like most affair relationships I guess, was filled with excitement and passion on one side and confusion and feelings of dashed hopes on the other. Yet there was never a doubt in my mind about how I felt about her. I loved Jessica and wanted to be with her.

At the same time, I also knew the relationship was terribly unfair to Debbie and my marriage. How can any marriage ever be healthy and whole when one partner is giving himself physically, spiritually, and emotionally to someone else? It can't. No marriage can survive under those circumstances. It's not possible.

Change is always difficult, but it's especially hard when it involves changing personal behaviors that you don't want to give up. Knowing what I needed to do wasn't the problem. Doing it was. Understanding the need for change and actually taking the steps to make it happen are two entirely different things.

I knew my resolve would be tested in terms of keeping my commitment to not see Jessica after our conversation, and I was right. There must have been a hundred times when I wanted to talk and started to dial her number, but I never completed the calls. I spent hours reading cards that I wanted to buy for her or writing emails I wanted to send, but I never bought or sent any of them. With the lone exception of a five minute call on her birthday, I remained committed to our 'no contact rule' as I tried to focus my energy on my relationship with Debbie. As the months passed, it became easier to do and I eventually grew used to being apart. I'm guessing the same was true for her.

In the end, of course, my marriage didn't work out. Debbie and I divorced six months later, victims of too much damage already done and too many problems to overcome. Ending my relationship with Jessica made it possible for Debbie and me to try, but it wasn't enough to keep us together.

Through it all, I learned a lesson; albeit one I would've preferred to do without. I learned that I have the power to change my behavior, not only when I want to, but also when I don't – even when my feelings contradict, even when I resist, and even when it hurts.

Change is possible. Always.

❀ ❀ ❀

Behavioral change – changing our personal habits, patterns, and behaviors – is always challenging. Even when we know the change is warranted and in our own best interest, it's still hard to do and many times we still resist. Why? Stubbornness and foolish pride probably have something to do with it, but they aren't the only reasons. A major reason we have trouble with these types of changes is because we are psychologically addicted to the habit, pattern, or behavior which needs to change.

Psychological addiction, or a dependency as it is often called, is extremely powerful. Just as a physical addiction affects the body, a psychological addiction affects the mind. We have habits, patterns, and behaviors that have become engrained in us over time, whether good or bad, and they become comfortable and part of how see ourselves or understand who we are. When we try to move in a new direction, our psyche rebels against giving up that which is familiar to us and we are constantly tempted to return to our old ways, no matter how dysfunctional they may have been.

I once read about a polar bear which was relocated to a zoo in northern Colorado. In the months prior to its arrival, the zoo embarked on a multi-million dollar building project to create a 'natural' habitat for the polar bear. Unfortunately, the construction took longer than expected and the habitat wasn't completed by the time the bear arrived. In the interim, the bear was housed in a large cage.

Unable to roam freely, the bear spent most of its time sleeping. Several times a day when it awoke, however, the animal followed a predictable routine. First, the bear would pace five or six steps in one direction until it reached the bars of its captivity. Then, rising up on its haunches, it would turn around and pace five or six steps back in the direction from which it had originally come. It repeated the process over and over again until finally, seemingly tired of the monotony, the bear laid down and went back down to sleep.

When the habitat was completed, the construction workers and zoo employees looked on excitedly as the huge crane lowered the bear cage into its brand new environment. Then the cage was opened and the bear was set 'free' to enjoy its new home, which included a temperature controlled climate, snow covered caves, and a pond stocked with fish. No one was prepared for what happened next, however. The bear exited the cage and walked toward the caves until, suddenly, it seemed confused by its surroundings and the people watching. Then it rose up on its haunches, turned around, and headed back toward the cage! The bear repeated the process a second time, almost as if its innate desire for freedom had somehow been replaced by an acceptance of its confinement, You see, the physical barriers to freedom were removed, but the psychological ones still remained, if only momentarily. After a few minutes, the bear did venture away from the cage and was able to experience a new and better life.

You and I are not unlike that polar bear in this respect; we too have had moments when we have allowed our psychological barriers to hold us back and imprison us, unsure if we should venture out beyond the imaginary cages we create in our minds. The good news is we can break free from the chains that bind us and experience new life after divorce if we manage change effectively and improve our lives. The only question is, will we?

Because psychological barriers are mental rather than physical, making behavioral changes are more about how we think than what we do. When we are able to mentally commit to the change we need to make, then our actions will naturally follow.

So what about you? What changes do you need to make to improve your life? More importantly, what is holding you back from making them? The cage is open and you have been set free. You have the power within you to change any behavior which needs to be changed and to go wherever you want to go. It's up to you.

Level #4: Managing Group Change

Group change is the most difficult of the four levels to manage. Whereas you are responsible for your actions in the first three levels and can educate yourself, change your attitude, or adjust your behavior, group change involves more people than just you. Since two or more people are actively involved with the change and directly affected by it, and because each of those people are driven by their own motivations and interests, managing group change can be tricky.

Stephen J. King

When I moved out of the house prior to the divorce, my entire family was affected by the change. Debbie and I always shared the responsibilities of the house, such as getting the kids ready for school, making dinner, or paying bills, but we couldn't anymore since we were in different homes. We were both thrust into the unfamiliar role of being single parents whenever the kids were with us.

Our children were affected too. The change forced them to get used to having two homes instead of one and, since only one parent was there at a time, they had to adjust their daily patterns and routines. Everything in their home life was different than it had been before and, as a result, like most kids whose parents end up in divorce, they had to grow up a little quicker than they should have.

To minimize the impact of these changes upon the kids, I rented an apartment five minutes away from the house and lived there for the first year after my divorce. The moved proved to be helpful for all us – me, Debbie, and the kids – because it made it easier for the kids to go back and forth whenever they needed to. Debbie and I also tried to coordinate our schedules as much as possible so we could share the responsibilities of driving the kids to school, practices, or activities.

The situation was far from ideal – then again, divorce never is – but we did our best to manage the changes together as a group. There were occasional frustrations when Debbie and I disagreed about something, or when one of us affected the entire family by making a decision without consulting the other, but that is often the reality of dealing with change at the group level. No one person controls every decision and no one has all the power.

Although it is impossible to control every detail at the group level because there are other people involved in the decisions, don't ever make the mistake of thinking that you have no control in the process at all. You do. You always do, even if it's only in the way you respond to the decisions made by others. As a general rule, the more you remain open and flexible in supporting the decisions of others and working for the betterment of the entire group, the more they will supportive of decisions you make along the way.

So what is the best approach to managing change effectively at the group level? The answer is found in the Golden Rule – "Treat others as you would like to be treated yourself". If possible, be helpful and support- ive of each person in the group, even when things don't go your way. Be kind, gracious, and compassionate toward everyone, and work toward solutions which are in the best interest of all. In the end, trying to build unity and harmony within the group is always better than being divisive and argumentative.

❋ ❋ ❋

Approximately two and half years after the divorce...

My former brother-in-law, Jeff, came over late in the morning just as he said he would. I didn't know why we were meeting, but I knew it must be important. In the three years since the divorce, Jeff and I had barely talked. He called the house a few times back in the days when Debbie and I were still trying to work on our marriage, but it was always to speak with Debbie and not with me. I did receive a letter from him once urging me to 'get right' with God. I probably would've been offended if it had come from anyone else, but I knew Jeff's heart and I was sure he was just trying to help.

Jeff is a good man. Married to Debbie's oldest sister, he is the quietest of my three former brothers-in-law. A successful doctor who is honest, hard- working, and extremely practical, Jeff is very conservative in his approach to life. Despite the fact we differed in our views theologically, socially, and politically, I always appreciated his perspective and his sincere desire to serve God based on his understanding of Scripture.

Jeff and his family came down from Alabama to visit Debbie for a week in late March. The timing seemed odd, especially since there were no holidays or special events happening, but I was glad that Debbie was going to have some time to spend with her oldest sister, someone she admired and respected.

While they were visiting, I took Josh and Amanda out to dinner on a Friday night. Jeff came out to talk to me when I brought them back to the house and asked if we could meet the next morning. He didn't say why, but we set a time to meet at my new condo, which I was still in the process of painting since I'd just purchased it the week before. I didn't even have furniture moved in yet.

When Jeff arrived Saturday morning, I set up two folding chairs in the midst of the clutter of paint cans and boxes, and he came right to the point. He told me his trip to Florida was more than a social visit. Unbeknownst both to me and the kids at that time, Debbie had decided to sell the house and move to Georgia by the end of the summer, and Jeff had come down to help her plan. The news caught me off-guard, but not nearly as much as his next statement.

Jeff said Debbie wanted to take the kids to Georgia with her. She knew Chris, our oldest who was 18, wouldn't go, but she wanted to take Josh and Amanda since they were still under her care according to the divorce agreement. She had determined, Jeff said, that it was in their best interest and would be the best thing for them.

I disagreed, and I was extremely disappointed that Debbie had sent Jeff over to my house to do the 'dirty work' for her, although I wasn't necessarily surprised. Debbie has a lot of wonderful qualities, but communicating with me wasn't one of them. What upset me the most was not that Debbie wanted to move, but rather that she wanted to take two of my kids in the process. The decision would have a tremendous impact on our entire family, not only now but in the future as well, and yet she hadn't felt the need to talk about it with me or the kids? To me, that was disrespectful and didn't make sense.

I think Debbie knew what my reaction would be, which was why she sent Jeff to tell me in the first place. She knew I'd given everything that I had to be close to my kids, and that I would continue to give whatever I had left – which honestly wasn't much anymore – to keep them close in the future. I'd always believed that the best thing for our children was to have both parents close and actively involved in their lives, and the kids had said repeatedly that they didn't want to move. Taking Josh and Amanda away from their older brother was one thing, but taking them away from me was quite another, and I wasn't about to just lie down and let it happen.

I understood why Debbie wanted to move. For her, there were too many bad memories in Palm Harbor, and I agree that she needed to get away and start over somewhere else. If she felt the need to go, then I was all for it – just not with the children.

210

Jeff and Debbie had obviously rehearsed what he was to say. He explained that they had reviewed the divorce agreement and felt I couldn't stop Debbie from moving, even if I wanted to. He also said that Debbie wanted to be fair and, as a result, was willing to restructure our financial agreement to lessen the alimony if I would agree to the move without a fight.

I wanted to laugh right out loud at the nicely worded bribe, but I didn't. I had lived the last three years of my life in financial chaos because of everything I'd given to Debbie in the divorce, which included far beyond the normal amount of alimony and support expected, and I sure wasn't about to let her sudden desire to be 'fair' determine my role as a father to my kids now.

I told Jeff to tell Debbie that I would seek legal counsel immediately. I also made it very clear that I would fight, right down to my very last penny I'd fight, to keep my kids with me. I honestly didn't know if I could prevent them from moving or not, but I was determined to do everything within my power to try.

The next few months turned ugly and were full of legal posturing and angry conversations between Debbie and me as she tried to convince me to just let the move happen. Throughout it all, the kids continued to maintain that they didn't want to go. As it turned out, Debbie was correct that the divorce agreement didn't prohibit her from moving, but in my mind the issue had much more to do with what was right for Josh and Amanda than what was legally allowed. My lawyer felt that we might, and he stressed the word 'might', have a case to keep the kids in Palm Harbor because of my relationship with them before, during, and after the divorce but, if we ended up in court, there were certainly no guarantees.

The end result? Debbie did sell the house and she moved to Georgia at the end of the summer, but only after we finally agreed that Josh would remain in Palm Harbor and live with me and Chris. I would have fought with everything I had to keep Amanda with me too but, after some deep soul searching, I determined that the best place to be for a 12 year old daughter to be was with her mother. Trying to remain positive about the move when Amanda and I were together was one of the hardest things I've ever done. She was too young to understand the dynamics of it all.

There is a line in a Melissa Etheridge song which says, "The only thing that stays the same is change". That is absolutely true. Debbie's decision brought a host of changes for everyone in our family and we were forced to adjust. But apart from the fact that my daughter was in another state – thank God for cell phones – and that our family was geographically split apart, things worked out about as well as they could.

Life happens. So does change. We adjust and move on the best we can, regardless of the circumstances or situation. It's really the only choice we have.

I've learned something, though. I have learned that every change, no matter how bad or difficult it may seem at the time, can bring about positive results if we do our best to manage it right.

Every change has the potential to bring about something good. I believe that, for my daughter, for my boys, and for me.

❀ ❀ ❀

The Fundamentals In Managing Change...

So you have had a few changes in your life recently, have you? And some of them probably haven't worked out like you thought they would or might. It happens. It's called life. Regardless of how well we adjust, there will always be good and bad connected with every change.

We are creatures of habit. We like to live within our defined parameters of consistent and predictable routines. Change threatens that consistency and causes us to stress and worry about the future. Being concerned with change is a normal human reaction, but if that concern turns into fear then it becomes a problem. Worse yet, if we don't address our fears, change can negatively impact us for years to come.

It was Franklin D. Roosevelt who once said "There is nothing to fear but fear itself". I agree, especially when it comes to managing change. Think about how many times you've missed an opportunity in life because you were afraid to make a decision. Or think about the times when something negative could have been avoided if you had just made a decision sooner. Or the times you've hesitated in making a choice because you were worried or afraid of what others might think, or what it might cost you, or what might happen if you chose wrongly, or any of a thousand other 'might's' which held you back.

Remember the basic premise of this chapter – the key to effectively managing change is to maximize the benefits while also minimizing its negative affects. In other words, the best way to manage change is to focus on the possibilities rather than to allow ourselves to be overwhelmed by the negatives which 'might' result. We certainly have to address the negative associated with any change, but our goal is to focus on and accentuate the positives.

We can't manage change effectively if we live in fear. We have to meet our fears head on and deal with the issues. It's the only way we take control of our lives and make the best of each and every situation.

Here is a brief guide to help you manage the changes which have been brought on by your divorce:

- **Accept that change is happening and move forward** – As you already know, divorce brings many changes to your life and some of them are difficult to deal with. The best thing you can do in those situations is to accept the reality of the change and move forward as quickly and as positively as possible. Not every change will work out well for you, but every change will work out better if you address the issues that need to be addressed right away and manage them effectively. You don't do yourself any favors by ignoring change or pretending it won't affect you. Accept change, make the best of it, and move on. To help with this, think about times in your life when you have reacted positively to change in the past. What did you do to adjust? How did you try to make the best of those situations? What lessons did you learn? You've managed change effectively in the past and brought about a positive outcome, even when the change was difficult and undesired, and you can do it again. Draw on your experiences of the past and look beyond the fears to focus on the possibilities.

- **Take the time to educate yourself** – We covered this earlier in the chapter, but it's worth repeating. There are people who have gone through what you are going through now and who can help you manage the changes you are dealing with. Do your research. There are plenty of resources out there about divorce and the issues it can create. If you need help, ask. If you are confused, talk with a friend or counselor. The more you educate yourself, the better prepared you will be to meet the challenges now and in the days ahead.

- **Create a plan to manage the changes** – Once you've accepted the reality of change and educated yourself on the issues, then it's time to make a plan to manage the change effectively. Work to maximize the benefits of every change as you also seek to minimize its negative affects. You know where you are now and where you want to be in the future, so figure out a way to get there. You may have to adjust your plan as time goes on as new challenges arise or other options become available, but you can't adjust a plan unless you actually have one. And whatever you do, remember to always, always, always be open to new possibilities. When one door shuts in life, another one usually opens somewhere else. You just have to have the courage to walk through it.

New horizons are in your future and opportunities which you have yet to imagine lie ahead! Keep believing and work hard to manage change effectively as you keep moving forward. Look for the positives in every change and, regardless of how dark the storm clouds may seem, search for the silver linings. They are there. They always are. You just have to find them.

It's Your Choice...

Divorce changes your life. Some of those changes are initiated by you. Others are forced upon you by the circumstances of life or by the decisions of someone else. Still other changes lie ahead.

You have a choice. You can accept the reality of those changes and work to manage them effectively ...or...you can ignore the changes occurring in your life and fail to address the issues.

I invite you to look beyond your fears and regain control of your life by managing change effectively. And I invite you to make the best of every change by maximizing its benefits and minimizing its negative affects. Look for open doors and silver linings. They are there. But as always, it's your choice...

For Your Journal...

- How do you feel about the changes which have occurred in your life since the divorce? Which have been the most difficult? Why? Which have been the most beneficial? Again, why? How would you describe your attitude as you have dealt with these changes?

- Make a list of 8-10 major changes which have occurred in your life since the divorce. Next to each, identify whether the change resulted from a decision that you made or by a decision that someone else made. Which of these changes have been positive? Which have been negative? Do you see a pattern?

- Ask yourself these questions for each of the changes you listed above: Have I managed the change effectively? Have I educated myself about the issues related to this change? Have I had the right attitude in dealing with it? Are there behaviors I need to change which could help me manage it more effectively?

- Lastly, create an action plan for each change on your list to help you manage it more effectively. Be sure to include steps you can take to maximize the benefits and to minimize its negative affects. Set a goal to find at least one new opportunity or possibility which could result in the future specifically because this change has occurred.

Chapter 9
The Greatest Power – Choice...

"I have set before you today life and prosperity, and death and adversity...
Choose life in order that you may live..."
– Deuteronomy 30: 15, 19b –

The greatest power within any individual is the power of choice.

Our ability to analyze a situation, to consider the options, and then to choose from among those options based on what we believe is the best decision for us, is what sets us apart from every other living creature on this earth.

You have a choice. You always have a choice. Regardless of the situation, circumstances, or conditions, you have the ability to decide your direction and what you will say and do. You may not like the options that you have in any given situation, but the fact is there are still options, which means you must make a choice. No matter what you are doing, when you are doing it, or where you are, you always have a choice. It's that simple.

Choices come in all shapes and sizes. Many are simple and relatively insignificant, like when we decide what to wear to work or where to eat for dinner. Others can be extremely complex and carry great importance, such as when we decide who to marry or what career to pursue. Sometimes we have the luxury of time before making a final decision, while others choices demand a split-second response. But in every case and at all times, the one constant is that we have the power of choice. There are no exceptions.

Because the power of choice is a gift bestowed upon us, we are free to choose how we live and who we are. We are not puppets somehow divinely controlled by God or some force of nature, nor are we predestined victims of an eternal fate. Rather what we are is children of God, created with a free will and given the opportunity to determine our own lot in life. Whatever else that may mean, it definitely means this – we are in control of our own destiny and we alone are responsible for the choices we make.

Embracing the fact that you are in complete control of your own life is incredibly empowering. You can choose to be who you want to be and do what you want to do. You can live however you want to live and pursue whatever dreams you want to pursue. You can make the choice to heal and move forward after divorce, to set out in a new direction, and to live with purpose, passion, and hope. You can...you can...you can... The reality is that, through the power of choice, you are totally, completely, 100% responsible for you!

When we fail to take that responsibility seriously or allow others to make decisions for us that we should be making ourselves, then we forfeit our power of choice. In the process, we let someone else control our destiny. Giving up control of our life, either directly or indirectly, is never a good place to be.

❀ ❀ ❀

Approximately one month prior to the divorce...

Debbie and I tried to keep our marriage together after the affair, but I'm not sure either of us really believed we could do it. It was right for us to try, especially given the fact that we'd been married for almost 20 years, and there were actually a few moments when I thought we might make it, but the combination of my guilt and her anger were just too much to overcome in the end.

When a married couple is affected by an affair and tries to stay together, the time eventually comes when they either have to address the issue once and for all and move forward together, or they have to decide they can't and go their separate ways. We seemed to be stuck in the middle of those two decisions during our attempt to reconcile. But the longer we went without any resolve, the less I believed we would spend the rest of our lives together.

One evening, five months after I had confessed to Debbie and after yet another conversation between us had spiraled out of control, Debbie barged into my office at home just after midnight and angrily threw down a stack of papers on the desk in front of me. She walked out without saying a word and slammed the door behind her.

There before me was a packet of information and financial documents which had to be completed to begin the process of divorce. Although I was unaware of it until then, Debbie had already hired an attorney and made her final decision. At that point, it was up to me to make mine.

The options were clear. I could choose to either fill out the paperwork and start the process of divorce, or I could refuse and keep fighting to save my marriage. Neither was too appealing at the moment, and I knew both of them would be filled with heartache for our kids and our family. But one thing was clear to me. Debbie had given up on me and on us. From her perspective, our marriage was irrevocably broken.

After staring at the papers in disbelief for who knows how long, I finally made the decision through a sea of tears and began filling out the papers that would forever change my life. I worked on the documents deep into the early hours of the morning.

❋ ❋ ❋

Be Proactive...

Years ago I went to a workshop promoting Stephen Covey's book, *The Seven Habits of Highly Effective People*. The book identifies seven 'habits', or principles, which Covey believes are essential for people to be happy, successful, and effective in life. If you've never read the book, I highly recommend it.

The first habit, and probably the one that is most important for anyone seeking to make a new beginning, is 'Be Proactive'. You've probably heard the words said many times before, but here is a summary of Covey's explanation as I heard it.

The habit 'Be Proactive' is based on a simple premise, which is to every stimulus there is a response. For example, a stimulus might be something someone says to us or does to us. Our response is what we say or do in return. When we are intentional about thinking through our options of what we might say or do, and when we make a decision based on what we believe is the best option or response to the stimulus at the time, then we are being proactive in our behavior. When we don't, such as when we say or do the first thing that comes to mind or we allow our emotions to control our response, then we are being reactive in our behavior.

Animals are a good example of what reactive behavior is all about. I once had a beautiful dog, a black Labrador Retriever named Shadow. When I came home and called Shadow in a loving or playful way, she would always come running excitedly with her tail wagging and ready to play. But if I raised my voice because she had done something wrong, or spoke sternly when I called her name, Shadow would hang her head and go into her cage to hide. The stimulus was the tone of my voice, and Shadow's response was based wholly on that stimulus, whether playful or stern. Her behavior was reactive.

People are different than animals, however. Whereas a dog is always reactive, we aren't, or at least we don't have to be. As adults gifted with the power of choice, we have the mental and intellectual capacity to analyze the situation, think about our options, and choose the best possible response at the moment. This is true regardless of the intent of the stimulus, the emotions involved, or the amount of time we have to respond. Even when we only have a split second to make our decision, the human brain usually allows us to thoroughly think through our options before responding. We have the ability to be proactive in any situation and at any time, and to determine the best course of action for ourselves and others. We can always choose to be proactive because we always have the power of choice.

Despite our ability, however, there are many times when we aren't proactive in our behavior. Sometimes we let our emotions get the best of us and respond reactively, or we choose not to intentionally think through our options or take into account the situation. When we do respond reactively instead of proactively, we subconsciously give up the opportunity to remain in control of ourselves and, thus, we don't make the best choice possible.

If someone speaks rudely or angrily to us, often times our immediate reaction is to want to shoot back a rude or angry response. But if we choose to be proactive, we can step back from our desires and analyze our options. For example, we may determine the best response is to remain silent, or to just walk away, so that things don't escalate. Or we may decide to talk things out with the person in an effort to determine why the individual is upset. Or we might choose to respond with empathy and kindness as opposed to anger. Or, in some cases, it's quite possible that we may decide to be rude or angry right back at the person, believing this is the best option after we have considered the factors involved. But whatever option we choose and whatever choice we make in this scenario, it will be because we have responded proactively, considered our options, and determined the best possible reply in this particular situation.

We don't have to respond reactively to people or to life. As we look at our future, we can choose to be proactive and to make good decisions in order to bring about the best possible outcome. Whether we are considering our response when someone speaks rudely or, on a grander scale, considering our response to the issues of divorce, the principle works the same. Once again we see that we are fully responsible for our lives, choices, and decisions, whether they be good or bad, or right or wrong. Nothing and no one can force us to respond reactively or to make bad decisions unless we choose to allow it. We always have the power of choice.

It seems that we live in a world where people often make excuses for their behavior. They don't want to be accountable for their choices and decisions when things go wrong. Instead, they try to pass the buck or pin the blame on someone or something else. They won't, can't, or don't want to admit that they have made a mistake.

We've all done it at one time or another. We learned how to pass the buck when we were children. Somewhere along the line as we grew up, we had the opportunity to blame our brother or sister for something that we did, for a choice we made, which turned out wrong or deserved to be punished. And we did! And sometimes it even worked! We weren't the only ones to do it, of course, and there were plenty of times when our brothers or sisters did the exact same thing to us. But the point is we all learned how to avoid facing the consequences of our actions when we were young. Unfortunately, the problem now is that we are all grown up and many of us still do the adult version of the very same thing.

Most certainly there are factors which influence who we are and how we act, such as how we were raised, our education, and our life experiences, but none of those factors are valid excuses for making irresponsible choices and decisions now. Regardless of our past, or the struggles and hardships we've been through, we have the opportunity right now to make good choices and take responsibility for our actions in both the present and future. Nothing we have ever done or will do changes that fact.

I made some bad choices when I was married. I'm not proud of those choices, but I am responsible for them. They were *my* choices and *my* decisions, and I am the one who is accountable No one forced me to do anything I did because no one could. It's embarrassing to say and painful to admit, but those choices were mine and mine alone.

As often happens when we make poor choices or bad decisions, I suffered the consequences of my actions personally and professionally. Most of my struggles since the divorce are directly related to the choices I made back then. It's tempting sometimes to try to pin the blame elsewhere, but I know better. My life, like yours, is the direct result of choices and decisions I've made along the way.

Of course the same principle applies when we make good choices and decisions in life and we experience the positive consequences which often result. I realize that I've made a lot of those types of choices as well, just as you have too, and positively affected myself, my loved ones, and many others. I am just as responsible and accountable for those choices and decisions just as I am the bad ones. So are you.

As plainly as it can be said, here is the bottom line – you are always responsible for your choices and decisions because you always have the ability to be proactive through the power of choice. If you embrace this truth and live by it everyday, only then will you have full control of your actions, your future, and your life. You choose your path, your fate, and your destiny through the power of choice. There is no greater gift.

The Choice Process...

A process occurs whenever you make a choice. Sometimes this process happens quickly, like when you have to make a decision immediately or on the spur of the moment, and at others the process unfolds over a long period of time. Either way, it works basically the same.

Most of us never think about the process we use to make our choices, but we should. A well defined, well thought out, understanding of the choice process helps to avoid ambiguity in our decision making and allows us to make positive choices consistently.

No system ensures that we will choose rightly all the time. After all, we are human and we do make mistakes. But if we agree that good choices usually lead to positive results, then we must also agree it is important to understand the process which gives us the best opportunity to make those good decisions on a regular basis.

Three simple steps provide us with a framework to make good choices on a regular basis. First, we identify the core motivations related to the choice. Second, we evaluate our options and determine the positives and negatives of each. And third, we make our final decision and move forward.

Step #1: Identify The Core Motivations Involved...

We do what we do in life because of our core motivations. These motivations drive our words and actions, and are central to nearly every decision we make. While several motivations may be vying for our attention at any one time as we examine our options, one will inevitably rise above the others and become the 'core' motivation which drives our final decision.

Many of our core motivations are good, right, and positive, and are obvious both to us and the people around us. Some, however, are not good, and we usually try to keep them disguised or hidden away. Whether good or bad, however, these core motivations affect every choice we make and, therefore, dramatically impact how we live.

Once again consider the example of an alcoholic. His doctor says he will die within six months if he doesn't stop drinking. At that point, he is faced with a choice, one that will ultimately be determined by his core motivations. The options are clear. Either he can keep drinking and die, or he can quit drinking and live. Assuming his core motivation is to live and be with his family, he makes the choice to give up the bottle. He may have tried to quit a hundred times before but was never able to do it, primarily because the core motivation which drove his decision back then was different than the one driving his decision now. Only when he had the proper motivation to do what needed to be done was he able to do what he really should have done long before.

Identifying the core motivations we use to make decisions is helpful for this reason – if we determine the motivation driving our decision is negative, selfish, or hurtful, then we can 'mentally override' the motivation through the power of choice and instead re-evaluate our choice based on what is good and right. In other words, the power of choice is always stronger than any motivation, feeling, or emotion, and it allows us to shift our thinking in order to make good decisions on a consistent basis.

The struggle for me to end my relationship with Jessica is a good example of how two core motivations can conflict with each other during the decision making process. While several motivations were at work in my life simultaneously during the affair, two in particular were especially important. First, I was motivated to continue my relationship with Jessica because I loved her and wanted to be with her. And second, I was motivated to remain married to Debbie because I cared for her and loved my children. There were other motivations which conflicted as well, especially those involving my moral and spiritual life, but these two core motivations drove almost every decision I made at the time.

In fact, they were the driving force behind my desire to keep the affair hidden. I didn't want to be put into a situation where I had to choose one over the other, which I knew would happen if Jessica and I were discovered. So instead, I chose to juggle things the best I could. When it all became too much for me and I eventually confessed, I then had to decide which of these two core motivations was really more important. My decision was to remain at home with my children and to try to rebuild my marriage with Debbie. As important as Jessica was to me at the time, the motivation to be with her was secondary when weighed against the option of not living with my kids.

It's important to recognize that core motivations influence all of our decisions, not just the important ones. Take, for example, something as simple as trying to decide whether or not to eat a bowl of ice cream. You want the ice cream because you know it tastes good, indicating that one of your core motivations is self satisfaction. But on the other hand, you may also worry that eating the ice cream will cause you to gain weight, indicating another of your core motivations is to maintain your personal appearance. Unless you mentally override one of those motivations through the power of choice, which you can always do, the stronger of these two will eventually win out and determine your final decision.

Our goal in this first step of understanding the choice process is to identify core motivations and to recognize the power they have in our lives. Furthermore, we want to do our best to make sure that our decisions are based on positive motivations rather than negative ones, such as selfishness, jealously, or greed. The key is to remember that the power of choice always gives us the opportunity to make the best decision, regardless of what motivations are vying to influence our choices.

Step #2: Weigh The Positives And Negatives Of Every Option...

You may be familiar with the Scales of Justice model that is used to symbolize the workings of our judicial system. The model consists of a scale in perfect balance with two bowls suspended by chains at either end. The bowls represent the opposing sides of any legal argument. Based on the 'weight' of the evidence imaginarily placed in each bowl, the scale will tip one way or the other and indicate the right decision which needs to be made for justice to prevail.

Thinking about this model can be helpful as we consider the various options we have related to any choice. We can mentally envision placing the positives of an option in one bowl and the negatives of that same option in the other. Once we have thought through every contingency and 'weighed' all the evidence, we can imagine the scale tipping to one side or the other, thus indicating the right decision for us to make in that situation.

You probably don't have a Scales of Justice model to carry around with you, but the good news is you don't need one. A simple pencil and piece of paper will work just as well. List the positives of any option on one side and the negatives on the other. Then determine a value, or weight, for each piece of 'evidence' based on its importance. Finally, add up the numbers on each side and see which way the scale tips. After going through this process with every option related to any choice, you should be able to determine the best decision for you.

As you weigh the positives and negatives of each option, make sure you factor in the impact of choosing that option upon those that you love. You are the one who must ultimately decide, but every decision you make has an impact on those around you. In other words, you are the center piece of the puzzle, but you aren't the only piece.

When you throw a pebble into a pond, ripples move out concentrically from the point of entry and create a 'ripple affect'. The ripples nearest to the point of entry are stronger and more intense than those that drift far away, and therefore have more of a direct impact on the surrounding environment. The farther away from the point of impact, the weaker the ripples are and the less impact they have. At some point, far away from where the pebble entered the water, the ripples cease altogether.

Every choice and decision you make has a ripple affect. Some of those choices are like pebbles which barely make a splash and barely have an affect at all, while others can be like boulders which generate huge waves and touch the lives of everyone you know.

My choice to become involved with Jessica was like one of those boulders. The decision impacted not only my own life, but also the lives of my wife and kids, my church, and the surrounding community. The force of the ripples I created was life changing, especially for those closest to the 'point of impact'.

Conversely, when I made the decision to stay in Palm Harbor after my divorce, there was a different kind of ripple affect created. My kids were positively affected because I remained an active part of their lives everyday. My Mom, who was aging and becoming more dependent upon me, didn't have to relocate to stay close to me. And my friends were happy just because they were my friends and wanted me to be around. Once again, a choice that I made directly impacted not only me, but also those that I loved.

Every choice has consequences. That lesson was instilled in us by our parents, and it is one we also try to pass along to our children. No one is 'an island unto themselves'. Every choice, every decision, everything we say and do, has an affect on someone else, whether directly or indirectly.

Understanding core motivations, weighing the positives and negatives of every option, and considering the impact of our decisions upon those we love are all vital keys to making good choices consistently. We may not always make the right decision, but we can always try. And if you hit an occasional bump in the road or, like me, you've made a few bad choices in the past, do your best to address the fallout, put it behind you, and focus on making good decisions in the days ahead. You can't change what has already happened, but you can always begin again through the power of choice.

❀ ❀ ❀

Approximately three years after the divorce...

The opportunity was tempting. Part of me wanted to jump in right away and see where it would lead. But another part of me – an older and wiser part tempered by life and the lessons I had learned in the past – said slow down and think it through. Starting a new church was something that I had thought about often, but it was no small decision in light of everything I'd been through.

There were a million questions running through my mind. Was it right for me? And if so, was this my opportunity to do it? If I started a new church, what would the affect be upon my family and the other people involved in my life? What were the risks? And what was motivating me to consider this opportunity now when I had passed on it before? Questions, questions, and more questions...

I had never been afraid to set out in a new direction in the past, either personally or professionally, but this decision was bigger than me alone. How would my boys be affected? They both lived with me now and had said many times before that I should consider starting a church in the area rather than driving 60 miles to my church in Bradenton, but I wasn't sure if they really understood all of the issues. And what about my Mom? She was aging and hadn't been able to make the trip to Bradenton recently, and I knew it would be easier for her to participate if I started a church nearby.

There were others to also consider. How would my congregation in Bradenton feel if I decided to leave to start another church? How would I feel leaving them, especially after everything they had meant to me as I healed after my divorce? And what would the members of my former church in Palm Harbor think if I began something new only a few miles away?

This wasn't the first time I'd wrestled with the decision, although the circumstances were much different before. Only a year after the divorce, a good friend had asked me to consider the possibility. He said he had the financial resources to make it happen and that he wanted me back in ministry. But back then I was still struggling spiritually and emotionally, feeling like I was unworthy to be considered a pastor again, and I decided the timing wasn't right. There were other reasons, too. I knew starting a church at that point would be hard for Debbie to deal with, and I was still confused about my relationship with Jessica. On top of all that, I didn't want to expose myself or my kids to the publicity that starting a new church might bring. As I said, the timing just wasn't right.

But two years had passed since then. I was now in a much different place emotionally and I felt good again. I'd been through counseling, dealt with my issues, and my spirit had healed. I felt like I had recaptured my passion and enthusiasm for life. I knew who I was and I'd rebounded professionally. I had a sense of purpose again. Life still had its share of problems, to be sure, but things were much better overall.

Other things had changed in the past two years as well. Debbie had moved to Georgia and was in the process of healing. My boys were living with me. I had purchased a home, a little two bedroom condo, and had a place of my own once again. And although things were still a bit rough financially, I was finally at the point where I could keep my head above water.

It was then that, quite unexpectedly, this new opportunity presented itself.

I went to a restaurant with a friend one day when a man suddenly came up and introduced himself. His name was Stan and, although I didn't recognize him at that moment, he had attended several of my services back when I was the pastor of the Palm Harbor church. He asked if we could set a time to meet later in the week. So we scheduled a lunch for the next day.

I didn't know why we were meeting, but it didn't take long for me to find out. Stan said he believed our paths had crossed for a reason and that, perhaps, it was even divinely inspired. Then he went on to explain that he had thought of me often since I resigned and had kept up with my whereabouts through a mutual friend of ours. Stan believed that I needed to be "back in the pulpit" of a church in the community and, because he had been blessed financially, he wanted to give whatever help he could in making that happen. He was willing to provide the support I needed in order to begin a new church in the Palm Harbor area.

I was flattered by his comments, and his invitation, as I listened patiently and allowed myself to dream. I didn't know if our meeting was providential or not, but I did believe then and now that God can use the happenstances of everyday life to bring about possibilities and opportunities. I couldn't help but to wonder if this was one of those times.

I haven't made my final decision on Stan's offer yet. My concerns in the present are different than my concerns of my past, but they are still concerns nonetheless. It would be difficult to leave my church in Bradenton and I'm happy and fulfilled in my work at Meals On Wheels. Yet at the same time, there is an excitement in my spirit which intrigues me and feels right, and a big part of me that would like to see this dream become a reality. The feelings are hard to ignore.

Wrestling with life changing decisions is always hard, especially when you know that what you decide will impact people you love. Whatever my final choice, I want to make sure that I make it for the right reasons and my priorities are in order. Thankfully, I have time to think about it. In the meantime, I'll just keep weighing my options and praying for a little help from up above.

It would be nice if we had a crystal ball which allowed us to see into the future. That way we would know in advance if we are making the right decisions or not. But, unfortunately, that isn't how life works. Then again, maybe that is why life is so interesting – we never really know what will happen next.

❋ ❋ ❋

Step #3: Take Control, Make A Decision, And Move Forward

Do you know the main thing which holds us back as we try to move from where we are to where we want to be? It's indecision, not surprisingly. The inability to make a choice, the failure to act and be decisive, is one of the greatest enemies we face as we move toward new horizons.

I have a good friend whose marriage fell apart a few years back. Her divorce wasn't particularly 'messy' as far as divorces go, but it was still tough on her. For twenty five years she had been a dedicated wife and mother, and she was successful at both, but she struggled to adjust to her new life after the divorce. It was as if she lost her way and wasn't sure of who she was. With no life partner and with her kids grown and living on their own, she wandered from job to job and from relationship to relationship searching for something she couldn't define. That something was a sense of purpose and identity.

Her general unhappiness and lack of direction, in my opinion, were directly related to her inability to make some important decisions. She had several opportunities to improve her life by making choices which could have brought positive change, but she always hesitated because she feared making the wrong decision or one she would later regret. Over time, the windows of opportunity began to close and, as a result, she remained stuck right where she was in the same situation.

I know the pattern well because I've been there myself. Maybe you have too. A lot of people, especially in the first year or two after divorce, are afraid to make any choices or decisions. With their confidence shaken and with feelings of uncertainty about their future, they withdraw into a shell and don't make any decisions at all for fear of choosing wrongly. What they don't usually realize is that the same fear which protects them from making bad decisions is also the one which holds them back from making the choices which lead to healing and a better life.

The only way to overcome that fear is to take control of your life, be decisive, and trust that you will make good choices. There's no magic to it. Use the steps in the process and believe they will lead you to the best possible decision at the time, and then make the decision without putting it off. Making the choices and decisions which lead to positive outcomes is the only way we can get from where we are to where we want to be. It's the only way we can move forward.

My son Chris had the rearview mirror of his truck fall off a few months ago. Until it was fixed, he had trouble seeing what was behind him as he drove. Instead, all of his attention was focused on what was in front. It may not be a safe way to drive, but it's a wonderful philosophy for living life.

Focus on what lies ahead. The windshield, not the rearview, is where our attention needs to be. Looking back can be helpful from time to time as we remember the lessons that life has taught us, but the best thing we can do for ourselves right now is to set our sights on where we are going. I know this – if we spend all of our lives looking back, we will miss the opportunities which lie ahead.

Improving your life begins with a commitment to make good and positive choices and decisions all the time and in every situation. Take control of your future and don't be afraid or hesitate. Follow the process. Identify your core motivations, weigh the positive and negatives of each option, consider the impact of your choices upon those you love, and then make a decision and go with it! You are the only one who can determine your future.

❋ ❋ ❋

Approximately a year and a half after the divorce...

I pulled into Philippe Park about 10:00 AM on a weekday morning. I'd been there dozens of times before, but this time felt different. I was on a mission. I'd come to renew my spirit – or perhaps better said, to find my spirit once again – and to seek some direction for my life. Things had been rough since the divorce and I needed to get back on track.

About a year before the divorce, I met with a member of my church who had recently gone through some dramatic changes in his own life. A couple of years earlier, and with the support of his wife and kids, he had determined it was 'God's will' for him to risk everything he had, including his house and 401K, to pursue a dream. As it happened, the new venture he was embarking upon turned out to be very successful.

Admiring what he had accomplished and intrigued by the risk he took, I asked him how it was that he determined God's will was for him to do what he did. I've never forgotten his answer.

He said that he went to his favorite spot and separated himself from everyone and everything for an entire day. While he was there, he read Scripture and prayed as he listened for the still, small voice of God, the one so often muted by the hustle and bustle of life, within his spirit. Eventually through that process, he determined God was calling him to follow his heart, to have faith, and to risk everything he had to chase his dream. Some people questioned his decision and his methods, but from his perspective he found the answer he was looking for.

I had thought about our conversation more than once as I went through my own struggles after my divorce. Our situations were entirely different – he was pursuing a dream and I was just trying to survive – but our desire to find direction from God was the same.

Thinking about our conversation back then, I pulled into Philippe Park and went to one of my favorite spots in the world – a shady, grassy, tree lined area right next to the water. Intent on discovering that still, small voice within my own spirit, I pulled out a folding chair and grabbed my Bible, a notebook, and a pen. I was there three hours, most of it spent reading, praying, and writing. It felt good.

I wish that I could tell you I came away from that experience with a grand master plan to 'fix' my life. I didn't. I wish I could tell you it was a life changing moment, or that I had a revelation or received a miracle, but it wasn't and none of those things occurred. What did happen, however, was almost as important to me.

I 'heard' my inner voice. Not audibly or verbally, like when someone talks to you in a conversation. But rather I felt it, deep within the recesses of my spirit. Call it God, the Holy Spirit, my conscience, or whatever you want, but the message was loud and clear. What I sensed was that I had to start focusing on the hope of my future and to stop living in the past. I'd been wandering in the wilderness longer than I should've been, and it was time for me to move in a new direction. I knew it was the only way I would ever be happy again.

The truth is that I probably didn't need to go to Philippe Park to hear that message, although I'm glad I did. I pretty much already knew what I needed to do before I ever got there. The difference that day, however, was that I actually decided to do something about it.

Maybe God did speak to me. I don't know. Or maybe it was just my own inner voice speaking a little louder than usual. Either way, I was able to make some decisions right then and there that I'd been putting off. It was time for me to let go of the mourning, grief, and pain, and to get back to living life again.

Looking back from the perspective of time two years later, I realized some-thing very important about my get-a-way day in the park. I had taken a few steps forward and one or two back as I tried to move on in the eighteen months after my divorce, but my real new beginning in life – the event which actually began my journey to new horizons – really started then...

❀ ❀ ❀

Everyone who has struggled through the pain of divorce eventually arrives at a watershed moment concerning their future. Either they have to choose to take control of their lives, set out in a new direction, and determine their own destiny, or they don't and allow the fear of failure to sink its hooks deeper into their soul.

No where is the power of choice more evident, or more important, than at the moment of that decision, for what is decided will ultimately impact their lives forever. I invite you to exercise the power of choice. I invite you to take control and to make good choices and decisions. I invite you to seek new horizons.

Creating A Personal Mission Statement...

Confucius once said "The journey of a thousand miles begins with a single step". He was right. Our journey of a 'thousand miles' – the journey from divorce to new horizons – begins with a single step as we commit ourselves to doing what we need to do to heal and move forward into the future with hope. Once we've made that decision, then it's time to create a mission statement.

You need a personal mission statement. Why? Because it will help you define your priorities and guide your actions in the days ahead. When your world spins out of control and life is moving in a million different directions all at once, your mission statement will be the tool which will help you to focus on what is really important.

Businesses learned the value of a well thought out mission statement years ago. Rarely does a company succeed nowadays without having a clearly defined mission which its employees all know and which reminds them of their ultimate purpose. When opportunities arise within the parameters of the mission, they are pursued with passion. And when opportunities arise which align, they are handled elsewhere or put off until another day.

The same concept applies for us on a personal level. When we have a clearly articulated, well defined mission, our purpose, passion, and goals become clear, and we won't waste time chasing after things which are insignificant or unimportant in our lives.

Think of your personal mission statement as a GPS for life. Just as a GPS guides your journey and keeps you moving in the right direction, so too will your mission statement. And if you find yourself in territory that is unfamiliar or, worse yet, if you get lost on the journey, your mission statement can point the way to get you back on course and moving in the direction that you want to go. In the end, just as a GPS will help you arrive at your destination more quickly and efficiently than if you don't use one, your mission statement will help you go from where you are to where you want to be with fewer 'wrong turns' and 'detours' along the way.

Throughout this book you have been invited to use the power of choice to take control of your life and make good decisions. To help you by providing the clarity and direction you need on the way to new horizons, I encourage you to craft your personal mission statement right now.

There is no right way or wrong way to create a mission statement, but let me offer two helpful suggestions. First, keep it simple and short, certainly no longer than a paragraph or two. Whittle down your thoughts to what is essential and important for you, defining the concepts and principles by which you want to live. Ideally your personal mission statement will be short enough for you to commit to memory.

Second, make sure your mission statement accurately reflects both who you are and who you want to be. This is the essence of what a mission statement is all about. It must reflect your purpose, passion, and heart, and capture the essence of your spirit. Goals define the 'what'. Values define the 'why'. But your personal mission statement is really about the 'how' – how you will think, speak, and act in relation to God, others, and yourself.

My personal mission statement is written below. I share it as an example of what a mission statement might look like when it is completed. Yours may very well end up being totally different from mine in terms of content or writing style – in fact, I expect it to be different – and that is okay. No mission statement is any better or worse, or more right or wrong, than any other as long as it truly reflects the mission of the one creating it.

With that in mind, I offer my mission statement for you to read. I'm proud of it not because it is creative or well written, but because it captures the essence of who I am and want to be.

This is my GPS to new horizons.

❀ ❀ ❀

My Personal Mission Statement

Acknowledging I am responsible for
my choices, actions, and decisions,
I commit to:

Live a life defined by grace –
being thankful for my blessings in all circumstances;
forgiving others as God has forgiven me;
respecting everyone, regardless of differences or beliefs;
encouraging others without criticisms and put downs;
laughing often and living much.

Live a life defined by love –
being honest in my relationships, even when it hurts;
helping others whenever possible, regardless of the personal sacrifice involved;
seeking to give more than I take always and everywhere;
caring for the least, the last, and the lost of society;
sharing my love for my family, friends, and others every day.

And live a life defined by hope –
trusting in Jesus Christ alone for my salvation;
growing in my faith and being a good example for others;
recognizing I am a child of God and a person of infinite worth;
focusing on the future rather than being consumed by the past;
committing to new horizons and inspiring others to do the same;

In all things grace, in all things love, in all things hope – now and forever.

❀ ❀ ❀

Again, remember your mission statement will probably look very different than mine because we are two different people. But whatever you do and however you do it, make sure your personal mission statement reflects the passion within your soul. Choose every word carefully, struggle with every phrase, and be proud of the finished product.

Now it's your turn. Find a quiet place where you can clear your mind, listen for that inner voice, and focus on what is important for you. And as you write, may God's blessings be upon you!

It's Your Choice...

Ironically, you have a choice about the way you make choices. You can choose to exercise the power of choice by identifying your core motivations, weighing your options, considering your loved ones, and making the decision to move forward ...or...you can fail to exercise your power to choose and allow the fear of failure, or someone or something else, to determine your fate. Either way, you are one responsible and accountable for your decision, and you are the only one who can make it. It's your choice...

For Your Journal...

- Do you believe that you always have a choice, regardless of the circumstances or situation of life? Why or why not?

- Identify an experience which turned out badly because you were reactive in your behavior rather than proactive. Now identify an experience which turned out better than expected because you were proactive instead of reactive. What were the differences between the two examples you chose? What caused you to be reactive in one and proactive in the other?

- Think about the process by which you've made choices and decisions which turned out well in the past. What were the core motivations that drove those decisions and how did you make them? Did you weigh your options? Did you consider the impact of your decisions on others? What did those experiences teach you and how can they help you make better decisions in the future?

- Summarize your thoughts, feelings, and emotions as you wrote your personal mission statement. Was it difficult to write? Why or why not? Does it reflect who you are and who you want to be? Does it define your priorities? Now that it is written, what will you do with it? How can it help you move in the direction you want to go?

Chapter 10
The Greatest Joy – The Journey...

There is an appointed time for everything
and a time for every event under heaven –
A time to give birth and a time to die;
A time to plant and a time to uproot what is planted;
A time to kill and a time to heal:
A time to tear down and a time to build up;
A time to weep and a time to laugh;
A time to mourn and a time to dance;
A time to throw stones and a time to gather stones;
A time to embrace and a time to shun embracing;
A time to search and a time to give up as lost;
A time to keep and a time to throw away;
A time to tear apart and a time to sew together;
A time to be silent and a time to speak;
A time to love and a time to hate;
A time for war and a time for peace.
– Ecclesiastes 3:1-8 –

Life is a journey – a long and winding journey. Birth marks its beginning and death its end, but the path in between is totally up to us. From our highest highs to our lowest lows, and from our greatest joys to our deepest sorrows, life is all about the journey.

Your journey is exactly that – yours. The people you've met, the places you have been, and the things you have experienced are unique to your life. They have shaped who you are today. No one has ever lived life exactly as you have, because no one is exactly like you. And just as your journey past has brought you to this place and time, your journey present will now lead you into the journey future.

Celebrate the journey. Cherish every moment, good and bad. Only then can you experience life as it is meant to be lived and strive for your full potential. No matter what happens, what you are doing, or where you are, remember the journey is always what you make of it.

❈ ❈ ❈

Approximately five months after the divorce...

I dialed the number, unsure if I even knew how to call someone in another country. The familiar voice on the other end let me know that I'd done it correctly. I hadn't seen Eric in almost ten years, but it seemed like only yesterday when we had shared the journey of life together.

Back in the day, some 25 years ago, Eric and I met at Vanderbilt Divinity School in Nashville, Tennessee. We both attended seminary there. We lived in the same dorm during our first year and quickly became friends. Then, in our second and third years of seminary, we rented a house and roomed together. We worked our way through school by waiting tables at the same restaurant.

I have a lot of great memories of our times together – playing guitars late into the night; having long conversations about women, school, and life; going out on the town and listening to music; and just doing all of the things that students usually do in college. It seemed like a good time was always waiting right around the corner. I'll never forget the time when Eric, who was from Michigan, came home with me to Florida during the winter break. He shocked my Mom by laying out in his bathing suit in 50 degree weather, trying to get a tan. Or the too many times when we rode home from work late at night on my motorcycle with Eric on the back holding a pizza in one hand and a six pack in the other. Or the time Eric hurt his knee as we were playing a pick-up basketball game and I had to carry his books to class and tote him around for the next six weeks while he was on crutches. Or the time...anyway, like I said, I have a lot of great memories from those days.

Eric heard about my divorce halfway across the world from a mutual friend. He emailed me soon after, just to let me know he was thinking about me and wanting to make sure I was okay. He asked me to call if I had the chance, and gave me his phone number in Australia, where he had moved shortly after he was married.

Renewing our friendship lifted my spirits. It felt good to talk with someone who was completely removed what I had been through. In fact, it was just what I needed. Other than the first few minutes when I explained what happened and we talked about the divorce, the rest of the hour was spent reminiscing, reliving memories, and catching up on life. I guess true friendship lasts forever, no matter how much time or distance comes in between.

As I hung up the phone, I thought about how my life, and really everyone's life, is marked by seasons through the years. Some seasons are happy and filled with joy, like the one I spent with Eric at Vanderbilt. And others are more difficult, marked by sadness and pain, like the one I was experiencing now. But all of them together – the good and the bad, the happy and the sad – somehow combined to form a collage of life. All of them were parts of my journey.

Seasons had come and gone for me since my years at Vanderbilt, and each one had been different and unique. I was smart enough to know that, just as surely as those seasons had eventually passed, this one would too. Soon the calendar of my life would change and I'd be able to put this terrible season of divorce behind me once and for all. Brighter days were coming. I was certain of it. I just had to be patient and keep on doing what I needed to do to heal.

I was at a crossroads in my life. Yes I had made some mistakes and paid dearly as a result. But whatever the future would hold, I knew this season was only one small part of the greater whole and I refused to let it define me. No life, mine or any other, can ever be judged on a single season, no matter how good or how bad it may be. Rather the value of life can only be measured by the sum total of our seasons; by all of the relationships and experiences – past, present, and future – which shape our journey.

Reconnecting with an old friend helped me gain a new sense of perspective. It also helped me realize this season, full of hurt and pain, was only temporary. One day soon a new season would dawn. I didn't know how, where, or when, but I knew it would happen. Life had taught me that...

❀❀❀

Stephen J. King

Seasons Of The Journey...

I've lived in central Florida most of my life. Every area of the country has its own unique benefits, of course, but I have to admit I love the weather and mild climate here. The thermometer rarely dips below 40 degrees in the winter and, while the heat and humidity of summer can sometimes be stifling, the gentle change of seasons rarely affects how I live or what I do. For many people in other parts of the country, that isn't the case, however.

Winters in the north, for example, are often cold and dreary, and make life more difficult to manage. People often choose to remain inside rather than to go somewhere and battle the icy roads and freezing conditions. Even nature itself seems to rebel as trees grow barren and the grass turns an ugly shade of brown. A good snowball fight with the kids or a day on the slopes can be fun, but by and large most prefer to stay at home where it's warm and dry.

Ah, but then the splendor of spring arrives. The sun seems to reappear in the sky as the temperatures warm. The birds begin to sing and the smell of new life is in the air as flowers bloom, displaying the full array of nature's beautiful colors. People rush to the great outdoors to ride bikes, take walks, or enjoy a barbeque in the back yard with friends and family. For many, it's their favorite time of year.

Eventually, however, the spring passes, just as the winter did before it, and gives way to another season as the 'dog-days' of summer arrive. After that comes the beauty and cool, crisp air of fall. Finally, after each season has run its course, the cycle begins all over once more.

If there is one certainty in nature, it is this – seasons change. Every season gives way to another in time, whether we want it to or not, and each is different and unique when compared to the one before. No season remains forever, regardless of how much we might wish that it would. It's the way of nature. And truth be told, it is the way of life as well.

Our lives are made up of different seasons, too. And like the ones in nature, each life season is different and unique from the one before it, and each presents a new set of circumstances, opportunities, and challenges.

242

Unlike nature, however, the seasons of life aren't based on a calendar or the weather outside, but rather on the variety of factors which make up our life situation at the time, such as our age, marital status, famiy, careers, or any number of other important things.

Some of life's seasons are short and only last for a while. Others can remain for several months or years. Some are determined by our choices, while others just seem to occur regardless of what we do or where we are. Sometimes the seasons of life are predictable, again like their counterparts in nature, but other times they come upon us suddenly and unexpectedly. Each can dramatically impact our lives.

A cold, dark winter season of life can come upon us quickly, when a loved one dies, or when we experience a personal trauma or tragedy like divorce. The beauty of spring, can come just as quickly, however, when the door is opened for a new chapter in life, such as a new relationship, new career, or new place to live. But whatever the season and however it manifests itself, the one thing we know for sure – the one great lesson we have learned from nature – is that this time will eventually pass and give way to another.

We want the good seasons to last forever, of course. Our hope is that the cold and dark of a difficult winter life season never appears. But life doesn't always work according to our plans. People change. Relationships and families change. We change. No one stays the same forever. It's just not possible. Life is always changing.

Maybe you are in the midst of a terrible life season now. Maybe the hurt and heartache of your divorce has brought on a difficult winter storm, more intense and more powerful than you ever imagined. Maybe even you've begun to question if this time will ever end.

If so, hang in there and don't give up, because I've got good news for you. One day soon, the time will come when you will be able to look back upon the darkness of this winter through the lenses of spring and new beginnings. I can't tell you when it will happen, but I can absolutely guarantee that it will. How do I know? I know because it happened to me and, more importantly, nature teaches us that it will. One season *always* gives way to another. Your task is just to hold on and make it through this one.

Spring always follows winter. That's just how it works. Don't ever forget that truth as you move forward to new horizons.

❋ ❋ ❋

A little over two years after the divorce...

The brisk North Carolina air sent chills through my bones as I stepped off the bus at 6:00 AM in front of our hotel. Tired from traveling all night with Josh and his soccer team, I couldn't help but to notice the breathtaking view in the east as the sun peeked through the mountains and darkness began to give way to the dawn of a brand new day.

Josh and I had traveled all night from Florida, along with 14 other members of the Palm Harbor Under 16 Club Soccer Team and their parents, to North Carolina to participate in the prestigious Raleigh Shootout Soccer Tournament. There were few things in life that I enjoyed more than watching my son play soccer at the competitive level. He was good – very good – and so was his team, and I'd been looking forward to the trip for months. The bus ride was long, but a few movies for the boys, some good conversation, and a couple of adult beverages for the parents had actually made it quite enjoyable.

For most of the trip, I sat next to my good friend, Jim Merrick. His son, Brent, had played with Josh on the same team for six years and they were also good friends. Like me, Jim was at every game and we watched most of them together. It wasn't unusual for us to take the boys out for a bite to eat afterwards.

Jim had a lot of qualities I admired. He was a good father, a kind man, and always respectful in the way he treated others. He was one of the first people to reach out to me when the divorce became public and my world fell apart. I'll never forget that about him.

Shortly after I divorced, Jim started a new internet company which was designed to battle fraud and identity theft, called Clickfirst.com. His motivation for starting the company was a personal experience he had a few years before in which he had been defrauded out of a large sum of money. He had a passion for what he was doing and wanted to help others avoid the same mistakes he had made. *Knowing that I had resigned from the church and well aware of my financial situation, Jim invited me to become a partner in the company without making a financial investment.*

Jim's invitation seemed like a God-send to me back then. I knew that starting a business wouldn't be easy, and it certainly offered no guarantees, but I also knew that building something from the ground up and helping people in the process was just the type of thing I wanted to do. I also figured it might be my best opportunity to get into something which would provide me with the money I needed to meet my obligations. So, a few months later, I took a huge risk and left my job at Metropolitan Ministries to become the managing partner for Clickfirst. Six months later, however, before the company ever really got off the ground and became fully operational, the investment monies stopped and we were forced to shut down.

The next four months were hell as I struggled to survive and desperately looked for work. At the time, it appeared my decision to leave Metropolitan Ministries for Clickfirst ten months before had been a terrible mistake. But in fact, in retrospect and with the perspective only time can bring, I realized just a year later that it had actually been one the best thing that could've happened to me at the time, although I couldn't have predicted the events that would eventually transpire for me when it happened.

I didn't realize it as I was in the midst of going through it, but working with Jim at Clickfirst gave me the time and space to heal and to regain my confidence after the divorce. Perhaps more importantly in the grand scheme of things, I would've never had the opportunity to became the Executive Director of Meals On Wheels of Tampa or the pastor at Harvey Memorial Church in Bradenton if I hadn't left my job at Metropolitan Ministries to work for Jim in the first place. Only because the business failed was I forced to look for something new, and only then were the positions at Meals On Wheels and Harvey Church available. If the events of my life hadn't worked out just the way they did, I would've never been aware of those opportunities and never applied for the two positions which are now the heart and soul of who I am.

Sometimes the greatest blessings in life are the ones we can't see or that don't work out the way we thought they would. Jim turned out to be one of those blessings for me. His friendship, then and since, really changed my life and, in a strange way, eventually led me back into the ministry and the work I love so much now. Life is hard to figure out sometimes.

The leaves were changing colors as we got off the bus in Raleigh that morning, and the unmistakable signs of fall were all around. Nature was at work once again and I felt blessed to see the seasons changing right before my eyes. I could sense the seasons in my own life were changing too. After a long and nasty winter filled with more heartache than I cared to remember, spring seemed to be coming fast. I could feel it. It was in the air...

✻ ✻ ✻

One day, when you're on the other side of this season and look back from the perspective of time, you'll discover the same thing I did. There are certain people who come into our lives, often unexpectedly and at just the right time, that seem to be sent from above. They know just what to say, or just the right thing to do, to help us through our weakest moments, when the hurt and heartache seem unbearable. They are the ones who make it possible for us to move from darkness to light, from winter to spring, from where we are to a new beginning.

Some people believe God puts these people in our lives at a specific time or for a specific purpose. Perhaps. I really don't know. Maybe that's what the writer of Hebrews meant when he said we've all "entertained angels unaware". What I do know though, is that these people are incredible gifts to us along the way of our journey. They lift us up when we've fallen, offer hope when things seem hopeless, and walk with us when others can't or won't.

Whether these people appear in our lives by happenstance or an act of God really doesn't matter. The important thing is that they're there, and I'm grateful for that. Thank you, Lord, for all of the 'angels' who have touched my life and joined me in the journey.

Every Moment Is A Gift...

I was 24 years old and ready for the best summer of my life. I had every detail planned. First, I'd take my final exams to complete my second year of seminary. Then, I would drive to Florida to visit my family and friends for a few days. And finally, I'd load up my car and drive across the country to work for four months as a ministerial intern in one of our nation's most beautiful national parks. I was sure the summer would be one of the greatest experiences of my life.

And as it turned out, I was right, although once again not for the reasons I anticipated or imagined. The summer was incredible and living in the park was spectacular. The scenery and amazing wildlife captured my heart, just as I thought it would. But so too did a beautiful, young woman from Auburn University. There among the winding rivers and picturesque mountains of the great northwest, Debbie and I met and fell in love. It was romantic, thrilling, and magical, all wrapped up into one, and it was a summer that forever changed my life.

Yet it almost never happened.

Six months before the summer began, I interviewed with the "Christian Ministry in the National Parks' (CMNP) for a summer intern position as part of my curriculum requirements at Vanderbilt Divinity School. I was accepted into the program a few weeks later and assigned to go to Glacier National Park in northern Montana when school ended. I couldn't wait for the summer to arrive.

When exams finished in late May, I went home to Florida for a few days, just as I had planned. The day before I was to leave for my week long trip across the country, however, the National Director of the CMNP program called me at my Mom's house. He apologized for the inconvenience, but he wanted to know if I would be willing to change my plans and go to Yellowstone National Park instead of Glacier. Evidently the person who was scheduled for Yellowstone had withdrawn from the program at the last minute and I was the most qualified to replace him.

It really didn't matter to me where I went one way or the other. I had mentally prepared myself to go to Glacier for months, but I didn't know anyone there and had no ties. In my mind, Yellowstone and Glacier were mirror images of each other – big, magnificent, and very, very cold – and if I could help the CMNP by changing my plans and filling a need, then so be it. I accepted the new assignment over the phone.

Here's what is interesting, and it's something I've thought about hundreds of times since that day. If I would've missed the call from the National Director, or if he would have tried to reach me just a mere 12 hours later after I'd already left, I would've ended up in Glacier that summer instead of Yellowstone. Since all of this happened before cell phones, texts, and emails were standard or even invented, the Director would have had no way to contact me while I was on the road and would've simply called the next person on his list to fill the void. If that would have happened, I would've missed out on my time in Yellowstone and I would have never met the young woman who, just three years later, would become my wife.

I've often wondered how my life might be different now if I would have missed that call. I'll never know, of course, but I'm certain that Debbie and I would have never met and fell in love. Consequently, I would've missed out on all the joys of our marriage in the good years and the pain of it in the bad. But the 'what if's' go far beyond Debbie. I would've also missed out on the chance to be the father of my three children. I would have probably married someone else later in my life and had other children, but they wouldn't be the three I have now and love so much. Who knows what else might have been different? I might have ended up with a different career, different family and friends, and living in a different place than I do now. The possibilities are endless.

It reminds me of a story I heard about a couple who was happily married for 30 years. Before they ever met, they lived in different parts of the country. Both of them happened to be vacationing in Japan at exactly the same time, although each was with a different tour group. As the story goes, both of their groups ended up at the same flower shop for the same presentation and, as the man moved closer to get a better view, he accidentally bumped into the woman. He politely apologized and, for a moment, the two shared a brief conversation. Then they went their separate ways.

After the man left with his tour group for the next destination, he suddenly decided to go back to the flower shop to talk further with the woman, hoping she was still there. The two ended up talking for over an hour as both of their groups went on without them. He asked her out that evening, she accepted, and the rest, as they say, is history.

What are the odds? What are the odds of two people from different parts of the country vacationing overseas and being at the same flower shop at exactly the same time? What are the odds of them bumping into each other? Or of the man leaving his group to go back and find her? Or that she was still there? Or of her deciding to let her group go on as she talked with a man she had just met? Think about how incredibly different their lives would have been for the last 30 years if any one of those things, or a thousand different others, had happened differently. In the span of a few brief moments, their lives became intertwined forever.

So what can we learn from stories like these? We learn that, in spite of our best efforts to plan and control every aspect of our lives, the journey of life is, and will always be, wildly unpredictable. We can control many things in our lives, but there will always be those that we can't or don't, no matter how hard we may try or how much time we spend figuring it all out. Unexpected moments, chance encounters, and random events will always dot the landscape of our journeys and forever impact who we are. I've had plenty of them – my summer at Yellowstone being just one example – and so have you.

Every moment, regardless of how random or insignificant it may seem at the time, has the potential to affect our lives dramatically. Each can create memories that will never be relived or recaptured in quite the same way. So cherish every moment, and recognize their importance. Separately and together they are the gifts which make up the journey on this wild, crazy, unpredictable ride we call life.

In his beautiful song entitled "The Dance", country singer Garth Brooks captures this perspective as he sings about looking back on a broken relationship from the past through the eyes of the present.

Perhaps the words can take on special meaning for those of us who have recently been through the pain of a divorce:

> *"And now, I'm glad I didn't know*
> *The way it all would end, the way it all would go;*
> *Our lives are better left to chance; I could have missed the pain,*
> *But I'd of had to miss the dance.*
> *Yes my life is better left to chance;*
> *I could have missed the pain, but I'd of had to miss the dance."*

Anyone who has ever struggled with a broken relationship can relate to the joy of 'the dance' when things were good, and the pain of the end when they weren't. The two feelings are forever tied together in our memory and, as we learn over time, it's hard to appreciate one without the other.

Maybe you've wondered what your life might be like if you had chosen a different path or married someone else along the way. It's only natural to think about. But the truth is, no matter what path you might have chosen, all of them would have been filled with both pleasure and pain. Yes, you might have escaped the heartache of the present if you would have married someone else, but you also would have missed 'the dance'.

Life has a way of eventually balancing out. The bad and the good, the rough and the smooth, the winter and the spring – they all come and go through the seasons of our lives. Our challenge, now and in the future, is to make the best of every moment, and to recognize it for the gift of life that it is. It's the only way to truly celebrate the journey.

Celebrate The Journey Past...

❋❋❋

A little over two years after the divorce...

The cardboard box was marked 'Old Pictures' and sat on the beat-up dresser tucked away in the corner of my storage unit. Tired from loading the car in preparation for my third move in the last two years, I decided to take a break and go on a quick trip down memory lane. It turned out to be quite a journey.

The first picture I pulled out of the box was of an old friend from high school named Richard Hladik. I hadn't seen Richard in forever, but the memories of our times together back in those days flashed through my mind. I thought about us driving his car to the high school state playoffs in Jacksonville, working together on a tobacco farm in Massachusetts for eight weeks in the summer after our 10th grade year, and whining and complaining as we cleaned the offices of the old Aetna building on Kennedy Boulevard with our first 'real' jobs for The Professional Janitorial Service. Those were good memories, all of them.

Then I pulled out my high school yearbook and leafed through the pages. I thought about old friends like Terry Digangi, Barry Klein, and Donna Kundick, and wondered what they were doing now. I looked at pictures of the cheerleaders and saw a shot of my first real girlfriend, Heather Black, with whom I 'went steady' for a full nine months. Then I saw a picture of the love of my life in my senior year, Peggy Mallory, the girl who I swore that I would one day marry. Reading all of the handwritten notes scribbled across the pages from classmates brought back memories I hadn't thought about in thirty years. I was amazed some of them were still rattling around in my head after all that time, but it felt good to reminisce.

Next I pulled out a bunch of pictures bound together by a rubber band. Most of them were of my best friends back in high school and college – Steve Dison, Mike Barber, Tim Murray, and Jim Marshall. There were shots of us in our cars, at church, or just hanging out and having fun. Only later in life did I realize how lucky I was to have those guys as friends. Our friendships remained to this day, but life didn't allow us to get together much anymore. What a shame. For all of us.

Other pictures brought still more memories. I thought about my teachers in school, Mrs. Wilson in the 3ʳᵈ grade, my Spanish teacher, Mr. Briejo, and my high school basketball coach, Herman Valdes, all of whom touched my life in an important way. I laughed out loud when I saw my prom picture and how funny I looked in my light blue, crushed velvet tux. And I thought of other random memories, like how excited I was when I got my first real kiss from Ellen Johnson in the 6ᵗʰ grade during a game of spin the bottle, or when I carved my initials into the balcony pew at First Baptist Church.

Soon my mind just wandered, thinking about all of the people who had once shared my journey. There were cousins, aunts, and uncles. Grandparents, many of whom were no longer alive. Friends from college and seminary, now scattered across the globe. Staff members, all of them creative and talented, who I worked with in ministry. And countless friends, church members, and others who were kind and compassionate.

Every memory linked to another as I thought about all of the places I had been and the experiences I'd had. A summer in Yellowstone. College at the University of South Florida. Seminary at Vanderbilt. Church retreats in North Carolina, Georgia, and Key West. Mission trips in Belize. Family vacations in Utah, Cocoa Beach, and Alabama. Cruises to the Caribbean and Mexico. Trips to Israel. And countless weekend getaways in places like New Orleans, Miami, and Atlanta.

I thought about more recent times too, and the people who had helped me and supported me after the divorce. Friends like Mike Reeser and Jim Merrick, both of whom were always just a phone call away. Bill and Marijo Carnes, and Fred Zinober, who opened their homes to me when I needed a place to stay. Jim Ferman, whose generosity allowed me to survive in that first year after I resigned from the ministry. Bill Johnson, Ron Harris, and Dennis Driscoll, who all lifted me up when things were at their worst. And Heath and Megan Schiesser, whose unexpected act of love and kindness really enabled me to take the first step on the path to new horizons.

Further down in the box were family pictures, mostly of the kids when they were young. I laughed at the funny faces they made in most of the shots and the outfits we had them dressed in back then. I took a little extra time to look at all of our annual family Christmas pictures, each one taken at a different location as the kids grew older, and each one representing another year that had passed in our lives. My favorite shots were of those at the beach and by the tree in our front yard. There were also plenty of pictures of Debbie and me as well, most of them during happier times, along with a beautiful photo of my mom which had been taken for the church directory. And, of course, there were about a zillion shots of our pets, including both of our Black Labs, each named Shadow, and our cats Blackie, Smokey, and Oreo.

By the time I reached the bottom of the box, my little break had lasted over an hour. Every picture represented a memory, and every memory had sent my mind racing in a hundred different directions. Each one reminded me of someone, something, or some place which had once been important in my life. The pictures symbolized my journey past.

As I resealed the lid and placed the box in my trunk, I wondered what other pictures would fill the boxes of my life in the days ahead. The memories from this box would always remain and be cherished – of that there was absolutely no doubt – but I knew they would be joined with others in the years ahead. Other people, other places, and other experiences would be a part of my life and, in time, would be just as special.

One thing was apparent to me, however. If there were more boxes to fill, it was up to me to go out and make those memories. No one could live my life for me. This this was my journey and nobody else's.

Feeling refreshed by my trip down memory lane, I started packing the car again just as my son pulled up in his truck to help. The newest leg of my journey, wherever it would end up leading, was about to begin. I was ready.

❈ ❈ ❈

Your journey past, like mine, is filled with wonderful memories which you will never forget. Some of those memories make you smile. Others, perhaps those more recently involving your divorce, are more difficult and bring sadness. But each of them, and all of them, has one thing in common – they are yours.

In the midst of your darkest moments – in fact, especially in those moments – remember the joys of the journey. Remember the people, places, and experiences that have touched your life and shaped who you are today. These are the gifts of life which you have been given and your blessings to cherish. They may not all be filled with roses and sunshine, but they are, and always will be, uniquely yours. Celebrate the journey past.

Live The Journey Present...

Live the journey present. Live fully in the right here and right now of this day and time, and make every moment the best it can possibly be. No matter what you do, who you're with, or where you are, seize the moment and live life to its fullest. Be present and engaged in every conversation and every experience, and never allow yourself to take one second for granted. Your yesterdays are gone forever and your tomorrows are yet to arrive, but this moment, here and now, is the one you are given to live. Make it count and live the journey present.

❊ ❊ ❊

Approximately six to eight months after the divorce...

Tuesdays were always special to me after the divorce. Those were the nights I got my mid-week 'fix' with the kids by taking them out to dinner and then back to my apartment. I had them plenty of other times too, like on week-ends, during our Thursday night one-on-ones, and when I ran them back and forth to practices for their friend's homes, but Tuesdays were dedicated to us being together as a family. They were often the highlight of my week.

As time went on after the divorce and my financial problems began to mount, however, Tuesdays become a concern. Eventually I arrived at the point where I worried about having enough money to take them out for dinner, even when it involved something as simple as a burger and fries. Sometimes I made a meal at home, but I'm not much of a cook and my usual diet of tuna sandwiches and tomato soup really didn't appeal to them. More than once I skipped meals during the week just to make sure I had enough to take them out to Sonny's, their favorite restaurant, for a barbequed sandwich. Sometimes I even borrowed from my Mom.

I tried to hide my financial problems from the kids, mostly out of embarrassment, but they knew I was struggling. All they had to do was to look in my refrigerator or see how I lived. Yet they never complained about where we ate or what we did, which I appreciated, even when it meant they couldn't do what they really wanted to do. Although they didn't fully understand my situation, they knew the issues were complicated.

One Tuesday evening after dinner at my Mom's house, I was driving the kids back to my place and we passed a putt-putt golf course. Josh asked if we could stop and play sometime, and Amanda quickly chimed in saying she'd like to play too. I'm sure both of them thought I'd say something like, "Sure. We can go sometime," as I kept on going.

Fortunately for me, however, their request came at a good time. I had just officiated a wedding for a friend the weekend before and he had given me twice the normal honorarium. He even mentioned that he wanted me to use it to do something fun with the kids. So, I decided to do just that and made a quick U-turn to head back to the course.

I could think of a hundred different reasons why we shouldn't have stopped – there was school the next day, the kids needed to finish their homework, we'd get home too late, it would cost too much money, etcetera, etcetera... – but there was one reason I determined we would. There had been too many times in the last few months when I had put life on hold and my kids deserved to have some good old-fashioned, spontaneous fun with their dad. I decided to seize the moment.

We had a great time over the next two hours, laughing and talking as we took full advantage of the opportunity. We scored a two on one hole and an eight on the next as we played goofy tricks on one another and seemingly hit every obstacle on almost every hole. When we were done, I realized I hadn't had that kind of fun with my kids for way too long.

As I said my prayers that night, I thanked God for my kids and our silly little game of putt-putt golf. I knew He had more important things to worry about in the world than me having a good time with my children, but I also knew that somehow He would understand. It just felt like the right thing to do.

I also made a request that night, one that God had heard me pray before. I asked Him to help me make the best of every moment I had with my children, no matter what happened in their lives or mine, and to give me the strength to be the example to them I needed to be. Once again, I knew He understood.

Thank you, Lord, for all of the little moments in life that make it special. Amen.

❋ ❋ ❋

I greatly admire my friend Mary. Her story is an inspiration not only to me, but to anyone else who has ever tried to start over in difficult times. She is an example of what can happen when someone decides to take control of their life and to address the issues which need to be addressed.

Mary went through a very ugly divorce a few years ago. There were all of the usual problems that one has when their marriage ends – financial challenges, relationship problems, feelings of anger, hurt, and resentment – but Mary also had another problem, one which was even more significant than any of those. That problem was an addiction, and she knew it threatened her future if it wasn't addressed.

Shortly after the divorce, Mary left her home town in the state of Washington and came to Florida to live with her mom. That's where I met her. Her goal was to start over and change her life. It wouldn't be easy, but she knew it was something that she had to do.

Mary entered a Twelve-Step Program – a program which offers guidance outlining a course of action for recovery from addition – shortly after she found a job. Things were tough for a while, especially since her children were in Washington with their dad and she wasn't able to see them as often as she wanted to, but Mary remained committed to her goals and did the things she needed to do to improve her life.

As of the time I write this, I'm proud to tell you Mary has now been sober and on the right track for more than four years. She has successfully turned her life around, and I believe is healthier physically, mentally, and emotionally than ever before. In addition, her kids have moved to Florida to live with her and she also fell in love and remarried just last year. It's wonderful to see good things happen to good people.

Part of the reason I have so much respect for Mary is that she had the courage to address the difficult issues in her life and to find a way to deal with them. She went through some hard times along the way, but she remained positive, persistent, and determined. And as a result, her dream of starting over has now become a reality. If you were to meet her, you too would admire her attitude and the appreciation she has for every moment. Mary is a great example of what it means to live in the journey present.

It's unfortunate, but too many people are weighed down by the problems of the past and unable to live life fully in the present. Rather than face their problems and address their issues head on, they are content to struggle along seemingly being miserable and unhappy. They become distant and withdrawn, preoccupied with the past and removed from life in the here and now. They have a restless spirit and no peace of mind, and you can almost feel their stress lurking just below the surface. It's a tough way to live. I know because I've lived it myself.

Divorce can cause these things, but it isn't the only reason that people fail to live life fully in the journey present. It can happen to anybody – married or divorced, young or old, rich or poor – and at any age or station of life. Whenever we allow worry and fear to control us and we fail to embrace the moment, we run the risk of just existing rather than really living. And make no mistake about it – there is a huge difference between the two.

To exist rather than to really live means that we waste our time waiting for life to happen rather than making it happen ourselves. It seems to me we wait enough in our lives already. We wait in checkout lines, traffic jams, and on the phone. We wait for the next meeting, the next paycheck, or the next big event. We wait and wait and wait, for somewhere to go, someone to love, or something to do. But if all we ever do is wait rather than to live life and treasure each moment for the gift that it is, one day soon we'll wake up and discover life has passed us by. That is a situation no one wants to be in. Life is meant to be lived, and it's up to us to seize the moment and live the journey present.

I don't want to only exist, and I'm sure you don't either. I don't want to just go through the motions of life, waiting for someone else or something else to bring me the peace and happiness I deserve. Instead, I want to make life happen now. I want to give life my best shot in every conversation and in every experience, regardless of where I am, what I'm doing, or who I'm with. I want to be fully alive here in the present and soak up everything this life has to offer. I want to live in the moment.

What does it mean to live in the moment? It means we focus on living today rather than waiting for tomorrow, next week, or next year. It means we commit to being fully present and engaged in everything we do, at the very time that we do it. And it means we dedicate ourselves to making every minute of every hour of every day the very best it can possibly be. That's what it means to live in the moment.

Living in the moment is about helping a friend in need, crying at a sad movie, or enjoying a conversation with your family. It's about laughing at yourself when you do something stupid, showing kindness to a stranger, or reading the same book to your kids for the hundredth time. It's about singing at the top of your lungs when your favorite song is on the radio, having a beer with someone you love, or enjoying a day by yourself. Living in the moment is about celebrating all of the simple pleasures, expecting something good to happen, and taking time to reflect upon the deeper issues of life. Ultimately, living in the moment is all about the everyday stuff of the journey present.

Time is a precious commodity, and certainly much too valuable to be wasted. Any moment, and every moment, has the potential to be special if we give it the attention that it deserves. So stop settling for less. Make every second count, no matter what life throws at you along the way. Live every moment like it's your last and make the best of it.

I invite you to live life fully in the journey present. I invite you to live in the moment. And in the process, I invite you to be fully alive.

Prepare For The Journey Future...

What happens from here? That is the real question, isn't it? Don't you want to know what your life will look like on the other side of divorce? Will you find someone new? Will you move to a new town, or maybe take on a new career? What will you do? Where will you go?

Each of these questions basically asks the same thing – what will happen in your journey future?

The truth is there is no way to know. The future is impossible to predict with any certainty because life has too many moving parts. You can make all the right plans and do all the right things, but you can't control everything. There will always be unexpected twists and turns in life, just as there always has been in your past.

There is one thing you can control, however, both in the present and in your future. I'm talking about your attitude. More than any anything else in life – more than what you do, where you go, who you meet, or what you accomplish – your attitude will determine the success of your journey future. Nothing is more important now and in the days ahead.

So as you prepare for the journey future, the real question to be answered here is what attitude will you choose to embrace as you live? Will you commit to living life fully in the present, or will you be content to let it slowly pass you by? Will you make the most of every moment, being fully present and engaged in every conversation and experience, or will you spend your time waiting for life to get better? Will you live with passion, purpose, and conviction as you grab hold of everything life has to offer, or will you settle for something less?

Robert Hastings wrote a poem about the journey of life entitled "The Station". It's long been one of my favorites and offers a wonderful perspective on life. Consider it as you determine your attitude for the journey future:

❊ ❊ ❊

"Tucked away in our subconscious is an idyllic vision. We see ourselves on a long trip that spans the continent. We are traveling by train. Out of the

windows we drink in the passing scene of cars on nearby highways; of children waving at a crossing; of cattle grazing on a distant hillside; city skylines and village halls.

But uppermost in our minds is the final destination. On a certain day, at a certain hour we will pull into the station. Bands will be playing and flags will be waving. Once we get there so many wonderful dreams will come true, and the many pieces of our life will fit together like a completed jigsaw puzzle.

How restlessly we pace the aisles...waiting...waiting...waiting...for the station. When we reach the station that will be it, we cry. 'When I am eighteen...When I buy a new Mercedes Benz...When I put the last kid through college...When I pay off the mortgage...When I get a promotion...When I reach the age of retirement...Then I shall live happily ever after.'

But sooner or later we must realize that there is no station; no one place to arrive once and for all. The true joy of life is the trip. The station is only a myth."

❀ ❀ ❀

"The true joy of life is the trip". Truer words have ever been spoken.

Life is ultimately about the journey, not a final destination. There is no magical station life at which we finally arrive where everything is perfect and we are happy all the time. That isn't how life happens. Instead, life is made up of a million little moments, conversations, and experiences, some filled with happiness and joy, and others with sadness and sorrow. Each one is different. Each one is unique. Yet somehow they join together to form a single journey – your journey.

Celebrate the journey. Make it special and live it large. Embrace every moment – past, present, and future – because they are your moments and yours alone. You've been through the harsh winters before, and you'll make it through this one too. Spring is coming. Better days are ahead. And new horizons are ever before you.

Life is all about the journey...

It's Your Choice...

I invite you to embrace life – to cherish the journey past, to live fully in the journey present, and to prepare for the journey future. You can choose to live life fully and to be present in every moment...or...you can choose to wait, and wait, and wait as life slowly passes you by.

You deserve to be happy. You deserve to celebrate life rather than to simply exist. The true joy of life is in the journey, and you are the only one who can determine yours. Wherever you are, whoever you're with, and whatever you do, embrace the journey. It's your choice...

For Your Journal...

- Think about your journey past. Write a list of the people, places, and experiences which have shaped your life and made you who you are today. Spend a moment reflecting on each of them and give thanks.

- Think about your journey present. Identify a time when you failed to 'live in the moment'. What happened and why? Were you stressed out, worried, or overwhelmed by your problems and fears? How might the experience have been different if you had been fully present and engaged?

- Allow yourself to dream about your journey future. What does it look like, and what people, places, and experiences does it include? More importantly, how will you choose to live? What can you do right now in the journey present to help you prepare for the journey future?

- Write a statement which defines the attitude you want to have as you move forward from here. Will you make your best effort to live in the moment? To make the best of every day? Will you embrace the journey – past, present, and future? Will you seek new horizons? What is preventing you from starting right now?

Chapter 11
The Greatest Ally – Attitude...

"I am convinced that life is 10% what happens to me
and 90% how I react to it."
– Chuck Swindoll –

Adapted from Peter Marshall's 'Keeper of the Springs'...

Once upon a time
a little town grew up at the foot of a mountain range.
The town was sheltered in the lee of the protecting heights,
so that the wind that shuddered at the doors and
flung handfuls of sleet against the window panes
was a wind with fury already spent.

High in the hills above,
a strange and quiet forest dweller served the people
as the Keeper of the Springs.
Unappreciated by those who never saw him,
the Keeper of the Springs daily patrolled the mountains and cleared away
pools of silt, fallen leaves, and foreign matter which
threatened to pollute the water.
Through his efforts, the spring waters ran uninhibited down the hills,
leaping over rocks and through the ferns and mosses,
until they joined with other mountain streams
to form a river of life for the people below.

Millwheels whirled by the power of the river and businesses thrived.
Gardens grew healthy and strong, and fountains
threw its waters like diamonds high into the air for all to enjoy.
Children played happily along its banks and
the townspeople enjoyed happiness, health and prosperity.

In due time, however, the City Council came to be ruled by
a group of hard-headed, hard-boiled, business men,
whose only intent was to save money by cutting the civic budget.
Said the Keeper of the Purse at a meeting one day,
"Why should we continue to employ this romance ranger
called the Keeper of the Springs?
I've never even seen him in all the years I've lived here,
so surely his work isn't vital to our community.
I say we build a reservoir and house our own water,
and rid ourselves once and for all of his salary and service."
Blinded by greed and unaware of the consequences,
the Council immediately dismissed the Keeper of the Springs
of his duties that very day.

Soon a reservoir was built and the basin filled,
but the water was neither as clear nor as pure
for the townspeople as it once had been.
In time a sticky, green scum formed on the surface of the basin,
and right away the delicate machinery of the mills clogged with slime.
Businesses shut down and panic gripped the community
as a foul and vile stench filled the air.
Within days an epidemic raged and the clammy, yellow fingers of death
brought sickness and disease to every home.

The Council called an emergency meeting to address the problem
and admitted its mistake to let go of the Keeper of the Springs.
The town leaders rushed high into the hills
to find the one whom they had taken for granted for so many years,

and humbly asked the Keeper of the Springs to return to his duties.
Filled with compassion for those he had served so long in the town below,
the quiet forest dweller accepted their apology
and immediately began to make his rounds once again.

Within a matter of hours, the springs began to flow cool and clear
down the mountains once more.
Sickness waned and the stench disappeared.
Life returned to the town as businesses opened their doors,
millwheels whirled again and gardens revived,
and children came back to play on the banks of the river.

Never again did the people
question the value of the Keeper of the Springs.
And the sparkling waters of life ran clear and pure
down the hills and mountains forevermore.

The end.

❊ ❊ ❊

You are the Keeper of the Springs. You are the one who is responsible, the only one responsible for clearing away the garbage and debris which threatens to pollute your life. No one but you can enable the springs of life to burst forth from deep within your soul to bring you the peace, health, and happiness you want and deserve. You alone are the Keeper of the Springs.

How do you clear away the garbage and debris? How do you remove the pain, hurt, and heartache of your divorce so the springs of life can flow clean and pure once again? And how do you form a river of life which can carry you right on in to new horizons? You do it by embracing a positive attitude, always and everywhere, that's how!

Stephen J. King

Choosing Our Attitude...

Divorce may be common nowadays, but its frequency doesn't lessen the devastating impact it has upon the individuals involved. I've seen people nearly destroyed by divorce, and I was almost one of them. Thankfully, in time I was able to pull myself together, heal, and focus on the things I needed to do to move forward. But it wasn't easy.

Forgiving myself was one of the keys, just as accepting forgiveness from others and granting forgiveness to others were also. Having the courage to address my issues through counseling, and in my Divorce Recovery class, was another. These things, along with many more, made it possible for me to start over as I healed mentally, emotionally, and spiritually. None of them would have been possible, of course, without my commitment to make good and positive choices consistently along the way.

Through it all, I believe that the most important decision I made was to work on my attitude. After struggling through a year and a half of life where it felt like I was existing rather than living, I made the intentional decision to embrace a positive attitude at all times and in all things, regardless of my circumstances or situation. It was only then that I was able to do what I needed to do to change my life for the better. Focusing on building a positive attitude was the best thing I ever did in terms of my healing and recovery.

Life may be all about the journey, but living life is all about attitude. Of all the decisions we make through the power of choice, none is as important in determining our success or failure as is our determination of what type of attitude we will embrace. Attitude affects everything, including what we say and do and how we live and treat other people. We can't always choose our feelings or emotions, and we can't always control our circumstances, *but we can always, always, always, choose our attitude in responding to the world around us.*

Think of your attitude as a filter for interpreting and responding to life. It's different from your DNA, your fingerprints, or the color of your eyes, all of which are predetermined before you were ever born. Rather attitude is a matter of choice, and it's one you make everyday. Because it is, we have the ability to modify our attitude or to change it completely at any time and in any situation.

Many things influence our attitude, including our family, friends, education, background, and circumstances, but none of them can ultimately determine it. Your attitude has only one master, and that is your power of choice. You choose your attitude, and you are the only one who can. No matter how difficult life becomes or how challenging your situation, you are responsible for the attitude you embrace. There are no exceptions. For you alone are the Keeper of the Springs.

❋ ❋ ❋

Approximately three and a half years after the divorce...

I laid Mark Barber to rest earlier this week. His memorial service was last Thursday. Sadly, Mark was killed just a couple of days earlier when he stepped off a curb while attempting to cross a busy six lane highway and was hit by a car. He died instantly. He was 51. God help me, but there are some things in this world that I will never understand.

Mark was the older brother of Mike, one of my best friends growing up. Throughout our junior high and high school years, Mike and I spent a lot of time together. Many times Mark was around and, a result, I got to know him pretty well back then, although I lost touch with him when I went off to seminary.

Mark was a good guy. In all the years I knew him, I can't ever remember a time when he was upset or angry at anyone. He was the definition of "laid back", always relaxed and seemingly without a worry in the world. Despite his rather quiet nature, Mark had this big, booming laugh that couldn't help but to make you laugh when you heard it. And he had a great smile to go with it. People often exaggerate the good qualities and ignore the bad of someone they love who passes away, but I don't believe I'm doing either. In my mind, at least in the years I knew him, Mark was a kind and gentle soul who was always friendly and considerate of others.

I hadn't seen Mark since I was in my early 20's, but Mike kept me posted on what he was doing whenever we got together. Mark lived a different life than most. He never married, never had children, never owned a home, and rarely had a car. The things that most of us consider to be important, even essential, in life, just weren't to him. In fact, for much of his life including at the time of his death, most if not all of Mark's earthly belongings could be fit inside a duffel bag. He fought a few personal demons through his adult years but, then again, haven't we all?

Mark eventually moved out west to Colorado, then to Utah, and then to New Mexico, always working odd jobs to provide just enough money for him to get by. He was an enigma in many ways. Mark loved people, yet he lived most of his life alone. He was friendly and outgoing, but at the same time shy and introspective. He once went down to Mexico by himself and pitched a tent on the beach for a few weeks just so he could spend time reading about the deeper issues of life and some of the different cultural understandings of God. As I said before, Mark lived differently than most.

While his death was tragic, the thing I'll remember most about Mark was how he lived, not how he died. He had a certain spirit about him, an attitude about life that was unique and positive, and that always showed a concern for others whether he knew them or not. During Mark's memorial service, Mike offered the eulogy and shared a story that captured the essence of who Mark was to me. Mike said he and his wife, Judy, treated Mark to a weekend at the beach for his 50th birthday. When they arrived at the hotel, two elderly couples, who happened to be staying in the room next to Mark, were just arriving as well. Mark introduced himself and they struck up a conversation. Later that afternoon, Mark brought each couple flowers that he had purchased after they met. Why? Because that was Mark. That was who he was and the type of thing he often did. There was no particular reason for his gift of kindness. He just wanted to brighten their day.

I've thought a lot about Mark and the legacy he left behind over the last few days. Mike was right when he said during the eulogy that Mark lived life on his own terms. There is something I greatly admire about that in him. More admirable still was the way he touched the lives of people who knew him – including me. I hope, when my day finally comes and they lay me down in the grave once and for all, I'll be remembered as fondly.

Rest in peace, Mark. You will be missed.

❀ ❀ ❀

An attitude which is positive and embraces life is always better than a negative one that doesn't. It really is that simple. A positive attitude is more productive and healthier for you physically, mentally, emotionally, and spiritually. You're fooling yourself if you believe anything else.

Given the choice between improving our lives with a positive attitude or continuing to struggle with a negative one, there isn't a person alive who would choose the latter. The good news is we are given that exact choice!

You and I can better our lives by making the choice to improve our attitude. Yours may be good already, but I'm willing to bet it can be even better. Constantly working to build a more positive attitude can help us to keep moving forward no matter what life throws at us, even when it comes to dealing with the issues of a painful divorce.

Please don't misunderstand – a positive attitude isn't a cure-all for all of life's problems. There will still be plenty of hardships and struggles along the way, and we will still have to focus on making good decisions if we expect to move forward. But nothing can help us bounce back quicker from adversity, or be mentally and emotionally stronger when things don't go our way, more than an attitude which is positive and optimistic. There is no greater ally as we set our sights on new horizons.

The Steps To Building A Positive Attitude...

If our attitude isn't what it should be or can be, or if it is holding us back from healing and moving forward, then it is our responsibility to change it. As we've already established, the power of choice gives us that ability. Reshaping or changing our attitude isn't easy because old habits are hard to break, but it can be done. We can build a positive attitude and improve our lives if we commit to the change, do the right things, and put in the time and effort.

So how do we change our attitude? The process begins by understanding this fundamental concept – *we are always in control of our attitude, and our attitude is never in control of us.* Once we recognize this truth, then the real work begins.

Step #1: Begin With The Proper Approach

Ask any pilot to tell you the most important part of successfully landing a plane and he will likely say it is the approach. Ask any football coach to tell you the most important factor in winning next week's game and he too will say it is the approach as he prepares his team for the next opponent. Ask any student studying for a test, or any business person anticipating a meeting, or anybody about to do anything of importance or significance, and they will all tell you the same thing. Our approach to any task usually determines its success or failure.

The same is true for us as we begin our task of building a positive attitude. Our approach is critical and it will ultimately determine whether we are successful in accomplishing our goal or not. If our approach is half-hearted or without conviction, or if we believe the task is too difficult and give up halfway through, then our attitude will remain just as it is and we will never see the improvement we desire. But if we are fully committed in our approach and work to build an attitude which is positive at all the times and in all circumstances, then nothing will be able to stop us. It all starts with the approach.

An important part of that approach involves the way we communicate with ourselves. Self-talk, as it is often called, is what we tell ourselves in our thoughts and through our feelings, or in that quiet voice deep within our spirit that no one else can hear but us. Learning to practice positive self-talk rather than negative self-talk is an important step as we develop a positive attitude.

When our self-talk is filled with criticism, pessimism, and negativity, or when we constantly tell ourselves that we aren't good enough, smart enough, or skilled enough to accomplish whatever it is we are trying to do, then our attitude is usually pessimistic and negative as well. Even when we do have the skills and abilities to accomplish a task, negative self-talk can convince us otherwise, many times causing us to not even try. The end result is that we remain right where we are and we are afraid to try anything new that might help us to move forward.

Conversely, when our self-talk is positive and filled with and affirmations and encouragement, that is also reflected in our attitude and how we live. The end result when this occurs is that we have confidence in ourselves, in who we are and what we can do, and we are usually unafraid to try new things which can help us to improve.

Children provide us with an excellent example of what the power of positive affirmations are all about. When a child is constantly affirmed by the significant people in his life – parents, teachers, siblings, and peers – that child reflects those affirmations in a sense of confidence which usually leads to success in whatever he chooses to do. By the same token, if that same child is constantly ridiculed, put down, or criticized by the significant people in his life, he is likely to feel inferior and hesitant to do anything outside of his defined comfort zone.

Positive affirmations work the same way for us as adults except there is one notable exception – the most significant voice for us in our lives is the one that comes from within ourselves. What we say to ourselves about ourselves is more important in determining our confidence and attitude than any other voice we might hear, even if that other voice is from our spouse, children, parents, or friends. Self-talk often becomes a self-fulfilling prophecy which dictates the success or failure of a task before we ever begin.

We need to teach ourselves positive self-talk skills. We need to affirm to ourselves the good things we do and the unique set of gifts, talents, and abilities we have. In reinforcing those traits, we remind ourselves that we possess a variety of positive tools and experiences which can help us accomplish almost any task and change, alter, or affect our situation for the better. Listening to the positive affirmations of our inner voice enables us to proactively focus on what we can do to improve our lives instead of on what we can't.

How do we develop self-talk skills which affirm the positive? We do it the same way we improve in every other area of our lives – we practice.

I once coached a junior varsity, high school basketball team which was made up of 15 and 16 year old boys. Our season got off to a rough start. We lost our first three games and plummeted to the bottom of the standings. After that time, however, we went on a long winning streak and ended up playing for the league championship. What caused the turnaround? There is only one answer – practice, practice, and more practice. We practiced the fundamentals every day and worked hard to improve our skills. The more we practiced, the better we played. The better we played, the more games we won. And the more games we won, the more confident our team became. By the end of the season, our players expected to win every time we walked out onto the court.

Practice can't make us perfect, but it will definitely make us better. That's true not only in basketball, but in every other discipline of life as well. Whether it is sports, music, academics, business, or anything else, the truth is the more we practice, the better we will become. We learn to play sports better by playing, read better by reading, dance better by dancing, and work better by working. In the same way, we learn to be more positive in our approach to life by being positive.

Building a positive attitude begins by affirming ourselves in the good things we do. It doesn't mean we ignore our mistakes and failures – we are all accountable for our actions and we need to work on correcting our shortcomings whenever possible – but it does mean that we refuse to let them dominate our lives. Instead, we can intentionally choose to focus on the things we do which are good, right, and positive, and we allow them to guide us into the future.

I know my mistakes and failures well, and I've shared them openly with you in the pages of this book. But I've also worked hard to address those issues in my life and to make them right. I will never discount or downplay their significance in my past, but I also won't let them dominate my life in the present anymore. Instead, I choose to focus on the many positive qualities I have which can help me be a better person in the future.

At the risk of sounding immodest, here are some of the positives I affirm regularly to myself. I am a good father to my kids and a good son to my mom. I'm a good friend who is always ready to help, talk, or listen. I have a big heart and I truly care about people, and I have a sincere passion and compassion for those who are less fortunate. I'm a good leader who inspires others through my example and enthusiasm for life, and I make a positive difference in my community. I am considerate and respectful of all people. I am intelligent, thoughtful, caring, and kind. I am sensitive to the needs of others. I am... well, you get the idea.

I want to affirm these positives in my life because I'm proud of them and they make me feel good about who I am and what I do. More importantly, they remind me of the gifts, talents, and abilities I have which I can use to positively affect almost any situation at any time.

You need to give yourself permission to feel good about you, who you are, and what you do well. It may seem odd to you at first, but remember you aren't being cocky or braggadocios because you're only affirming these things to yourself.

You already have the gifts, talents, and qualities which can help you build a positive attitude and improve your life, you just have to remind yourself of them every now and then. Focus on the good and positive within, and let them be your guide into the future. If you really want to improve your life, the approach makes all the difference.

Step #2: Do The Little Things

I have a rusty old coffee can in my closet at home. I'm not sure how long I've owned it, or even where it came from since I'm not a coffee drinker myself, but that can has survived every move I've made since the divorce. If you saw it, you would probably tell me to throw it away. But I won't. Why? Because that rusty old coffee can reminds me that, with persistence and a little patience, the little things in life often add up to something big.

I use the coffee can for my spare change. Every day when I get home from work, I empty my pockets and make my little deposit of pennies, nickels, dimes, or quarters. Each deposit, on its own, is small and seemingly insignificant. But over time, those coins add up and continue to

Stephen J. King

accumulate. When the can gets full, I usually dump it out on the table and wrap the coins as I watch a ballgame or listen to music. I'm always amazed at how much money I have when I'm done. Most times those little, daily deposits end up adding up to a sum of well over $200. It really is true – the little things in life can add up to something big!

We need to remember that lesson as we work on building a positive attitude. It's the little things – the words we say, the things we do, and the way we treat other people – that eventually accumulate over time and add up to something big. If we take the right approach by focusing on our positives rather than dwelling on our negatives, and if we do the little things that contribute to a positive attitude every day, we will soon be amazed by the sum total of the result.

Here are a few examples of the 'little things' we can do on a regular basis to help us build a positive and optimistic attitude:

- **Look for a way to help someone everyday** – This is a great place to start. Wherever you are – whether at home, work, or out in the community – and whatever you are doing, look for a way to help someone everyday. Run an errand for a friend. Help a family member with a chore. Volunteer at a non-profit organization in your neighborhood. Hold the door open for a total stranger or lend a hand to an elderly person who needs help loading their groceries. Somehow, somewhere, and in some way, make it a point to go out of your way to brighten someone else's day. They will be grateful for your kindness and you'll feel good for helping them. It's a win-win situation! But be warned, helping others is addictive. Once you start, it's hard to quit. It's a great way for you to start building a positive attitude.
- **Give thanks for your blessings everyday** – Before you go to sleep at the end of your day, say a prayer and thank God for all of the good things in your life. This not only provides you with the opportunity to focus your mind

on positive things, but it also is a great way to make sure that you don't take your blessings for granted. Besides that, praying regularly is also a subtle reminder that you are never alone on this journey we call life.

- **Find something to laugh about everyday** – I recently heard a statistic that regular laughter adds 5-7 years to our lives. I'm not sure how anyone is able to gauge that in quantitative terms, but there's no doubt that laughter improves the quality of our lives. Find something to laugh about every day, even in the worst of times. Watch a funny movie or your favorite show on TV. Read a joke or talk with someone who lifts your spirits. We've all heard it said that "laughter is the best medicine" and, true or not, it is definitely good for the soul!

- **Share your love with those you love everyday** – This 'little thing' may just be the most important one of them all. Make it a point to tell your children that you love them. Call you parents, your grandparents, or your brother or sister just to let them know you were thinking about them. Thank a friend for being a friend. Send a card to someone who is going through a difficult time or that you haven't seen in a while. One way or another, find a way to show your love for your family and friends. The more you do it, the better you will feel and the more you'll want to do it in the future. And don't be surprised if they begin to share that same feeling right back at you! That's usually the way it works and I guarantee that it will make you feel good.

- **Take care of your body everyday** – Eat right and get plenty of rest. Make it your goal to live a healthy lifestyle. Don't worry about indulging every now and then, but make it the exception rather than the rule. Find time to walk, work out, and exercise regularly. You'll not only feel good physically, but you'll feel better mentally too.

You'll also discover that you have more energy and your stress will go down. Make it a priority to feel good!

- **Take care of your spirit everyday** – Make it a habit to read something inspirational or to listen to something uplifting every morning as you enjoy your cup of coffee. Listen to one of your favorite CDs on the way to work, or read a devotional thought right before you go to bed at night. What you feed into your spirit makes a difference in your and attitude. The old saying, "garbage in, garbage out" is true, but so also is its corollary. If you fill your mind and spirit with positive thoughts each day, then positive thoughts are what will also come out!

- **Do something for yourself everyday** – In this world of busy schedules and more things on your 'to do' list than you can possibly accomplish in one day, it's important to find some time for yourself to rejuvenate your spirit. Have lunch with a friend. Call someone you haven't seen in a while just to say hi. Find a quiet spot at the beach or the park to 'get away from it all' for a few minutes. These little 'mini-vacations' in the middle of the day will help keep you sharp and stay balanced. They'll also go a long way in helping you build a positive attitude.

Add more 'little things' to the list if you wish – anything that is positive and lifts your spirit is appropriate – but the key is to make sure that you do at least some of these things every day. If you do, it won't be long until you too see your little, daily deposits add up to something big.

One addendum to my coffee can story. I've started a new tradition when I cash in my change. I've committed to use the money only for things that I enjoy or that will help someone else. In other words, I won't use it for things like bills or groceries. Instead, I want to use the money for things like taking my kids out to eat, buying a gift for someone else, or doing something I couldn't afford previously. I encourage you to try it. By the way, coffee cans are optional.

Despite all of our efforts to take the right approach and to do the little things we need to do to build a positive attitude, there are still bound to be times when we get discouraged. Challenges and setbacks happen in life and, when they do, it seems they can take the wind right out of our sails. It happens to all of us.

How we respond to those challenges and setbacks, however, is what will determine their lasting impact upon our lives, either positively or negatively. We can either respond by dwelling on the pain and continuing to let them bring us down or hold us back, or we can respond by learning what we can from the experience and continuing to look ahead to the future with hope and optimism.

The irony is this: certain setbacks in life, like divorce for example, can actually help us and produce positive results in the long run. They are painful to go through at the time, but these same setbacks often open up a whole new world of opportunities and possibilities for us in the future if we can just remain strong and keep a positive attitude. We may not be able to understand this truth as we struggle through them, but it becomes evident as time goes on.

My divorce was a horrific personal tragedy, and certainly the most difficult setback I've ever experienced in life. Yet as I look back on it now, three years removed from that time, I can see several good and positive things have resulted. I learned valuable lessons about life, love, and friendship, some of which I would've never learned otherwise. The communication with my kids is more open and honest than ever before, and our relationships are as strong as they've ever been. I dealt with personal issues I needed to deal with, and I was set free from the pain and struggles of my pre-divorce situation. I met new friends who now are incredibly important in my life. And I had the opportunity to write this book – a project that is near and dear to my heart – which I hope will inspire others to new beginnings and new horizons.

Did I ever envision that any of these things would happen three years ago as I was going through the turmoil of my divorce? No, I didn't. I couldn't have imagined them then, because there was too much happening and too much pain at the time. But they all did happen eventually, and they were only made possible because I experienced the setback that I did at that time in my life.

Every setback, every failure, and every mistake, no matter how difficult or disappointing it may be at the time, has the potential to result in good if we deal with it appropriately and keep a positive attitude.

❋ ❋ ❋

Approximately three years after the divorce...

I had lunch this week with two of my favorite people in the entire world. Cathy Smith and Cindy Vann are about as good as they come. Both are special people and special friends to me, and each of them have played an important part in my journey.

Cathy is a successful businesswoman who is incredibly generous and philanthropic. She and her husband Bob are highly respected for who they are and what they do, and they support a variety of worthwhile causes throughout the community. Cathy is also the past President of the Board of Directors at Meals on Wheels of Tampa (MOW) and was a member of the Search Committee which eventually hired me to lead the organization as the Executive Director.

Cindy is also an incredible person who is very gracious and generous. A stay-at-home mom who is active in her church, Cindy has volunteered for MOW by delivering meals to the elderly for over 15 years. She is the current President of the Board at MOW and was also a key member of the search committee which eventually hired me.

The three of us spend a lot of time together discussing our mission at MOW, which is to serve the homebound and seniors of our community, but I'm also grateful our friendships extend beyond work. We are personal friends too and have shared some wonderful times together. I baptized Cathy's children and granddaughter last Christmas, and I'll have the honor of performing her oldest daughter's marriage this summer. I've also spent some great times with Cindy and been over to her house to have dinner with her husband and family. Both of them have been a listening ear for me as I've gone through the ups and downs of my struggles related to the divorce.

Cathy and Cindy each have their own unique gifts, but in my mind they are the same type of people and a lot alike. They are both strong leaders who have raised wonderful families, and both of them have an unmistakable passion for life that is contagious. Their positive attitudes affect everyone they come in contact with and everything they do.

As we sat in the restaurant waiting for our food, I thought about the fact that I would've never met Cathy or Cindy if it had not been for the long and winding path my life had taken. It was only because of my resignation and divorce that I eventually ended up at Meals On Wheels in the first place. My life could have gone in any of a thousand other different directions if I had made different choices along the way, but it didn't and I didn't. All the good and bad of my journey, all the experiences I had along the way, some-how combined to bring me to this particular place in time. And if things hadn't worked out exactly as they did, the end result would have been that I would've never met two people who I now consider to be among my greatest blessings in life.

As I tried to wrap my mind around it all, I started thinking of other friends and experiences I might've missed out on too if my life had taken another path. I would've never had the opportunity to pastor my church in Bradenton and, as a result, would've never met Diane, Scott, Todd and Rose, Stan and Michelle, or any of the other friends I have there. I would've never worked with people like Morris, Rod, and Emily at Metropolitan Ministries, or Scott, Rosalie, and the staff at MOW. I might've never recon-nected with old friends like Eric or Terry, or never made the new ones I've met like Alex and Christine. In all probability, none of these people or expe-riences would've ever been a part of my life if my past hadn't happened just the way it did.

I don't pretend to have God figured out, and I certainly don't understand how this life works sometimes. And I don't know how much of our journey results from chance and how much from choice. But I do know this – if I think about the people and places that I enjoy and value most in my life right now, very few of them would've ever been possible had it not been for the setback I experienced three years before which I thought, at the time, ruined my life. I've learned that good things can result from even the most difficult of circumstances and experiences in our lives, and that there really is a silver lining in every cloud. Sometimes we just have to look for it.

Cindy and Cathy are two of the silver linings in my life. I wanted to tell them about what I was thinking, but it wasn't appropriate at the time. Maybe I should have anyway. Hopefully I'll have other opportunities.

Perhaps this is one of them. Thanks, Cathy and Cindy, for who you are and how you live, and the special way you both have touched my life. You guys are the best.

❀ ❀ ❀

People say, "That which doesn't kill you only makes you stronger". I think they may be right because it sure seems true for me. Maybe for you too. I've learned we can make it through anything, including the pain and heartache of divorce, if we just keep a positive attitude and look for the silver linings along the way.

Like most other things we've talked about in this book, it is a choice. In our darkest moments, we can either look to the light or allow the darkness to envelop and consume us. Do yourself a favor. Keep doing the things you need to do to build a positive attitude. You'll be glad you did.

Step #3: Live Expectantly

Having the right approach is important in building a positive attitude. So is doing the little things which help to lift your spirit every day. But if you really want to enjoy life, you need to learn to live expectantly.

❀ ❀ ❀

Approximately three and a half years after the divorce...

I cried at church this morning. I didn't cry because I was sad or because something went wrong. Rather I cried out of admiration and respect for a living saint in our congregation who taught me a lesson about life.

From all appearances, the order of the worship service this morning looked pretty much like any other Sunday. We sang the hymns, prayed the prayers, and read the Scriptures, just as we always do. And, as usual, there was a place for 'Special Music', which is normally a time when there is a solo or duet right before I preach. I usually use the time to clear my mind and mentally go through my sermon, but not today. This morning my full and undivided attention was on the singer.

Carmen has been a member of my church in Bradenton for years, well before I ever arrived there as the pastor. If I had to guess, I'd say she is in her early-80s, give or take a few years. You rarely see Carmen without a smile, even though she has had more than her fair share of aches and pains. It's obvious the years have taken their toll on her and it's becoming more difficult for her to walk, even on her good days, as her movements are slow and measured. Even so, Carmen has a great attitude about people and life. She is always upbeat and encouraging, and she has a gift of making others feel special just by the way she talks to them. Everyone in our church loves her.

This morning, Carmen sang a song entitled "They Could Not", which has always been one of my favorites during the Easter season. She knew the song by heart and it was obvious to me that she'd sung it many times before in her younger years. Something else was apparent to me, too. Though the tone and quality of her voice had faded some through the years, her passion for the message had not.

As she sang the final verse, Carmen dramatically pumped her fist and spread her arms open wide, almost as if she hoped her voice could deliver a powerful crescendo to match. But it just wasn't possible for her to do anymore, yet it didn't really matter. The tears were already flowing for me and the rest of the congregation as she finished the song, and everyone in the sanctuary stood and clapped. The beautiful part of it all was that I knew in my heart they were applauding the singer herself as much as the song.

The truth is I've heard "They Could Not" performed better many times before at other churches by singers who were younger and more talented than Carmen. But in all my years in the ministry, not one of them had ever delivered the message with as much passion, with more heart or more soul, than I heard it delivered with today. Carmen wasn't just performing a song – she was offering a living witness to her faith through music. And I was blessed to be there to see it.

The funny thing is I really don't think Carmen was surprised by the response she received when she finished singing. In fact, I bet she expected it, because that's how Carmen lives – expectantly. She expects the best from life and always looks for the good, and that message is communicated through everything that she says and does. She may not be able to sing like she did long ago, but the years sure haven't changed her attitude.

The great thing about Carmen is that her way of living expectantly has rubbed off on the other people in our church. It's a beautiful thing to see. Because Carmen expects the best from herself and from life, I've seen others begin to do the same.

I've noticed life usually works that way. When we expect good things to happen, they often do. And when we don't, then they usually won't. Living expectantly is an attitude about life which is easy to see in those who embrace it. I'm thankful Carmen is one of those of people.

I want to be one too.

❋ ❋ ❋

Live expectantly. It's a powerful phrase, but it's even more powerful as a way to live life.

To live expectantly means we expect the best from ourselves, from others, and from life in every situation and at all times. It means we do the very best we can, whenever we can, and then we trust that the results will follow. To put it simply, living expectantly is about expecting the best out of life rather than settling for less.

To live expectantly doesn't mean that only good things will happen, or that life will always turn out the way we want it. This is unrealistic and impossible. But living expectantly does mean we always strive for the best life has, no matter where we are, what we're doing, or who we are with, even when we are in the depths of our most significant struggles. When we continue to look forward with hope and anticipation, and we expect good things to happen, it shows in our attitude. And when we don't, well, that shows too.

Have you ever noticed how often we get exactly what we expect to get out of an experience, regardless of whether those expectations are positive or negative? It's true in almost every area, whether it involves a meeting at work, listening to a sermon at church, or eating out at a restaurant. Our expectations often predetermine how we will think about our experiences one way or the other. Life works the same way.

When we approach life with a 'doom and gloom' mentality which expects the worst to happen, usually it will. On the other hand, when we live expectantly and approach life with a positive attitude, our focus is on what can go right rather than on what might go wrong. We still have the same challenges in life, but we respond to them differently with a positive attitude because we expect the best to happen, which inevitably produces a better outcome.

I want to live expectantly. I want to expect the best out of myself and out of others at all times, and I want to shoot for the very best life can offer in every situation. Don't you? I also believe that God wants us to live expectantly. Deep down in our soul, I have no doubt that He would much rather us live with the hope of what can happen rather than with the fear of what might.

People who live expectantly seem to me to be happier and healthier than those who don't. They are more satisfied with life, more content in the here and now, and more excited about the future. Their lives seem richer, fuller, and more abundant. Why would we ever want something less than that for ourselves?

Understand that the choice to live expectantly doesn't depend on our circumstances. Circumstances change but our decision to expect the best doesn't have to. Nor does living expectantly depend on our finances, the amount of possession we have, or our life situation. Rich and poor alike have the ability to look forward to the future with optimism, anticipation, and hope. There is only one requirement needed to live expectantly, and that is to embrace a positive attitude which expects the best out of life. That is what seeking new horizons is all about. It's simply a better way to live.

Step #4: Take Time To Relax And Enjoy The Moment

John Ortberg, a well-known pastor and author, once spoke at a clergy conference that I attended several years ago in Leesburg, Florida. I remember that I enjoyed listening to him, but the truth is I've forgotten most of what he said by now. There was one story, however, that I still remember and probably always will. Perhaps it was because it involved his children and, as the father of three kids myself, I could relate to the experience. Here's the story.

One evening at the Ortberg home, John drew the parental assignment of giving baths to his three young children, Johnny, Laura, and Mallory. To make things 'easier' and save time, John decided to put them all three of them in the bathtub together. When Laura finished her bath, she dried off to put on her pajamas, just as she was supposed to do, as Johnny and Mallory continued to play in the water. John then turned his attention to getting Mallory out of the tub next, so she too could get ready for bed. Mallory, however, had other ideas.

Instead of drying off when John handed her the towel, Mallory did what the Ortberg family has since affectionately named the "Dee-Dah-Day" dance. The 'dance' consisted of running around in circles, in this case soaking wet and naked, while singing "Dee-Dah-Day, Dee-Dah-Day, Dee-Dah-Day" over and over again. Most nights John enjoyed this little ritual and watching his kids have fun but, unfortunately, this wasn't one of those nights.

Annoyed that Mallory was ignoring his instructions rather than doing what she was supposed to do, John decided he was in no mood to watch her "Dee-Dah-Day" around the bathroom with water flinging in every direction. In a moment of frustration to which every parent can relate, John raised his voice at Mallory and said in his firmest, parental tone, "Mallory, hurry!" And that was exactly what she did!

Mallory began to run in circles even faster and started singing even louder. Of course, brother and sister thought this was hilarious and the more they laughed, the faster Mallory went. John said that he suddenly realized he was in the middle of a mutiny of three, and decided to take control of the situation once and for all. With more than a hint of anger in his voice, John said, "Mallory, knock off the Dee-Dah-Day stuff and come over here right now so I can dry you off".

Then Mallory asked the age old question which has plagued parents from the beginning of time. "Why?"

I'll never forget Ortberg describing his thoughts at that moment. He was busted and he knew it! He had no good answer for Mallory's question, other than the old, parental default, which is "Because I told you so, that's why!" He had nowhere to go, no work that he needed to do, and no deadlines to meet.

Even worse, there right in front of him were his kids having fun as his daughter "Dee-Dah-Day'ed" her little heart out, dancing away with the unbridled joy that only a child can have, and he had ordered her to stop. Why? Because he was irritated? What else in the entire world could possibly be more important at that very moment than watching his kids celebrate life?

John realized right then that he almost missed an incredible opportunity to seize the moment and create a memory. But to his credit, and much to the delight of Mallory, Johnny, and Laura, he didn't! Instead, he stood up from beside the tub and ran over to join Mallory as they danced and sang right in the middle of the wet bathroom floor!

There is an important lesson in this wonderful little story. Sometimes we all need to just stop, relax, and enjoy the moment. We need to stop our hurrying and running around, and to put away our insatiable desire to just finish what we are doing so we can move on to the next item on our to-do list. We need to recognize the opportunities right in front of us to "stop and smell the roses". I wonder how many times I've missed the chance to 'Dee-Dah-Day' with my kids, my family, or my friends. I really don't think I want to know.

We all get stressed out or frustrated from time to time. And we all have moments when we feel like we are wound a little too tight or overwhelmed and exhausted by life. Especially then, we need to learn to step back from the madness and just relax. Life doesn't always have to be as serious as we make it out to be.

So we come back to where we started – you are the Keeper of the Springs. You are the only one who can clear away the garbage and debris which threatens to pollute your soul and drag you down. And you are the only one who can enable the springs of life within you to come bursting forth. It all begins with your attitude.

I promise you this – if you approach life with the right attitude and do the little things that you need to do to be positive every day, and if you live expectantly and take the time to enjoy the moment when it arises, you'll be a better person because of it.

Chuck Swindoll, a gifted teacher, pastor, and author, says it this way:

"The longer I live, the more I realize the impact of attitude on life. It is more important than the past, than education, than money, than circumstances, than failures, than successes, than what other people think or say or do. It is more important than appearance, giftedness, or skill. It will make or break a company...a church...a home. The remarkable thing is we have a choice every day regarding the attitude we will embrace for that day. We cannot change our past...we cannot change the fact that people will act in a certain way. We cannot change the inevitable. The only thing we can do is play on the one string we have, and that is our attitude. I am convinced that life is 10% what happens to me and 90% how I react to it. And so it is with you – we are in charge of our attitude."

He's right – life is 10% what happens to you and 90% how you react to it. Your attitude determines your life, not the other way around. Be positive, expect the best, and celebrate life! And if you dare, do a "Dee-Dah-Day" dance with someone you love!

It's Your Choice...

The choice is yours. You can choose to have a positive attitude and to live expectantly as you move into the future with hope...or...you can choose the opposite and expect the worst.

The quest for new horizons is about more than just overcoming challenges. It's about embracing a brand new attitude, a fresh perspective, even a new reality. It's about moving from fear to anticipation, and from frustration to expectation. But once again, only you can make the decision. After all, it is your life, your attitude, and your choice...

For Your Journal...

- As you think about your divorce in relation to the story of the Keeper of the Springs, with which character(s) do you most identify? The Keeper of the Springs who was no longer wanted by the people he served? The townspeople who were negatively affected by the decisions of others? Or The Keeper of the Purse who was responsible for the crisis in the first place? Why?

- What does it mean to have a positive attitude? Do you have one now? How can your attitude be improved? Are you willing to do what you need to do to build a positive attitude? Why or why not?

- Cite an example when having a positive attitude helped you to deal with a situation. Now cite an example when having a negative attitude made a situation more difficult. In both examples, what factors influenced your attitude? What caused you to choose the attitude you did?

- Make a checklist of the items in the "Do the Little Things..." section of this chapter. Commit to doing at least three of these things every day for the next week. Add other items to your list as you please.

- What does the phrase "live expectantly" mean to you? How would it change your life right now if you were able to live expectantly? Do you believe that you can, and that it will make a difference in your life? Why or why not?

Chapter 12

The Greatest Resource – Hope...

"I believe that imagination is stronger than knowledge – myth is more potent than history – dreams are more powerful than facts – hope always triumphs over experience – laughter is the cure for grief – love is stronger than death."
– Robert Fulghum –

I believe "hope always triumphs over experience" too...

❀ ❀ ❀

A little over two years after the divorce...

Two years had passed since I'd last seen most of the people gathered for the seminar. As they entered the Community Center that evening, I'm sure many of them, like me, were thinking about the last time we had all been together, which was a hectic and painful Sunday morning when I resigned as the pastor of the Palm Harbor United Methodist Church. So much had happened in my life since then – a divorce, a bankruptcy, three moves to different homes, a brand new career, a new church...

Everyone at the seminar was there upon my personal invitation. About a month before that date, I sent out brochures announcing the two hour seminar, called 'New Horizons', to a select group of people from around the community. I had decided to put the seminar together as a way of telling my story and sharing the lessons I had learned. I also hoped it would inspire others to make a new beginning in some area of their own lives. Since it was the first time I'd spoken publically in Palm Harbor since leaving the church,

I was a little nervous about the type of reception it would receive, but I felt strongly about the message.

The set-up for the event, thanks to good friends who coordinated the registrations, the sound and video, and the refreshments, was perfect. I greeted each guest individually by name as they entered, sharing a hug or handshake with most of them. I knew that I was ready, both spiritually and emotionally, to share the trials and tribulations of my journey with these who had once been an important part of it. I stood up to begin at 7:00 PM.

For me, the next two hours were incredible, as I hope and believe they were for those that attended as well. Struggling between laughter and tears, I talked openly about my mistakes, the divorce, and the many struggles I had faced since. But it was what happened next that really made the evening special, for it then that I focused on the message for which 'New Horizons' was created.

Using a mixture of personal stories with videos and music, I talked about the life giving power of hope, which I believed was the only thing that got me through the last two years of my life. It was an important message for me to share but, knowing the circumstances of some of those who were gathered, I knew it was also important for them to hear. The power of hope, I said, was the only thing that saved my life. Furthermore, that same power transcended my situation and was available to anyone, anywhere, and at any time, who ever felt beat down or discouraged by life.

Hope was there for me, I told them, even when I was too stubborn to accept it or too blind to see it. It was there in the love of my family and friends who never gave up on me, even when I'd already given up on myself. And it was there when I finally allowed myself to receive God's amazing grace and the love and forgiveness He alone could offer. And it was also there, day after day and time after time, in the kindness of people who loved me, helped me, and supported me. The power of hope, I said, is always present for anyone who needs to try again and make a new beginning.

After playing an emotional music video which challenged everyone to examine their lives, I closed the evening by inviting anyone who needed to start over in an important area of their life to come forward and light a candle as a symbol of hope. Not a single person remained in their seat. Standing together in prayer with our candles lit was a moment I will never forget.

The message of 'New Horizons', both then and now, is that hope always has the power to offer us a new beginning in life. No matter what we've been through or will go through in the future, and no matter how desperate our lives become, hope is always there to inspire, encourage, and lift us.

In all, over a hundred people attended the 'New Horizons' seminar that evening. Some, I'm certain, were just there out of curiosity or to see how I was doing. Others, perhaps, were there out of a personal need. But regardless of why they were there, they all left with the same message – the power of hope can change your life. They left with something else too – the story of a prodigal son, one whom they knew well, who once was lost, but now was found.

Some people say you can't go home again. They're wrong. I did and I'm glad. For me, 'New Horizons' affirmed everything I already believed in my heart. Grace, love, and forgiveness are more than just words. The power of hope is both present and eternal. And new beginnings are always possible.

❄ ❄ ❄

The Importance Of Hope...

Hope is a simple four letter word, but it is filled with purpose, resolve, and passion. The life giving power of hope has graced every soul of every person, from the greatest leader to the lowest servant, who has ever walked this earth and is infinitely stronger than any feeling, sentiment, or emotion. It's been said that a person can survive for thirty days without food and three days without water, but only three seconds without hope. Based on the experiences of my life, I believe it's true.

I've never studied psychology, but I can certainly testify to the power of hope in my own life. In the darkest moments of my journey – when I felt lost, alone, and without purpose, or when I just wanted to give up or give in to the pain altogether – it was only hope that gave me the strength to go on. Even when I didn't know it, even when I couldn't feel it, and even when I wouldn't recognize it, hope was alive deep within my soul. And because hope lived, I was able to live as well.

I've also seen the power of hope in the lives of others many times in my years in ministry. Whether it was the eternal hope of an elderly woman as she held the hand of her dying husband for the final time, or the healing hope of a parent who sat in a hospital as her son struggled with his addiction, or the hope of a better tomorrow as a family dealt with an unspeakable tragedy, it has always been present. Hope can never be fully defined, but it is unmistakable in the lives of those who depend upon it.

The dictionary says hope is "an emotional belief in a positive outcome related to events and circumstances within one's personal life". That's a good start, but it doesn't go far enough because, subjectively speaking, hope is so much more than we can ever define. It's impossible to convey its importance to our lives – spiritually, mentally, and emotionally – in a single statement.

Hope drives us, motivates us, and inspires us. It empowers us to persevere when times are tough and beckons us to a vision of a brighter day, even when all the evidence around us points to the contrary. Hope may lie latent for a week or a month or a season of life, seemingly shattered by the hurt and pain of our circumstances, but it is never buried. Its flame may flicker, but it is never snuffed out. For, you see, hope is life itself.

Whatever you're going through and whatever you feel or believe, inscribe this truth upon your heart – the life giving power of hope is always present and always available. Like the air you breathe, hope offers life. Like the roots of the giant redwood, hope nourishes the soul. And like the blessed light of the early morning sun, hope eventually breaks through the darkness and illumines your path to new horizons.

Hope never dies.

❀ ❀ ❀

Approximately a year and a half after the divorce...

Of all the places in the entire world, the moment occurred in aisle two of my local Publix supermarket.

It was late in the afternoon and most of the other shoppers were anxious to get home after a long day at work. Unfortunately, getting home from work wasn't an issue for me. I'd been unemployed for three months, ever since my attempt to start a business with a good friend had gone bust. I had no job and, more importantly, no source of income. I was in deep, deep trouble.

I had sent out dozens of resumes and called everyone that I knew, but I kept running into one dead end after another. The whole process was wearing on me, and I was becoming increasingly frustrated and discouraged. I tried to keep my spirits up, but I had just about run out of options.

Most of my life had been spent as a pastor in the United Methodist Church, which I loved and enjoyed. Ministry was more than just a job to me; it was my calling in life, and one that I pursued with purpose and passion. Only after resigning from the Palm Harbor church did I realize how much I missed it. Because of the events which led up to that time, I had already conceded to myself that I would never pastor a church again. The hole in my heart was hard to fill.

I'll never forget how I felt as I surrendered my credentials to my District Superintendent in our final meeting. The ordination certificates were made of nothing but paper and ink, but they represented so much more to me. They were a symbol of my identity, of who I was and what I'd done for the last 25 years of my life. And they reminded me of all the people and churches I'd been blessed to serve. When I finally handed them over, it was as if I was giving up a piece of my soul. Maybe I was.

I had often regretted my decision to leave the ministry. Hindsight is always 20/20, I guess, but if I would have known then that Debbie and I would eventually divorce just six months later anyway, I would've probably made a different decision. In all likelihood, I would have accepted the Bishop's offer to go on suspension, receive counseling, and then examine my options at a later date. But that's not how it worked out. Because Debbie insisted I leave the ministry if we were going to try to stay together, I did *what I did back then. As a result, almost two years later, I was still scraping to get by.*

As I searched for a can of tuna in the second aisle at Publix, I suddenly heard a familiar voice call my name. "Steve, is that you?" Before I could answer, Edgar was already making his way through the shoppers toward me with a big smile on his face.

Edgar is a kind and gentle man with a very stately appearance. He also happened to be a long time pastor at a church in the community. We didn't know each other well, but our paths had crossed several times during our years in ministry and we had gradually struck up a friendship. Like most people in churches in the area, Edgar was well aware of what had happened to me. I hadn't seen him since.

We exchanged the normal pleasantries as other shoppers maneuvered their carts around us until Edgar finally grabbed my arm and pulled me to an open spot in the aisle. He said he didn't know if he would see me again, so he wanted to take this opportunity to share a few thoughts. Since he was still holding my arm and nearly had me pinned up against the shelves, I really had no choice but to listen to him.

He told me I needed to get back into the ministry. I was a gifted pastor who inspired people in their faith, he said, and he believed that the church needed people like me. While he admitted that he couldn't begin to understand what I'd been through, the one thing he was sure of was that God's love was bigger than any of it. I may have made some mistakes, he pointed out, but God's call upon my life had never changed. He even went on to say that he thought I was just "wasting my time" if I tried to do anything else.

Then Edgar almost started preaching to me. Right there in the middle of Publix, he began to tell me about people like Moses, David, and Peter, all of whom had made big mistakes but had been restored by God's grace. Finally, as at last he released my arm, Edgar told me that everyone he knew was hoping I would one day make the decision to be a pastor again. The challenge, as he perceived it, was for me to forgive myself and move on with life.

I knew in my heart that everything Edgar said was true and right, including the part about God's call on my life, despite what I had done to mess it up. Yet none of it lessened my guilt or took away the fear. The thought of going back into the ministry scared me and, despite his kind remarks, I wasn't sure that I had the courage to do what I needed to do to try again.

Before Edgar left to get back to his shopping, he pulled out a pen tucked away in his shirt pocket and wrote down his phone number. He asked me to call him later that evening, saying that he wanted to check out something first. He knew a pastor in Bradenton who was leaving his church to move up north and Edgar wanted me to apply for the position. The church would be far enough away to give me a fresh start, he said, yet also close enough for me to remain in the area.

I did call Edgar later that evening and, as it turned out, two days later I officially applied for the position of pastor at Harvey Memorial Community Church in Bradenton Beach. I interviewed with the Trustees a week later and told them my story. Then, after two weeks of 'trial sermons' before the congregation, I was offered the position. I accepted, but not without some hesitation.

It's now been eighteen months since the day I ran into Edgar on aisle two of Publix, and I've realized something during that time. The nudge I felt that day within my spirit at Publix – the nudge I'd tried to deny and ignore as I continued to struggle and find my way after the divorce – was something that I eventually had to act on. Until that point, I'd allowed myself to be controlled by my fears instead of guided by my hope. But no more. I'm back where I belong, as a pastor leading my church in Bradenton and doing exactly what I was meant to do.

Being in a small church with limited resources is unlike any other experience I've ever had in the past, but the beauty of it is that the people are wonderful. And really, in the end, that's all that really matters.

My congregation has taught me some important lessons over the past year and a half. I've learned that the joy of serving a church doesn't depend on how many people are in the pews, but rather the joy comes in simply sharing the journey of faith together with others. And I've learned that people who live by grace renew the hope of someone who has been lost and wandered in life, even if that person is their pastor. Most importantly, I've learned that to love and to be loved, regardless of your struggles, failures, and mistakes, is the greatest blessing of all.

I'm thankful that my God is a God of hope. I'm thankful that He believes in things like second chances and new beginnings, and that He never stops believing in us, even when we aren't quite sure we believe in ourselves. Even when we want to quit or give up, He doesn't and won't.

It's still hard to believe that it took a trip to Publix for me get back into the ministry and learn those valuable lessons in my life. It just goes to show you, you never know...

❋ ❋ ❋

If we agree that a hope for the future is vital to us as we move forward, then we must ask the question, "What do we do when we feel hopeless?" In those moments when our dreams are shattered and the worries and fears have taken control and are ready to consume us, what can we do to restore within our spirit the life giving power of the hope?

I've wrestled with these questions after my own divorce and the one thing I can tell you is that there are no easy answers. I wanted to believe life would get better, to believe that there was always hope, but I didn't know if I could. What I learned, however, was that the only way to really keep hope alive was to never give up, never stop trying, and never stop dreaming.

Hope Principle #1: Never Give Up...

Never give up! Never, ever, give up! No matter how bad things get or how desperate they become, don't ever give up! The single greatest thing you can ever do to keep hope alive is to never, ever, give up.

I learned long ago that the power of a message is only as good as the listener and his or her desire to receive it. In other words, if we believe that never giving up is a message of truth that can change our lives for the better, then we will act upon it and see the results. But if we close ourselves off to the message – if we aren't open to hearing it or aren't willing to act upon it – then it will have no real impact or value upon our lives. The message to never give up is crucial if we want to have hope, and it's one that we need to both hear and act upon.

One of the most incredible speeches I've ever heard was delivered by the late Jim Valvano, who was the basketball coach at North Carolina State University several years ago. Jimmy V., as he was often called, is probably best known to basketball fans for coaching his undermanned North Carolina State Wolfpack team to a 'miracle victory' over the heavily favored Houston Cougars in the NCAA Basketball Championship back in 1983. As impressive as that accomplishment was, it paled in comparison to the impact Valvano had upon millions of viewers just a few years later as he courageously fought against the demon of cancer.

Valvano's final public appearance occurred before a national television audience at the Espy Awards in 1993, in an auditorium packed with his family and friends. With the cancer ravaging his body and slowly sapping his strength, Valvano offered an amazing and inspirational speech which was filled with hope, humor, and passion. He talked about the love and devotion of his family, and the importance of making time every day to think, to laugh, and to cry. And he spoke about the precious gift of life and encouraged everyone to never take it for granted. Then, in an emotional moment filled with tenderness and pain, he concluded his speech with these words:

"Don't give up. Don't ever give up... Cancer can take away all my physical abilities, (but) it cannot touch my mind, it cannot touch my heart, and it cannot touch my soul. And those three things are going to carry on forever...God bless you all."

Having finally met the foe he couldn't defeat, Valvano died just a few months later at the young age of 47.

That wasn't the end of his legacy, however. Because of his courageous example in fighting against the dreaded disease which has taken the lives of so many, that evening ESPN announced the creation of the V Foundation in his honor. Dedicated solely to cancer research, this foundation continues to grow and has already funded hundreds of projects, physicians, and scientists in an effort to unravel the mysteries of cancer. One day, hopefully in the not too distant future, because of the efforts of

Jimmy V., The V Foundation, and many others, a cure will be found. No one knows how or when it will come, but there is hope on the horizon.

The message to never give up is important for those battling life threatening diseases, but its application goes way beyond just that group. In fact, the message to never give up is universal in its application. It's meant for anyone and everyone who is struggling with difficulties and challenges of any kind, including those related to divorce, and at any time and any place, regardless of the circumstances. Whatever life brings – be it disease, divorce, or something which is less significant but challenging nonetheless – the message urges us to keep fighting, keep going, and keep trying no matter what. It's the only way to keep our hope alive. And it's the only way to make it through to the other side of the problem.

Never give up became a personal mantra for me when I decided to change my life, deal with my issues, and set my sights on new horizons. In those moments when I felt sorry for myself, or when I questioned whether or not it was worth it to go on – and there were plenty of both of those moments – I thought about Valvano's words. If he and others could be courageous and keep on fighting in facing death, then I could certainly do the same in facing life. As it happened, the message to never give up played an important role in my healing and recovery as it renewed my hope and helped me move forward.

The truth is we can deal with any circumstance in life if we never give up and are committed to finding a solution. It doesn't mean that life will be any easier, but facing our fears and fighting through them is always better than giving up. Ultimately, when we make the decision to never give up, we are choosing life, hope, and healing over defeat and death.

I don't know the obstacles in your life. I only know what I've been through. I don't know how discouraged, frustrated, or overwhelmed you are right now; again, I only have my own experiences to draw upon. But I do know this – if you never give up and you keep on fighting through your hardships and problems, and if you make the decision to focus on the hope of what can be rather than the pain of what is, you'll make it through your struggles and come out to experience better days on the other side.

Keep hope alive. Keep pushing forward, and keep seeking new horizons. Whatever happens, whatever trials and tribulations come your way, keep fighting to persevere and overcome, no matter what. It isn't always the easy way, but it is always the best way. Most of all, never give up. Don't ever, ever give up.

Hope Principle #2: Never Stop Trying...

We don't 'try' to struggle in life. We don't 'try' to become discouraged or depressed, or to have bad things happen. And we certainly don't 'try' to bring physical, mental, or emotional pain upon ourselves. Yet despite our efforts to avoid these things, sometimes they happen. Once again, they're part of life.

One thing is sure, however. While we don't try to bring problems and bad times into our lives, the only way we can improve our situation once they're there is to 'try' to make things better. Problems don't just go away, and life doesn't just magically fix itself. It's up to us to work as hard as we can to change the situation, address our issues, and resolve them. It's up to us to try.

Never stop trying means we commit ourselves to a continual and sustained effort to make life better. Whereas the message to never give up is about attitude, the message to never stop trying is all about effort. Without trying to change our situation and to get back up, regardless of how many times we've been knocked down, our lives simply won't improve.

Never stop trying. Do everything you can, however you can, wherever you can, and every time that you can, to make things better. Never give in and never quit. Stay focused on the goal to move forward and improve your life.

Hope without effort will wither and die. But hope with the commitment to never give up and never stop trying enables us to overcome our challenges, persevere in hard times, and eventually realize our dreams. Never, ever, stop trying.

❀ ❀ ❀

One year and seven months after the divorce...

"Steve, on behalf of the Board of Directors at Meals On Wheels of Tampa, we want to offer you the opportunity to be our next Executive Director. Congratulations!"

The words were like music to my ears. After what seemed like an eternity of searching for the right position, my efforts had finally paid off. My patience was tried many times along the way, but I knew the offer to lead Meals On Wheels was a testimony to my persistence and the power of hope.

Three months earlier, at a time when I was both unemployed and discouraged, I went to lunch with an old friend, Judith Lombana, who was the Director of Development for the Museum of Science and Industry (MOSI) in Tampa. Judith had always been well connected in the community, and my hope was she might be aware of a non-profit organization which could use someone of my gifts and talents. She said she didn't know of any at the moment, but she would keep her ears open and do whatever she could to help. Being a good friend, I knew she would.

When we finished lunch, Judith wanted to take me on a tour of the Museum's newest exhibit. To be honest, I didn't want to go. I was anxious about my situation and I just wanted to go home and spend the rest of the day feeling miserable all by myself. In fact, the last thing I wanted to do was to look at a museum exhibit when I should have been scanning the want ads for work. I tried figure out a way to bow out gracefully, but Judith wouldn't take no for an answer. So, regrettably, I agreed to go.

After the tour, which took about 20 minutes and was actually quite enjoyable, we walked back to Judith's office and she took a moment to read a fax left on her desk by mistake. The fax announced that Meals On Wheels of Tampa was currently searching for a new Executive Director. Judith asked me if it was something I might be interested in and, of course, I was. She said that she knew a Board member there, a wonderful philanthropic woman named Amy Shimberg, and offered to call her on my behalf. She did and the result was that Amy and I set an appointment to meet for later in the week. Things went well and, soon after, I began the formal interview process with the search committee.

But learning about the opportunity and setting the wheels in motion was only half the battle. With over 100 applicants for the position, some from as far away as Alaska, the hiring process took three months to complete. I interviewed with the Search Committee and Executive Committee on three separate occasions, basically doing everything I knew to do to keep my name in front of them, including sending timely emails to the President of the Board and asking friends to write letters of recommendation before they even asked. I knew in my heart that I was the right person for Meals On Wheels. I just had to convince them. Finally, at long last, I received the call from Cathy Smith, who was the President of the Board at that time, and was officially offered the position. I accepted on the spot.

In retrospect, after working at Meals On Wheels for a while and realizing the position was everything I hoped for and more, I thought about how close I came to missing out on the opportunity. If I had given in to my feelings and not taken the tour with Judith at MOSI, I might've never seen the fax or ever known that the position was open. It reaffirmed to me the importance of taking action and following every lead, no matter how small or insignificant it may seem, because you just never know where it might lead.

Here's what I've learned – good things may come to those who wait, but good things come even more to those who do what they can to pursue them. Jesus said it this way, "Ask, and it will be given to you. Seek, and you shall find. Knock and the door will be opened unto you." (Matthew 7:7) Pretty smart guy, that Jesus.

Whatever you do, never stop trying.

❋ ❋ ❋

The scene was precious. Driving through my old neighborhood on the day after Christmas, I watched a young father run slowly along side of his daughter as she tried to ride a bicycle for the very first time. With one hand on the handlebars and the other on the back of her seat, the father called out instructions and shouted encouragement every step of the way. But as soon as he let go, she became frightened of riding alone and gently fell into the grass next to the sidewalk with the bike. As I continued up the street, I watched in the review mirror as the father picked up the bike and the little girl got back on to try again.

My mind flashed back to a time long ago when I, too, had run along side my daughter trying to teach her to ride. Riding a bike was easy for me, of course, because I'd done it all my life. But for my daughter Amanda, like the little girl I saw with her father on the day after Christmas, riding solo for the first time represented a tremendous challenge. Trying to maintain balance and control the bike as it wobbled back and forth without Dad holding on to the back was a scary proposition indeed.

I wanted to take away Amanda's fear, but I couldn't. No matter how much I wanted to help her, she had to eventually get to the point where she could ride the bike on her own. I couldn't do it for her, and neither could anyone else. If she was going to go where she wanted to go on her own, she had to learn how to take control of the bike and maintain her balance. Most of all, she had to conquer her fear of falling. She had to learn the important lesson that if you do fall down, it only means that you get right back up and try again.

In time, Amanda did learn to ride her bike, just as her brothers, Josh and Chris, did before her. She overcame her fears because she didn't stop trying. If she would have quit or given up, because it was too hard or she had fallen too many times, Amanda would've never experienced the opportunity to control the ride and claim her independence. And if that had happened, she would've never been able to go to the places that she herself wanted to go. But she didn't stop trying and she didn't quit. And neither will you.

If your experience is anything like mine, you have several people since your divorce who want to give you advice. That's a good thing, whether you actually use their advice or not, because it means they care and I'm sure you appreciate their concern. But ultimately, you have to learn to 'ride the bike' on your own and experience life after divorce yourself. No one can do it for you, even if they wanted to, because no one is you and no one but you lives your life.

Just as you learn how to ride a bike by riding, you learn how to live through divorce by living. And yes, there will be times when you fall and it hurts. There may even be times when you want to quit because you are afraid of falling again. But you won't quit. You can't. Not if you want to be happy and move forward in life once again. You have to keep trying, keep going, and keep living. If you don't, you'll never come to realize the joy of controlling the ride on your own.

I can tell you this with absolute certainty. If you don't give up and you are committed to keep on trying no matter what, the time will soon come when you will be able to maintain your balance and enjoy life once again. And when it does – when you conquer your fear of falling and learn to control the ride yourself instead of letting it control you – you'll discover a wonderful world of opportunities and possibilities ahead.

Whatever happens in life, just keep trying. Through all the tears and heartaches, through all the setbacks and frustrations, just keep going. When you fall down, get back up and try again. And if you fall again, keep trying until you succeed. Soon you will be able to go wherever you want to go and do whatever you want to do as you ride right into new horizons. No matter what – never, ever, stop trying!

Hope Principle #3: Never Stop Dreaming...

One of the best things about children is that, in their eyes, nothing is impossible. Their imaginations are unlimited and free and, as a result, so are their dreams. They believe they can live in outer space or build a city under the sea, or that they can become whatever they want to become in life, whether that is an astronaut, a dancer, a professional athlete, or the President of the United States. They entertain thoughts of the miraculous because, from their perspective, nothing is beyond the realm of possibility.

We would do well as adults to learn a lesson here from our children. The reality for most of us is, as we get older, our dreams seem to shrink. Instead of entertaining thoughts of the miraculous, reality sets in and life hits us upside the head with its hurts and heartaches. As a result, we begrudgingly learn to settle for the ordinary rather than pursuing the extraordinary. Simply put, we settle for less.

It doesn't have to be that way. We can still dream dreams and let our imaginations run wild and free every now and then. Even more, we can make those dreams a reality and do extraordinary things if we apply ourselves and keep reaching for the stars. As the children teach us, we need to learn to focus on why our dreams can happen rather than on only why they can't.

Divorce is one of the experiences in life that can shatter our dreams and leave us settling for less. None of us ever dreamed of being divorced when we walked down the aisle on our wedding day. That wasn't how life was supposed to turn out. Yet it did. And because it did, the pain of our experience has caused us to be hesitant, unsure, and cautious. We're afraid to believe again, to trust again, and most certainly, to dream again. The last thing we want to do is open ourselves up to the possibility of more hurt and pain in the future.

But don't you do it. Don't you dare let your dreams fade away and die just because you've fallen on hard times. Especially now, as you begin again in the aftermath of your divorce, your dreams are more important than ever. They may be different than they once were, and they may lead you in directions now that you never anticipated in the past, but don't you dare quit dreaming of what you can be and what you can do. In fact, I challenge you to dream dreams that are bigger and grander than ever before, and to set your sights on doing everything that you can to achieve them.

Dreams come in different shapes and sizes, but they all have one thing in common – they represent hope. So let your imagination run wild. Don't be afraid to dream new dreams which inspire you to a greater sense of purpose and calling. For when your dreams are alive, hope is alive. And when hope is alive, all things are possible to those who believe.

Never give up! Never stop trying! And never, ever, stop dreaming!

❊ ❊ ❊

Approximately two years and four months after the divorce...

I was sick and tired of the whole thing – sick and tired of struggling with every word, with how to say what it was that I wanted to say, and with writing and rewriting every story. I'd been working on this book for several months, but I thought seriously about tossing the entire manuscript in the garbage and deleting the chapters from my hard drive. I just wanted to be done with it.

After all, who would ever want to read my book anyway? How could I possibly inspire others to seek new horizons after divorce when I had such a difficult time finding the way there myself? In my worst moments, I actually thought of myself as the fool for believing I could publish this book. And even if I did, how would I feel if it turned out to be a failure or people didn't like what I'd written? Was it worth the risk of putting myself out there for everyone to see just so I could hopefully help someone else?

Maybe, I thought to myself, it would be best for everyone, including me, if I just gave up the dream and went on with life as it was. That would be the easiest thing to do. In the grand scheme of things, I was just one more person who had experienced the pain of divorce and who had a difficult time bouncing back. What was so special about that?

Every time I sat down to write these pages, those were the questions and doubts which crept into my mind. I tried to ignore them most of the time, but it was impossible for me to do for very long. No matter how much I wanted to keep believing in the dream and to see this book through until the end, the fears and uncertainties were always there.

It isn't easy to pursue a dream alone. You can do it, of course, but it's helpful when someone is there to share your dream and support you along the way. I'd never written a book before, and there were times I was overwhelmed by the work involved. Inspiring people through the spoken word was something I was used to as a pastor, but inspiring people through the written word was an entirely different undertaking altogether.

Despite my insecurities, there was no doubt of my transforming moment in the process. I can tell you the exact second when my thoughts shifted from 'I'm not sure I can finish this project...' to 'I will absolutely get this book done...' Call it a defining experience, a moment of truth, or whatever you want to call it, but I know very well the encounter which spurred me on and eventually inspired me to continue to chase the dream. And as it seemingly has so often happened in my life, the moment occurred when I least expected it.

One day, as I was blankly staring at my computer screen – writer's cramp, I think they call it – my oldest son, Chris, stopped in for a visit. That, in and of itself, should have been a sign something special was in the works, because it wasn't every day that my 18 year old son popped in unless he needed gas for his truck or something to eat, especially since he was living 30 minutes away from me at the time.

Somewhere in the conversation, Chris asked me how my book was coming along. I told him honestly that I wasn't sure, and asked if he wanted to read a few pages to give me his impressions. I was pleasantly surprised when he said that he did. He pulled a few pages from the manuscript, including one part which included a story about him, and began to read. For the next few minutes, there was complete silence as I watched his eyes. When he finally finished, he said "I really like it, Dad. It's good. I think you should definitely keep on writing".

That was it. That was my 'defining moment'. I knew right then that I couldn't stop, even if I wanted to, because Chris's affirmation wouldn't let me. Here was my own son – someone who had been at the epicenter of all the pain and heartache of which I was writing – and he was telling me that he liked it and to keep going. His words were enough to keep me chasing the dream.

Soon after the conversation with Chris, I made two critical decisions about the book which had been holding me back from moving ahead. First, I made the decision about who and what I wanted to include. My intentions were never to hurt anyone – Lord knows there has been enough pain involved with my story already – but I had to decide if I would include certain stories and conversations that might prove to be uncomfortable for me or others. I was especially concerned about several of the vignettes, since all of them are extremely personal, but I decided that I must include them if my book was to be authentic, genuine, and honest.

The second issue decision I made was even more important because it involved my kids. While writing about my struggles, my greatest concern was always about how it would impact my children. They know how much I love them – of that there is no doubt – and I've been honest in answering their questions about Jessica and the events which led to the divorce. But like any parent, I also want my kids to be proud of me. They have been through a lot and I certainly didn't want to add to their load. Yet, at the same time, I wanted them to know the depths of my sorrow and remorse, and to understand the resolve within my spirit as I tried to correct my mistakes and begin again. The end result was I decided to let it all hang out and write about my highs and my lows just as they happened. I knew I had to for this book to have integrity. My hope then and now was that they would see in me the model of grace, love, and forgiveness to which I have so often referred to in this manuscript.

With those issues finally resolved and Chris's words fresh on my mind, I started writing again, and again, and again; each time with my dream ever before me. The questions and doubts still lingered, but my perspective had changed. I realized then that the worst mistake I could make was not to fail in what I'd written, but rather the worst mistake I could make would be to have never written it all.

I had to complete this book, for myself if not for others. It is my story, my journey, and ultimately, my dream on the road to new horizons.

❀ ❀ ❀

The Power Of Belief...

Jesus said, "All things are possible to him who believes." (Mark 9:23).

His statement might test the limits of our faith, but the essence of His message is absolutely true. At the end of the day, the quest for new horizons is about *you* believing in *you*. It's about you believing in your dreams, your abilities, and your future. It is about you believing in what you can do and who you can be. And it's about you believing in the power of your new beginning. Without you believing in you, it's only a matter of time before you become discouraged and want to give up. But if you believe in yourself, then "all things are possible to him who believes..."

Maybe you've had a difficult time believing in yourself lately. Maybe your confidence is shaken by the divorce and it has caused you to doubt or question yourself and who you are. Maybe you've felt beaten beat and stressed out, and you are having a hard time feeling hopeful about the future. If so, I understand. I've been there too. But keep the faith, and don't give up hope. If you believe in yourself and never give up, never stop trying, and never stop dreaming, your new beginning has already begun. I assure you that better days are coming right around the corner.

If you are struggling, however, the question becomes: What can you do to build, or perhaps rebuild, your confidence so you can believe in yourself once again? It's an important question.

Lyle Schaller, who was considered an expert in the field of church growth, once talked about growing churches and how they perceive themselves. Every growing church he has ever attended, he said, had one common trait – they all had a positive self image. How did they develop that positive self image, especially at a time when so many other churches are just struggling just to survive? They did it by focusing on what they did well and on their possibilities for the future rather than focusing on their limitations. Instead of complaining about what they didn't have or what they couldn't do, these churches celebrated the good things they were doing and planned to build on those things as they moved forward. The positive energy created by that synergy perpetuated itself and carried over to their worship and programs, leading to growth and expansion.

The beauty of this model is it doesn't only apply to growing churches, but to growing people as well. We've already discussed the importance of focusing on good and positive things as a way of building our attitude, but we also see here that it can also help us build our confidence and a healthy self-image.

The truth bears repeating. The key to developing confidence and a positive self-esteem is to refuse to let our negatives define who we are. Instead of dwelling on what we didn't do, can't do, or aren't able to do, we instead choose to celebrate the good we are doing and will continue to do in the days ahead. When this is our approach, our focus naturally shifts from problems to possibilities, from disappointments to dreams, and from 'I can't' to 'I can'. The end result is we are able to move into the future with hope.

Have you ever seen a tiny flower growing up through a crack in a sidewalk? And if so, haven't you wondered how something so fragile and frail could possibly blossom amidst the concrete barriers which logically prevent it from growing? The answer, of course, is that even with imposing obstacles all around, the tiny flower was still able to receive the light and nourishment it needed to grow. Otherwise, it would never become what God intended for it to be.

You know what? You too will find the light and nourishment you need to grow if you spend your time focusing on the hope of the future rather than the mistakes of the past. Regardless of the obstacles and the barriers, believe in yourself and never give up, never stop trying, and never stop dreaming. It's the only way you can become what God intended you to be.

And if you get down or discouraged along the way and need a little inspiration to help you make it through, just look to the children. They teach us not only to live in the moment, but to transcend it, and to believe in the hope that tomorrow will be better than today.

I believe that too. Life will be better tomorrow than it is today, for both me and for you.

Believe It Anyway...

Music has always been a source of hope and inspiration for me, just as it probably has been for you too. Some songs take us back to another time and place, or have that special ability to lift our spirit or touch our heart. If I didn't know better, I'd think that certain songs were written just for me.

One of those songs is "Anyway", by Martina McBride. Maybe you've heard it. Its lyrics paint a picture of hope and describe everything I've communicated in this chapter. Unfortunately, reading the lyrics alone won't really do the song justice. It's much better when you 'feel' the passion as it is being sung and listen to the music. I hope you have the opportunity to do just that sometime soon.

Nevertheless, believing that you, like me, want to be inspired to a greater hope which never gives up, never stops trying, and never stops dreaming, I offer you the lyrics and message of Martina McBride's, "Anyway".

❀ ❀ ❀

"*Anyway*"
(*By Martina McBride*)

You can spend your whole life building something from nothing,
one storm can come and blow it all away; build it anyway.
You can chase a dream that seems so out of reach
and you know it might not ever come your way; dream it anyway.

(Chorus)
God is great, but sometimes life ain't good,
and when I pray it doesn't always turn out like I think it should;
but I do it anyway. I do it anyway.

This world's gone crazy and it's hard to believe
that tomorrow will be better than today; believe it anyway.
You can love someone with all your heart, for all the right reasons,
and in a moment they can choose to walk away; love 'em anyway.

God is great, but sometimes life ain't good,
and when I pray it doesn't always turn out like I think it should;
but I do it anyway. I do it anyway.

You can pour your soul out singing a song you believe in
that tomorrow they'll forget you ever sang;
sing it anyway. Sing it anyway.
I sing, I dream, I love, anyway.

❀ ❀ ❀

Never give up. Never stop trying. Never stop dreaming. And may the life giving power of hope be yours, lifting your spirit and encouraging your soul, now and forever! Amen.

It's Your Choice...

Hope is that special something deep inside your soul which helps you persevere in hard times and live expectantly as you move forward. You can nourish and grow the hope within your soul by making the choice to never give up, never stop trying, and never stop dreaming ...or...you can choose to let it wither away by settling for less. Either way, once again, it's your choice...

For Your Journal...

- What does the word hope mean to you? Think of a time when you were sustained by hope. What role does hope play in your life now? What can you do to nourish and grow the hope within your soul as you move toward new horizons?

- Where is the message "never give up" most applicable in your life right now? Why? What steps can you take to live that message as it relates to the area you've identified?

- Where is the message "never stop trying" most applicable in your life right now? Why? Again, what steps can you take to live that message as it relates to the area you've identified?

- As you think about the message "never stop dreaming", what dreams do you have for your future? What resources (time, money, effort, etc.) are you willing to commit to make those dreams become a reality? How do you begin?

- Do you 'believe in yourself' right now? Why or why not? What negatives have you allowed to define you? Make a list of the positive things happening in your life. What steps can you take to focus on these things in order to let them define you as you move toward new horizons?

Chapter 13
On The Way To New Horizons...

"I seek new horizons – to live at peace with my past, to be content in my present, and to look forward expectantly to my future..."

I thought long and hard about how to end this book. I wanted the ending to be positive and uplifting, and to inspire hope as you make a new beginning. I wanted it to encourage you as you chase your dreams, never give up, and never stop trying. Most of all, however, I wanted it to move you to action. You can take control of your life once again and make it to new horizons.

This final chapter is more of a beginning than an ending because your journey, like mine, will continue long after you're done reading. The only question left to answer is which way will it go?

As I've said often throughout this book, I can't make the decision for you, but I can certainly invite you to join me in the quest for new horizons. And so I will. Knowing the challenges of divorce, the hurt, heartache, and struggles I invite you to a new beginning.

❋ ❋ ❋

The Invitation

I invite you to join me on the journey to new horizons.

*I invite you to address the hurt and emotional pain of your divorce,
and to heal and move forward with life.*

*I invite you to forgive and to be forgiven,
and to look to the future with hope.*

*I invite you to live a life of grace and compassion
at all times and in every situation.*

*I invite you to embrace the power of choice
and proactively take control of your life.*

*I invite you to accept change and make the best of it,
and to use it as a springboard for your new start.*

*I invite you to develop a mission statement
which reflects who you are and who you want to be.*

*I invite you to embrace the journey – past, present, and future –
and to celebrate where you've been, where you are,
and where you are yet to be.*

*I invite you to live every moment to its fullest and to be fully alive,
and to cherish every conversation and experience.*

*I invite you to approach life with a positive attitude
and to live expectantly as you move into the future.*

*I invite you to never give up, to never stop trying, and to never stop dreaming,
and to nurture the hope within you.*

I invite you to a new beginning...

❁ ❁ ❁

Here is what I know – if you do the things in the invitation above, the day isn't far off when you'll begin to feel better and move forward. Just as darkness always gives way to the light of a brand new day, your hurt and heartache will fade giving way to the dawn of new horizons ever before you.

❋ ❋ ❋

Approximately three and a half years after the divorce...

As I relaxed at the causeway watching the sun slowly sink into the Gulf of Mexico, I thought about the many times I'd been here before for different reasons. In that first year after my divorce, I used to come here at all hours of the night and day to cry, grieve, think, and pray. Somehow back then, I always felt better being next to the water. It was my sanctuary.

Memories of those troubled times a few years before were all around me. I sat just a stone's throw away from the very place where I cried uncontrollably on the day I moved out of the house. A little farther down the beach was where I released the balloons on a brisk, windy day as I tried to let go of my pain. And across the road, under the palm trees in the sandy area, was where I came more than once in the middle of the night with a six pack of beer as I battled depression. They were painful remembrances – all of them – and I was glad those days were behind me.

I still came to the causeway regularly now, almost four years after the divorce, but it was for no other reason than to enjoy myself. Sometimes I watched the sunset or enjoyed a grouper sandwich with a friend. At others I rode my bike to the park at the end of the road or just sat in a chair by the water as I worked on my book or prepared a sermon. And every now and then, like on this particular day, I came just to kick back and relax as I gave thanks for my blessings.

Life had finally settled down and things were good. The healing power of time had combined with my own efforts to get better and had made it possible for me to begin again. I was in a good place now, content with who I was and who I had become. After a difficult season of life which lasted almost two years, I had recaptured my passion for living and was excited about my future.

I had many reasons to be grateful. My kids were healthy and doing well. Both of my boys were living with me. And even though I missed seeing my daughter everyday, somehow cell phones, text messages, and airplanes had seemed to lessen the distance between us since her move to Georgia. Debbie and I still had an occasional disagreement, but they were fewer and farther between now and the move away from Palm Harbor had helped her heal. I was glad for her because she deserves to be happy. My Mom, well into her eighties, was still healthy and relatively active. And though there were times I still wished things had turned out differently, Jessica and I were content in our friendship and realized our futures would be spent apart rather than together.

Things were also going well professionally. I was happy in my work at Meals On Wheels and at my church in Bradenton, and both gave me the sense of purpose I needed and desired in my life. I still had a few financial problems here and there, but they weren't anything like they once had been, and I was glad that I could continue to support my Mom and Debbie. I was at peace, and it felt good to feel good about life again.

My experience over the past few years had taught me many things, like good things really do happen to good people who work hard and stay positive, but sometimes they just take a while; and every problem has a solution, even if it's not the one we hoped for, and addressing that problem is always better than ignoring it or putting it off; and the difficult times in life really do define your character, and often bring with them opportunities that couldn't have happened otherwise. Most of all, I learned that a new beginning really is possible and new horizons really are reachable if you keep striving and never give up.

My life looks very different now than I thought it might just a few years ago, but I've also discovered the valuable lesson that 'different' doesn't necessarily mean worse. I'll always miss certain things about my old life that I can never replace, but there are also many wonderful things in my life now that I wouldn't trade. All of it only confirms what I've always believed – my journey has always been, and always will be, exactly what I choose to make of it. For better or worse.

I stayed at the causeway until the golden sun, like a fireball out on the horizon, was almost out of sight. Darkness would come soon. Then the light of a brand new day called tomorrow. Life had taught me that. The Gulf waters were beautiful and serene, just like I felt myself. Thank you Lord.

❋ ❋ ❋

I believe *New Horizons* can be helpful to anyone who has gone through the pain of a divorce, but I also realize that no two divorce situations are exactly alike. We all have our own unique set of issues, struggles, and problems, and whoever reads this book will interpret the stories and lessons I've shared through the lens of their own experience. In other words, the value of each is relative for every person based on their own personal circumstances.

Yet, I also believe that certain truths in life are not relative, and that they apply to all of us equally and at all times, regardless of who we are or what we've been through. The three truths below fall into that category. We've touched on them all at one time or another throughout in this book, but not exactly in the way that I share them now. These three truths represent the core of what it means to seek new horizons, and I invite you to make them your own.

Truth #1: An Ending Is Always A Pathway To A New Beginning

This is the foundational principle of *New Horizons*. It is particularly relevant for those of us who are seeking to start over after the tragedy of divorce.

An ending of any kind – whether chosen or forced upon us, desired or unwanted, good or bad – is always a pathway to a new beginning. There may be times we wish the ending had never occurred or that it had happened in some other way, but one way or another every ending prompts us to move in a new and different direction than we have traveled in the past.

Stephen J. King

The end of one road compels us to choose another to continue the journey. The end of a job forces us to find new ways to support ourselves. And the end of a marriage requires us to adapt and adjust to a new way of living as we move forward into the future. Whether we expect these endings to happen or not, every one of them is ultimately a pathway to a new beginning.

Many of my endings in the last few years have been painful. The break-up of my marriage was one. My resignation from the United Methodist Church was another. Moving out of the house and apart from my kids was still another, as were cutting off my relationship with Jessica and declaring bankruptcy. I mourned and grieved these endings because each represented a 'death' of sorts to a part of my life which had once been important.

Yet at the same time, each of these endings also forced me to set out in a new direction. Although I didn't want any of them to happen when they did, it was always my choice as to how I would react. I could allow these endings to ruin my life, or I could find a way to adjust and move forward. Some of the choices I made during that process were good and some weren't but, either way, I was the one – the only one – who could determine the impact they would have upon my life.

The reality is the 'yesterdays' of my old life are gone forever, whether I want them to be or not. The good news, however, is that my 'tomorrows' are ever before me. And those tomorrows – the people I meet, places I go, and experiences I have – will have only been made possible because of the endings which preceded them. Paradoxical though it may seem, even our most tragic endings, like divorce for example, are ultimately pathways to new beginnings.

This truth shouldn't surprise us. The theme occurs often in the Scriptures. Only through the sacrificial death of God's Son was forgiveness and life eternal made possible for the world – a tragic ending which led to a new beginning. Only because of the crucifixion was the resurrection able to be a part of the redemption story – again, a tragic ending which led to a new beginning. And only in 'dying to self' and having faith in Christ are we able to experience the abundant life Jesus promised – yet another tragic ending leading to a new beginning. The list could continue.

Dee Dee Rischer draws a powerful analogy which helps us to understand this truth in yet another way:

❀ ❀ ❀

"The morning my son Luke was born, I held his tiny body
and considered the journey he had taken in the last twenty-four hours.
I tried to imagine that change as he experienced it –
the inexorable pressure of muscles pushing him
into some strange and completely unknown passage,
his body at the mercy of larger forces bearing down on him.

Overnight, his body and world were radically altered.
He now must breathe air, not water.
He has to use his mouth for nourishment, no longer
relying on a connection to my body.
In his sleep, he flails his hands through the air,
startled not to hit the solid, comforting wall of my body.
After living only in warm darkness,
he experiences light, coolness, and the touch of other skin on his own.
Nothing can prepare him for this new life which must be,
quite simply, unimaginable.

Had there been a companion watching my child's journey from the womb
side, he would certainly have seen that process as death, not life.
Only when viewed from this side do we recognize and name it as birth.

The transformation my son has experienced
can only be matched by that other great passage in our lives – our death...
We see death from this side – and it is terrifying.
But our faith allows us to claim the promise:
What appears to be death is a portal to a life transformed."

❀ ❀ ❀

"What appears to be death is a portal to a life transformed." What a beautiful statement.

May the 'death' you have experienced in the ending of your marriage be a pathway to a beautiful new beginning and 'a life transformed'. Amen.

Truth #2: The Caterpillar Only Becomes A Beautiful Butterfly Through The Process Of Change

❋ ❋ ❋

Approximately three and a half years after the divorce...

It was Easter Sunday morning and I'd been asked to preach the annual Sunrise Service on the beach at Anna Maria Island. The Sunrise Service at Anna Maria is a wonderful tradition in which all six churches on the island gather together to worship on Easter as one, along with hundreds of other guests and visitors from around the community. I felt honored to be delivering the sermon.

Easter represents all that is good and right about the Christian faith. It affirms the good news of a risen Savior and celebrates God's love, grace, and forgiveness, while also challenging us to move beyond our indifference to experience a faith marked by promise and hope. The first Easter may have happened 2000 years ago, but its message and meaning are still as fresh and as relevant for us today as they were then.

Because the Easter message is so significant and attracts more people in worship than on any other Sunday of the year, pastors usually strive to be at their very best that day. I'm no exception. While I hope to make every sermon I preach special, I always work extra hard on Easter to prepare a message which is creative, inspirational, and memorable.

As I sat on the makeshift stage at the beach before the 1000 people from across the island who were gathered, my mind drifted back to another Easter Sunday morning I'd preached years ago at the Palm Harbor Methodist Church. On that morning, I had tried to communicate the message of resurrection and new life by doing something unique and unusual. I began my sermon without speaking as I silently carried a small wooden box to the altar, knowing that the congregation was curious as they watched me. I placed the box upon the altar, right in front of the cross, and stared at it for several moments before turning around to face the people and begin talking.

"He is risen!" I said as I opened with the traditional Easter greeting, to which the congregation responded back as one, "He is risen indeed!" I then started to develop my message by focusing on the fears and the doubts of the disciples, which I envisioned they must have had after watching Jesus, their leader, die on the cross. I imagined their questions out loud. "If Jesus really was the Son of God, where was God during the excruciating pain of his crucifixion? If God was so powerful, mighty, and loving, why didn't He do something? Why did Jesus have to go through His death on the cross in the first place? If God was God, couldn't He have changed things or found another way to bring salvation and accomplish His purpose? It just didn't make sense.

There were moments, I confessed, when I too felt like the disciples. I'd had my own share of fears and doubts, and times. I didn't understand how life works or why things happened. Why was there so much senseless pain and suffering in the world? Why was there things like cancer, AIDS, and dementia? Why were there shootings on school campuses, or earthquakes, hurricanes, and tsunamis which wiped out entire cities? Why did God allow 9/11 to happen? Couldn't He have stopped it if He truly was God? I knew that I was supposed to trust God in all things and at all times, I said, but sometimes that was difficult for me. Where was God when my Dad died or when I prayed for him to be healed? Why did innocent children die in this world? If God was so loving and kind, why did so many bad things happen to good people? Why, why, why...? I'd certainly had my doubts on the journey of faith, and I knew most people in the congregation could relate to exactly what I was saying.

Then my sermon shifted as I moved in a different direction. I said that, in my heart, I knew there would always be questions in this life which I couldn't answer or understand, but the great hope of Easter – which was that one day this world will end and all of us will spend eternity with God – superseded all those doubts and questions. In the midst of everything I didn't know, the one thing of which I was certain was that Jesus, God's Son, had died for my sins and rose from the grave to prove that He was who He said He was. The trials and tribulations of this life, at least as far as I understood them, were simply a means to an end.

I closed by drawing an analogy comparing the struggles of a caterpillar as it is changed and transformed within the cocoon in order to become a beautiful butterfly, to the struggles that each of us experience in this world as we are changed and transformed into becoming the people who will be with God eternally. Then, with the congregation's full and undivided attention, I slowly walked back to the altar in silence and retrieved the small wooden box I had placed on it as I began. When I opened it, I heard the collective gasp of the peoples as two dozen brightly colored butterflies were joyfully released into the air.

The message I hoped for had been received. Just as the butterflies that danced majestically throughout the sanctuary at that very moment could only become the beautiful creatures God intended them to be through the process of change and transformation, so it was for us as well.

What I didn't know that day – what I couldn't have known back then as I released the butterflies at the Palm Harbor Church – was how significant the analogy would become for me just a few years later in my own life. After my divorce, I was the caterpillar crawling along the ground and needing to change and transform. It was the only way I could become the creature God intended for me to be all along.

When I was finally introduced at the Sunrise Service and stood up to preach, far removed in both time and distance from the Easter Sunday at Palm Harbor long ago, only a few people at the beach knew my story. But it didn't matter because, as important as it was to me, it wasn't my story they had come to hear. Instead, they had come to hear The Story – the story of the greatest Good News of all; the story of a risen savior; the story of Easter.

The message of Easter transcends all of our pains, hurts, and struggles, and all of our doubts, questions, and fears. It offers us the hope of a new tomorrow and assures us that we can, and we will, be transformed into the people God has called us to be. Easter is an invitation to new life for all who are willing to receive it. Best of all, the story of Easter is for anyone who ever has lived or will. That includes you and me. The longer I live, the more I realize that is the greatest Good News of all.

The next time I'm invited to preach the Sunrise Service at Anna Maria Island, I think I'll take along a box of butterflies...

❀ ❀ ❀

The butterfly is a powerful symbol of new life. The reason, of course, is because of the amazing change which occurs within the cocoon as it transforms from an ugly caterpillar into one of God's most beautiful creations.

Transformation isn't possible without change, for butterflies or for people. I settled for being a caterpillar for too long after my divorce, crawling along in life and struggling to get from one point to the other, instead of changing and allowing myself to be transformed into something new. It was only when I decided to improve my life and to make the changes I needed to make that I was able to heal and begin my journey to new horizons.

Change and transformation are important for you too as you begin your journey to new horizons. The bottom line is that you can't, and you won't, move from where you are now to where you want to be in the future without considering the possibility of change. Sometimes change is difficult, painful and even scary, but in the end it's the only way that real and lasting transformation occurs.

You can change your life. You can transform it into something beautiful and new, and become the person God intends for you to be. You don't have to continue to crawl around, discouraged and disheartened by the circumstances of your divorce. Make the commitment to change what needs to change to improve your life and get started now. And in the process, may your desire for a better life lead to the day when you, like the butterfly, will spread your wings and fly!

Stephen J. King

Truth #3: You Are Loved

❀ ❀ ❀

Once upon on a time, a wicked witch kidnapped a beautiful young maiden with long, golden locks of hair, named Rapunzel. To hold her captive and prevent her escape, the witch locked Rapunzel away, deep within a distant forest, in a tall tower with no doors or stairs and with only a single window at the top.

The wicked witch came to check on Rapunzel and harass her every day, and brought just enough food and water for her to survive. Upon her arrival to the tower, the wicked witch would always angrily command Rapunzel to toss her long hair out of the window so that it would fall to the ground. The witch then used Rapunzel's hair to scale the walls of the tower and enter in through the window.

Feeling unwanted and unloved, Rapunzel lived a miserable life and cried herself to sleep each evening. Trapped by the walls of her prison on the outside and the hopelessness she felt within, her only comfort was to use her beautiful voice to sing the songs of happier days long ago.

As fate would have it, one day the King's son rode through the forest and heard the sweet, melodic sound of song echoing through the trees. Desiring to meet the person with a voice so lovely and pure, the handsome Prince followed the sound of the singing until he came to the tower, just as the wicked witch was also arriving for her daily visit.

Remaining hidden in the trees, the Prince watched from afar as the wicked witch issued her command, "Rapunzel, Rapunzel, throw down your hair" and scaled the tower to enter in. Disgusted by the witch's nasty appearance and angered by wretched tone with which she spoke to Rapunzel, the young and handsome Prince vowed then and there to rescue the young damsel in distress he had never seen.

As soon as the witch left, the Prince galloped upon his white stallion and rushed to the tower as he called, "Rapunzel, Rapunzel, let down your hair", and then scaled the tower and entered in. Their eyes met for the first time *and, seeing her own beauty in the reflection of his eyes, Rapunzel and the young Prince fell magically in love.*

The Prince rescued Rapunzel and returned with her to his kingdom, freeing her from the bonds of her captivity and the wicked witch forever, and the two of them enjoyed the rest of their days together and lived happily ever after.

The end.

✽ ✽ ✽

The story of Rapunzel is only a fairy tale, but fairy tales endure because they contain an element of truth. This one is no different. What is the truth contained within this fairy tale? Love has the power to set us free. It's a good lesson to remember.

Maybe you, like Rapunzel, have also felt trapped and imprisoned by your circumstances. Maybe the imaginary chains of loneliness and fear, of sadness and pain, have kept you bound, feeling hopeless and alone, and have held you back from living life. Perhaps there have even been times when you've wondered if a '...happily ever after' is even possible. If so, take heart, because I've got good news for you. You are loved and that truth really does have the power to set you free.

I can't promise a 'Prince Charming' to come along and magically sweep you away to a kingdom of eternal happiness, but I can tell you that you have people who love and care about you in your life right now. And, if you allow that love to lift you, it has the power to break the chains which bind you and to set you free!

I know this. Your family loves you – your kids, your mom and dad, and your brothers and sisters. Your friends love you, too, and they want to help and are willing to do whatever it takes. Most importantly, I know that God loves you, just like you are with all of your hurts, pains, and problems, and I'm absolutely certain that He wants the best for you.

One of my favorite passages of Scripture comes from the Apostle Paul as he writes to the church in Rome. Paul, who led a difficult life himself that was filled with hardships, struggles and problems, wrote these amazing words of hope and assurance:

"For I am convinced that neither death,
nor life, nor angels, nor principalities,
nor things present, nor things to come, nor powers,
nor height, nor depth, nor any thing else in all creation,
will be able to separate us from the love of God..."
(Romans 8:38-39)

He was right. Nothing can separate us from the love of God. Ever. When we understand this truth and claim it as our own, we will experience a peace and a purpose in our lives which is unmatched by any other. No power in this world is greater than love. And no love in this world is greater than God's is for you. That is the truth of the Gospel, and that truth shall set you free.

God loves you, even when you don't feel it. He wants the best for you, even when you don't understand what the best thing is for yourself. You are His child and you have His promise that He will never leave you or forsake you. Whatever happens in your life, wherever you go and whatever you do, don't ever forget that He loves you. Always.

If I could grant you one blessing above all others as you begin your journey to new horizons, it would be this – may the love of God fill your soul, guide your journey, and set you free. Amen.

The End (Or Better Yet, The Beginning)...

*It was one of 'those moments', **the kind that you know you will never forget.***

I left home before the dawn to get down to Bradenton early for my morning church service. My sermon still needed a little work – well, okay, a lot of work – and I was hoping to be inspired by parking at one of my favorite little spots down by the water. As it turned out, my drive across the Skyway Bridge provided all the inspiration I needed.

The Skyway Bridge is a signature landmark of the Tampa Bay area. It's a long structure which spans the waters that connect Tampa Bay with the Gulf of Mexico. The 10-12 minute drive across it, especially early on a Sunday morning when things are peaceful and quiet, is always one of my favorite times of the week. On this day, since I had left earlier than normal, I arrived at the bridge just as the morning sun was beginning to rise in the east.

It's hard to describe what I experienced as I drove across the bridge that morning. With the cool, fall air whipping through my windows and the peaceful waters of the Gulf looking like a sheet of glass for as far as the eye could see, the sun was reflecting gloriously off the clouds above and displaying the splendor of the morning colors. Although I knew it couldn't be true, I was tempted to believe that all of the forces of nature had somehow decided to suddenly converge to create the amazing scenery just for me.

That's when 'the moment' happened. There, right in front of me, appeared the crystal clear outline of the horizon, illumined by the incredible light of a brand new day. It was as if everything I had written about and worked for the last three years of my life was somehow miraculously and spectacularly confirmed within my spirit. The new horizon lay ahead and all I could do was keep moving toward it. It was a moment I'll never forget.

Life gives us those moments every now and then – moments which seem to transcend the ordinary and remind us we have a greater purpose and a higher calling in life than to just exist.

To me, the symbol of new horizons is all about hope. It's about living life fully, being fully alive, and dreaming big dreams. It's about embracing the journey, looking forward expectantly to the future, and constantly working to improve your life. And it's about celebrating God's love in good times and bad, being grateful for family and friends, and giving thanks for the grace which leads to healing and being made whole. In the end, new horizons are ultimately about believing in the power of new beginnings.

The truth is new horizons appear every day, whether we ever take the time to see them or not. Sadly, I've missed a few in my day. Maybe you have too. If so, too bad for both of us. But the good news is others will come, and they will always give us the opportunity to participate in them. And when we do – when we set our sights on new horizons and experience their power in our lives – they will always, always, always invite us to the blessed hope of a new beginning.

I wanted to remain in the moment on the bridge forever, but there was no way I could. It wasn't possible because I had to move on. Yet somehow I knew deep down in my heart that there would be other moments to come – moments just as inspiring and just as beautiful. In fact, I was absolutely sure of it. My quest for new horizons guaranteed it...

May the blessings of life rain down upon you and flood your soul. May the peace of God be your constant and ever present companion. And may your worries be few and your new horizons bright. Now and forever! Amen!

It's Your Choice...

Your final choice is one of the most important you will ever make. You can choose to seek new horizons and to celebrate a new beginning...or... you can choose to remain in the hurt, pain, and confusion which you are experiencing now.

My hope is this choice really isn't a choice for you at all. You have the ability and the power within you to change your life, to make a new beginning, and to seek new horizons. As it has been, is, and always will be, it's your choice...

For Your Journal...

- As you think about the past, what 'tragic' endings in your life have evolved into new beginnings? What endings have recently occurred in your life which may lead to new beginnings right now or in the future? What steps can you take to make those new beginnings happen?

- In what areas do you need to change and transform to improve your life? What is your biggest personal challenge or struggle now in the present? What changes can you make to transform in this area? Are you willing to make them? Why or why not?

- Make a list of the people who love you and offer a prayer of thanksgiving for each. Write a note or send a card to those who have touched your life in special ways.

Your final assignment: Wake up before the dawn and go to your favorite outdoor quiet spot. Write down your thoughts and feelings as you experience the light of a brand new day and look out upon the horizon.

Made in the USA
Charleston, SC
30 July 2012